Shakespeare AI³ :

Soul of the Iconcurchaic Age

Shakespeare AI³ :

Soul of the Iconcurchaic Age

M. D. Veritas

Bon Ton Republic Publications

2020

(hindsight…foresight)

Shakespeare AI³

= Active Inference

(3ᴿᴰ wave artificial Shakespeare intelligence)

cover: *Iconcurchaic Angel* (w/Lin Emery's sculpture "*Flight*")

(*Iconcurchaic = iconic + current + archaic*)

quotes: Dante, *Purgatorio*, canto 27, from lines 134-42;
    -Anthony Esolen, translator
  Rainer Maria Rilke, *Sonnets to Orpheus*, from #29;
    -Edward Snow, translator
Guillaume Apollinaire, on coining words like cubism & surreal
Pablo Picasso, on "finishing" a work of art
 grateful acknowledgments of previous publications:
Xavier Review, Xavier University, N. O. LA:
  print: I*n St. Jerome's New Orleans Study* (after Albrecht Dürer)
  poem: *A Crown of Flowers* (early version of *Floral Crown*)
Maple Leaf Rag (Anthologies), Portals Press, N. O. LA:
  poems: *Adam's Blessing* (early version of *Yeats's Last Paradigm Vision*)
        Maxine's Review (early version of *Her Unburdened Prescience*)
        Resurrection Visitation (early version of *Resurrection Epiphany*)
        Song of La Belle Orleanna (early variation of *La Belle Orleanna...*)
frontispiece & all art work/photos unless otherwise noted by Manfred Pollard:
Würzburg Residence, ceiling mural, *Myth of America,* by Giambattista Tiepolo,
 drawn from published photo of Wolf-Christian von der Mülbe, Dachau, in
 Heaven on Earth: Tiepolo Masterpieces of the Würzburg Years, Peter Krückmann
Catholic Passport, 18, photo by Karl Dietz, passport photographer at Staging Area
studio, U. S. Army base, Bremerhaven, Germany, 1970
Vivian at Barkhausen, Germany, 1968, photo by unknown German teacher
Vivian photos in Bremerhaven American High yearbook by Randolph Williams
Manfred photo in Panama Canal Zone by John Constantine

Trilogy: Volume 1:
Numbers of the 154 *Shakespeare's Sonnets* for allusions are in
brackets beside titles and poem numbers in the 1-21 crowns,
a 3 sonnet epiphany crown and 4 sonnets. The sonnets were
consecutively planned for allusions in a same numbered sequence.
Order changes were made after revisions as explained in appendix 1,
Coverdale Psalm allusions between equal =signs= are also in 3 crowns.
Shakespeare Sonnet allusions are in *italics* in each line
& all *allusions* are used or repeated only as many times as in the source,
i.e. the Bard's #40 has 10 *love* uses, my poem noted takes all 10 as allusions.

Volumes 2 & 3:
Shakespeare sonnet numbers for allusions are beside titles ( ).

photos, prints © 2020 Manfred Pollard
text Copyright 2020 M. D. Veritas™
ISBN-1: 978-1-7328146-0-8
all rights reserved Bon Ton Republic™ Publications, New Orleans
mdveritas52@gmail.com

The musicality of Shakespeare has been a feature of his language for over 400 years, along with the philosophical and spiritual take on the passage of time and contents of life making up the imagination coming to grips with personal and social history that consists of our "ages" in evolving/revolving cycles. The ancient Greeks sang about it in plays & epics. This book is a tribute to the "operatic" voice of the Bard once referred to as "the soul of the age" and coins a new word, "iconcurchaic" to express a timeless tribute, a labor of love in this age.

"(The New AI) essay is a delight. I do not pretend to follow all the threads but was compelled by the artful stream (or perhaps eager torrent) of consciousness. This stream emanates the physics of self-organizing, sentient systems, through the structured composition of Shakespearean prose and back again to the author's inference about his own (natural) intelligence. I particularly liked his conclusion: "my work fits the theory as a predicted outcome in itself." This has all the beauty of Quine's desert landscape and echoes the (almost tautological) simplicity of all great existential ideas – from quantum mechanics to natural selection. I was also taken with the word "iconcurchaic". I fully endorse the proposal that it should be in the dictionary (it is now in my spellchecker). If we have words like "Google," as semantic celebrations of epistemic foraging, we should certainly have "iconcurchaic". This word is particularly fitting for the free energy principle, which has basically been around since the days of Plato –and keeps enjoying renaissances –in one form or another – in the writings of Kant, Helmholtz, and a host of great thinkers of the 20th century. It is now iconcurchaic – in the 21st century –as underwriting the promise of 'third wave' artificial intelligence. And perhaps "Shakespearean active inference."
-Dr. Karl Friston, Oct. 2, 2019, Physicist/Psychiatrist, Scientific Director, Functional Imaging Labs, Uni. College London

Thank you for sending me your beautiful drawing of Tiepolo's ceiling above the Würzburg Residence staircase, focusing on the Apollo center and America. It is your own work and of course you may reproduce it in your book without asking anyone else for permission. Your wonderful translation of the fresco into a line and contour drawing shows just how much Tiepolo's principal structure here is one giant Rococo cartouche furthermore framed by his four parts of the world. It also reminds me of both Tiepolos', father and son, marvelously light and sketchy etchings.
-Dr. Christiane Hertel, Aug. 20, 2019, Professor of Art History, Bryn Mawr, author, *Pygmalion in Bavaria*

...hundreds of pages and drawings. Your output is amazing! I can compare it to a book of poems and drawings by James Stevenson -- whose work I followed for years in *The New Yorker* before his death. Stevenson's book is 61 pages, published In Singapore by Greenwillow Books. The poems each only four to twelve lines accompanied by a colorful watercolor picture, can remain in memory as an aphorism or mantra. Very different from your appendix of Shakespeare's 154 sonnets and the Bible's 150 psalms. You are a singular artist and researcher! Thank you for sending the latest evidence!
-Dr. Lin Emery, July 9, 2019, International Artist, on the color books of the *Shakespeare AI* series

LUX ET VERITAS

To Muses S. A., V. M., M. C. & P. H.

& Dr. L. E., Dr. H. B., Dr. K. F., Mr. R. A., Mr. W. M.,

Mr. & Mrs. G. & J. C. & Ms. D. B.

Well-wishing All Eternal Happiness

for Who Will Set Out Adventuring Here...

Contents

Shakespeare AI³: Soul of the Iconcurchaic Age (trilogy)

II Un-lost

Dante's Lost Book: Limbo

Inferno Sancti {6} *(50-56)*

1) Inferno Sancti
2) Simonized Church
3) Bishop's Endgame
4) Last Unleavened Way
5) Priceless Inheritance
6) Rabbi's Beloved Companion's Trust
7) Savvy Grace

Infallible Politics Uncrowned {7} *(43-49)*
1) Re-quested Ring Unsealed
2) Recycled Encyclicals
3) Sequestered Gestations
4) Catacomb Conclave
5) Sexual Taxation of a Holy Stimulus
6) Unsexed Politics
7) Feral Government Tamed

Crown of Creation {8} *(57-63)*
1) Passover
2) Unleavened
3) Pentecost
4) Trumpets
5) Atonement
6) Tabernacles
7) Last Great Day

Shrouded Crown {9} *(64-70)*
1) On the Shroud
2) Relic Shroud
3) Shrouded Belief
4) Translation Shroud
5) Entered Shroud
6) Love's Shroud
7) Stumbling on the Shroud

III Visitation

Floral Crown {10} *(29-35)*
1) *Symmetrical Flower*
2) *Leonardo's Cathedral Pod*
3) *Blossomed Mind*
4) *Floral Gift*
5) *Spiritual Bridal Bouquet*
6) *Floral Rapture*
7) *Floral Miracle*

Oracular Oaks {11} *(78-84)*
1) *Breathing Oaks Dream*
2) *Oracle's Enigma*
3) *First Oracular Oak*
4) *Oracle Oak's Diviner*
5) *Rebooting Oracular Oak*
6) *Rebooting Melchizadek*
7) *Oracular Oak Husbandry*

Ars Ironica Corona {12} *(71-77)*
1) *Moral Combat*
2) *Ars Ironica*
3) *Encyclopedic Britannica*
4) *Embracing New Knowledge*
5) *Clearing the Canon*
6) *Physical Metaphysics*
7) *Recycled Books*

Angel Trumpets {13} *(85-91)*
1) *All for your Everything*
2) *Time Heals and Wounds to Heal*
3) *Spirit Guide*
4) *Incarnadine Mind*
5) *Divined Family*
6) *Great Catch*
7) *Body's Heir*

Under the Orbital Lilac Tree

IV. Curvism

Com-Pounded Chinese Shakespeare Shavings

Dust Crowned Quintessence {14} *(92-98)*
1) *Jot and Titillate*
2) *When God Particles Collide*
3) *Einstein's Curvism*
4) *Hamlet's Dust*
5) *Mystery Guessing*
6) *Flash Life*
7) *Mirror Crown*

E=MC Crowned {15} *(99-105)*

Crop Circle Chronicles {16} *(106-112)*

Corona Poetica: Curvism {17} *(113-119)*

Byzantium's Renovation

A Unified Field Ballad

V. Orpheum's New World

Overture: Visions of Vivian

Libretto:

Apollo's Muses: Act 1 {18} *(120-126)*
1) *Sonnet Rings*
2) *Relentless Wonder*
3) *Harvest Feast*
4) *Following Apollo*
5) *Supernatural Bridge*
6) *Symphonic Spheres*
7) *Summer Rings*

Orpheus Transformed: Act 2 {19} *(127-133)*
1) *Oracular Oak*
2) *Musical Temple*
3) *Ethereal Wind*
4) *Disappearing Here*
5) *Godhead Grapes*
6) *Nightly Count*
7) *Her New Name*

*{ } on the right, crowns numbered {1} through {22} followed by 4
    epilogue sonnets w/ allusions
( ) Shakespeare Sonnet numbers for allusions *(in italics)*
    -continues through other vols.

Vol. 2, Recycling the Circle: Sonnets, Odes & Katanas

II. The Iconcurchaic Age

Vol. 3, Romance Languages: the Oddest Odyssey

"The most terrifying thing is to accept oneself completely."
--Carl Jung

Intro: Lux Volupte's Calm Harbor (67)

I. Unique Muses

1. Here Comes Lady Merlot (144)
2. Pretty Please Winged Nike Muse (33)
3. The Muse's Ritual Fruit (34)
4. Upstaged by the Muse (35)
5. Pen & Paper Muse (41)
6. The Muse's Slave (42)
7. Sleepless Muse (133)
8. Love's Overthrowing Muse (134)
9. Lover's Vow (40)
10. The Muse takes Root (145)
11. Music Appreciation (36)
12. Hope's Mirage Muse (37)
13. Thief in the Night Music (38)
14. Muse of Savvy Grace (43)
15. Your Brilliant Light (44)
16. Preparing for her Arrival (135)
17. Iconcurchaic Muses Garland

    1) *Domestic Muse* (136)
    2) *Muse's Wherewithal* (45)
    3) *New Old Muse* (146)
    4) *Begging the Muse Pretty Please* (39)
    5) *Black and White Silent Muse* (46)
    6) *Muse's Engagement* (47)
    7) *Righteous Muse* (48)
    8) *Love-seated Muse* (49)
    9) *Painting the Muse* (137)
    10) *Love Interest Muse* (138)
    11) *The New Model Muse* (50)
    12) *At the Muse's Liberty* (147)
    13) *Everything about the Muse* (51)
    14) *On Doom's Edge with the Muse* (52)
    15) *The Muse's Garland* (53)

2. Romantic Dialects & Odes

    1) *A Grown Child Seizes Time*

    2) To the Hunt (57)

    3) *A Ballad for La Belle Orleanna*

    4) Deva Demoed in a Dream (58)

    5) The Music Room Goddess Dance (59)

Prints

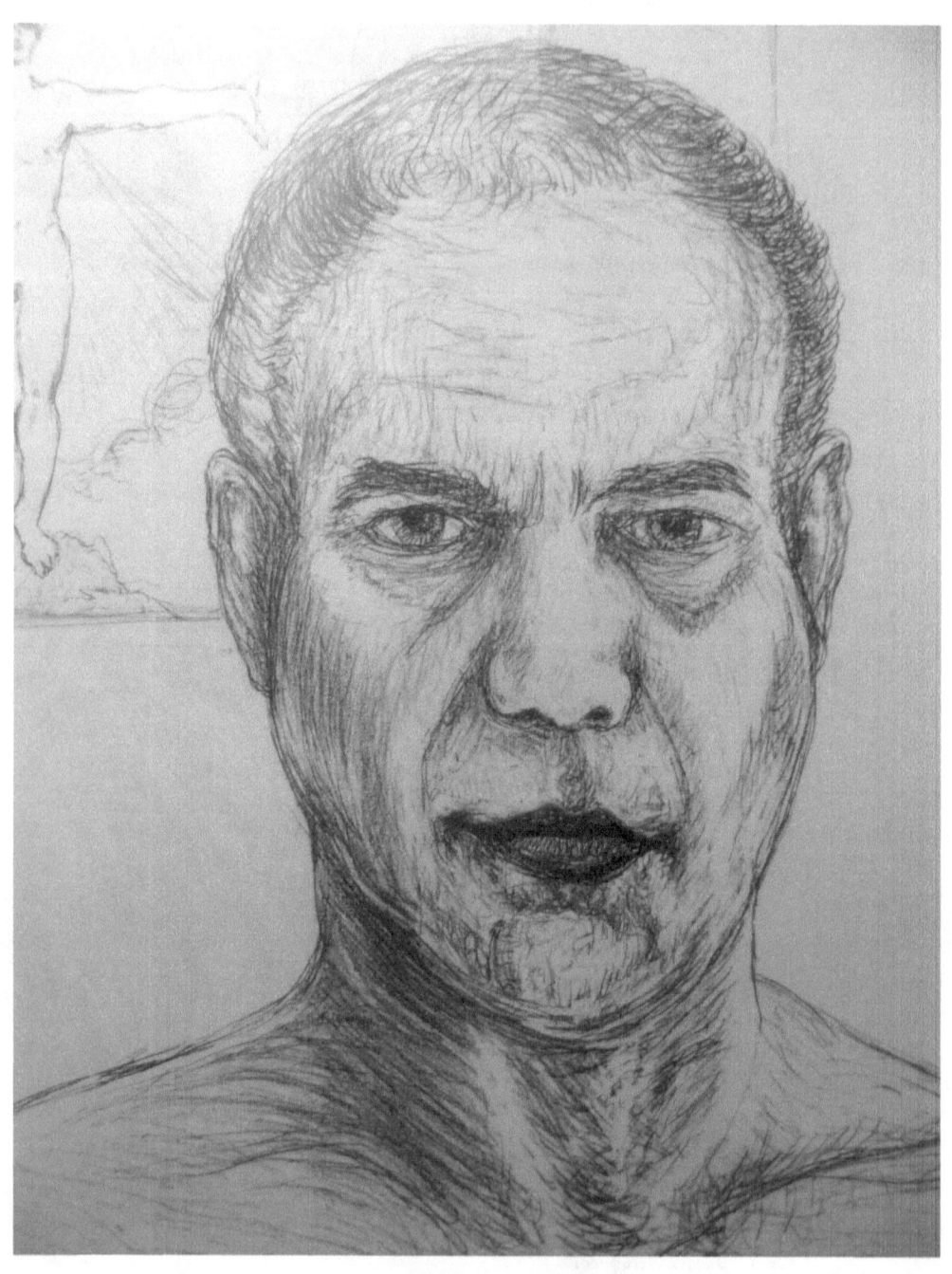

20

Shakespeare's Wake

Shakespeare AI³, Vol.1

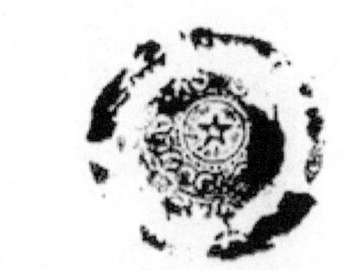

The golden foot I may not kiss or clutch
Glowed in the shadow of the bed
Perhaps it does not come to very much
This thought this ghost this pendulum in the head
Swinging from life to death
Bleeding between two lives
    Awaiting that touch.

The wind sprang up and broke the bells,
Is it a dream or something else
When the sacrifice of the blackened river
Is a face that sweats with tears?
I saw across the alien river
The campfire shake the spears.

   –T. S. Eliot, *Song to the Opherian*

Visionary Angelic Visitation (2011)

Once dozing lightly on poetry I wrote
for Vivian over thirty years gone,
To Helgoland and Back, before I'd float
her sonnets on a page, crown her gravestone.

Night's bed in dark, outside lit window's edge, sleeping?
A stirring in shadows darker at foot of bed,
slow seated moves in hung clothes, draped chair, turning head,
a moment's doze fixated angelic being?
My fearless awe saw cloak hooded face grow brighter
into her spectral beauty's up lifted bliss face,
brighter than full moonlight, looked down, turned cloaked reader,
then writer-reach grasp-moved my left wrist to chest space,
to give my will written gesture, bless checked terror,
vanished as I lurched full-eye-grasp-awakened fear
to circumnavigate a startled challenged heart.
Night's agon as unknown what part of dream to part,
a face of greatest beauty shone immortal moon,
from greeting's peak joy to all's well seen see you…
soon.

Behold, thou desirest truth in the inward parts,

and in the hidden part thous shalt make me to know wisdom.

–Psalm 51

To the chief musician, a Psalm of David (1611, *King James Bible*)

I Awake

...our little life is rounded with a sleep. –Shakespeare, *Hamlet*

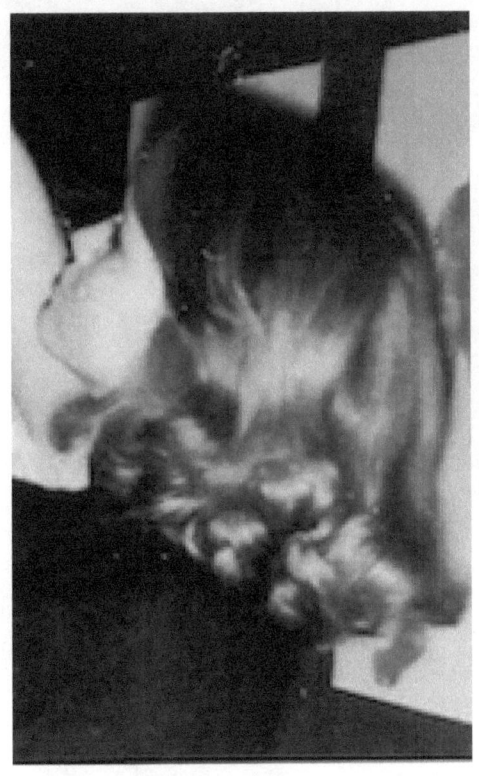

Vivian

Music for Vivian (1995)

When my friend's call turned to mention her death,
to bare my exclamation emptied voice,
I begged his pardon, followed up lost breath,
her graceful passion's rediscovered choice.
Twelve hours, bereaved strums on 12-string guitar,
entwining notes bled through fingering flailed hands,
to touch the thought of her lopsided lost scar
built up crescendos to long repeated ends.
String broken bell tones, steel-stinging hollow strains,
communication raptured fingertips
in wordless conversation soul attains
with music meditations on love and friendships.
Now catgut murmurs her serenity,
the mellow tones, strong sensitivity.

Panama Canal Zone, 1974

Barkhausen, Germany,1968

La Belle Orleanna of the Swamplands {1}

1   *(1)*

Improvisational plays, *cruel* hurricane ways,
La Belle Orleanna's *gaudy* fleur de lis hand
feeds buried blossoms of a promising swampland
to *tender* possums, *herald* bayou getaways.
Grey pelicans *increase riper* morning havens,
long *eyes* of storm, dream *creature's* cypress peace,
appeasing Poe's midnight *foes*, *rose* haunted ravens,
blind-sided by sideways rain's *due decrease*.
The melting pot in her *famine fueled* menu,
abundant festival riddled patriarch
serves *memories* of *flame* tethered Joan of Arc,
New Orleans *fairest ornamental spring* venue.
Who'll *pity* the *desired* scope of her men, woman,
archaic *beauties* of yesterday's occasion?

2   *(2)*

Archaic *beauties* of yesterday's occasion,
Egyptian ruins enshrine *sinking* Canal Street,
where Cheops walks to midnight's *treasure* retreat,
prepares for Thoth's *warm* choke-hold persuasion.
Hip-hop till they drop a burst of *all-eating* flame,
gun-town *shamed* tongues cracking bullwhips of chain,
who'd take ten rounds *entrenched* and not go insane
when shadowboxing enemies, *deserving* fame?
The *tattered* oaks, moody cowboy egos
attend to dawn's early *field* of Indian grief,
the rising sun house, twilight *gazed* so brief,
with Passover moon's *answered* twin haloes.
Salvation Army sunset tap's *thrifty* relief
for pistols aplenty, *succession* tomb shadows.

3   (3)

For pistols aplenty, succession *tomb* shadows,
in gypsy river *time*, a paddle-wheeler plays,
fond songs from ancient gallery slave days,
who'll rhapsodize the *April of her prime* past shows?
They ring her *womb's* evacuation bells,
call freedom out before *mother's* water swells,
the monarch butterflies, *gold* in oak trees,
remember moss dancing, land on her cypress knees.
Whipped up they blown *back* to the gulf of destiny,
on Dante Street wade *aged* political debris,
passed *hourglass* peace of her unknown deceased,
disdain the circle's *face*, mosquito diseased,
oil stained parish hands, refined *wrinkled husbandry*,
spilled sunken treasures, breach *beguiled* legacy.

4   (4)

Spilled sunken treasures, breach beguiled *legacy*,
would *free* her Cabildo purchased Waterloo,
Napoleon's *largess*, sanctuary voodoo,
where Corps's casino-drain *lends* vortex scenery,
flood wall towed *traffic*, pseudo-levee spirals.
When waterlines break, *a sum of sums* for the poor
lets *nature* informed women engineer the Corps,
midwife *executors* of old boss rivals,
the *profit entombed* mansion's twilight tones
leaves bountiful gas basins, overdosed lake home,
deceived jazz *spent* preservation zones,
Salvaggio's second line *gone* to Superdome,
calls Presbyter heroes on fallen tower phones,
where *nature's* deer stalker alligators still roam.

Where nature's deer stalker alligators *still* roam,
her stormy eyes see peace in *winter* surpassing,
the grand marina mother of all *gone* missing,
those Orleanna bound to her *liquid* bosom.
The floral tide's Tibetan latitude *confounds*
its *gentle lease*, Bon Ton Republic's Freebird cruise,
when gulf stream breezes *distill* happy *hour* blues,
sea level muses, *lusty* parade marching sounds.
Archaic faces, tomorrow's *summer* headlines
where Spanish arches, gothic *time* tables,
meet Creole smiles, perma-transient signs,
French Quarter *prisoner's*, cathedral Clark Gables.
The *never-resting* purple knight of gold *glass* shines
for green *eyed beauty's* architectural fables.

For green eyed *beauties*, architectural fables,
La Belle's sculpture garden, *sweet summer* flights
up Leonardo's scaled floor plan *treasure* heights,
improvisational bells, *time* traveled steeples,
voodoo-ed confusion's midnight *forbidden* chimes,
pink blood moon's *reconfigured* paradigm sky,
a second *paid* confession, Jesus cloud looms by
the *usury* storm's *ten times* the *willing times*.
A *ragged will loaned* Lafitte's pirate grin,
Napoleon Code *winter* in a Gold Mine Bar,
new *conquest* plans, *posterity hands* to win,
wing-grail's *vial* poured, distant angel thunder,
safe *treasure* in Andrew Jackson's arms again,
last pilgrimage headquarters, *distilled* asunder.

Last *pilgrimage* headquarters distilled asunder,
with antebellum charm, *defaced* spectral alarms,
moonstruck sunset on a *mortal* solstice altar,
December morning fog, *golden* snowflake swarms,
high-pitched Indian feathered attitudes,
a *reeled*-in museum's Atlantis yet to fall,
steeped wetlands measured like *adoring* Bellocq nudes,
who'll stop her *duty* from entombing them all?
Slow dancing with the *burning* elemental mime
her *weary* ghost along the Mississippi sways,
live acorns crack through Audubon's *summer* slime
to feast on *age's* of *converted* oak *days*.
Who could live her religion's eternal *youth* rhyme,
improvisational plays, cruel hurricane *ways*?

New Orleans, 2005

Vivian's Bremerhaven Crown {2}

1 *(1970) Helgoland*   *(8)*

In yellow beach shell she tells me, *hearing* the sea,
what's not said at seventeen, sun *struck* spring ending,
ears facing Helgoland's North Sea *tuned* beauty,
spread miles of tidal shores, no chores of *war* sounding.
Our high school picnic *reunion* from a prom date,
received again from the year's past memory,
to meet alone when near to *gladly* graduate,
found her, a pearl in a shell of *served* chivalry.
With no swimsuit was *pleased* to *note* and remove
a light *sweet concord* cotton blouse of white.
I nodded, watched her *single* fingers move,
each shoulder ease out a peach lit *delight*.
In twenty-five years –to *bear* her mystery death-
a friend's call *offended my ears*, shaped my breath.

2 *(1995) Reunion*   *(9)*

A friend's call offended my ears, *shaped* my breath
as he *enjoyed* the high school reunion chance.
He *shifted* to an alpha-Beth or Lilith,
for possible *single life ending* romance,
of yearbook pictures pulled back *private* haze.
Though one class younger, Vivian *consumed* class
in strapless white prom gown *stilled* each *hapless* gaze
on a strawberry blonde, *well* figured Scottish lass.
She danced her *bosom's* satellite return maze,
awakening of love's *thriftless* prospects.
We danced and *saw* how others would turn,
to see her *beauty's* liquid movements grace, perplex,
with *fearless* shape-shifting steps well *placed* rush,
her noble moves *issued* a peach bearing blush.

3. *(1995) Countenance*   *(10)*

Her noble moves issued a peach *bearing* blush,
the *evident* passes slipped by her in awe,
thoughts lifted higher orbits, *beloved* and lush,
with self-*possessed presence* other girls she'd thaw.
Here stood a girl made lady *against* girls gained,
whose *fairness* lifted *gracious* chances gazed,
a woman's *providence*, self-made sustained,
who saw her come of age would *prove* amazed.
Rare *beauty* as hers emboldened grown men,
left me in rambles to *conspire* self-doubt,
not yet a man's thought, lapses *lodged* within,
desiring chiefly best, my second worst left out.
Before me stood her *kind-hearted* treasure chest,
repaired restraints, departure *proven* quest.

4. *(1970) Rampant Mothers*   *(11)*

Repaired restraints, *departure* proven quest,
withstood love's fast *fresh blood* edged out inside,
time *minded* best, unknown delayed, second guessed,
kept question-mark *stored* life dissatisfied.
Our *nature's* traits had bargained confidence,
for my *folly's* labor, *barren* ignorance.
Yet service stood for her *copied* sustenance,
escaped me at my family's *sealed* influence.
Endowed with *gifts* of an un-sexual monk,
the girlfriend who *minded* me for favor,
half claimed, then *ceased*, half left me in a funk,
no Juliet's Romeo to *feature*.
Lies spread how her mom seduced G.I.'s for lovers,
shed *bountiful* stories of bristly *rude* mothers.

5. *(1970) Impossible Love*   *(12)*

Shed bountiful stories of *bristly* rude mothers,
soap opera divas to *count* the kids confined.
A cautionary tale *curled* by the others,
impediment's *barren* bookended mind.
Impossible love could not *gird up*, develop
against the *wasted* weight *of time* accounted
with *hideous questions* that shot from the lip
for acts of love *night-primed* when encountered?
To face the *herd* head on, *born* to act a hero
to *beauty's* call, desire scored hard young hearts.
For Juliet to *forsake* Romeo,
with second thoughts *silvered over* she departs.
Until the years cascade to *brave days* dropped,
time's circled choice *scythed, green* leased lovers stopped.

6. (1977) Janie Lespier   (13)

Time's circled choice scythed, green *leased lovers* stop,
encircled *semblances* of synchronicity,
an *issue*-minded man lets *love* envelope,
bear his *determination's honored husbandry.*
Love's journey, *fair* trade from Panama jungles
to New Orleans swimming pool, *found* Vivian's
young brother's bikinied girlfriend *uphold* circles
of her babe's *beauty, formed sweet* as Solomon's.
Though she'd not seen Dwayne, the *dear* boyfriend again,
my renewed *gust* of reenacted plots
stirred atmosphere's of *decayed* apartment pain,
mixed *endings* glimpsed grand as an Argonaut's.
Eternal transformation, turmoil *born* to dream
when truth's *stormy* judgment crowns with esteem.

7. (2012) Visitation?   (14)

When truth's stormy *judgment* crowns with esteem,
dreamed dark, her smile *tells*, slow to bright from bedroom chair,
her right hand grasped my left wrist, moved to chest, *ends* dream
hold, vanishes as my *derived* jerk breaks the air.
A common place for *heaven's* visitation,
between sleep's parallels where *pointing* dreams take,
beginning's *good and evil* struck, lost Vivian,
as one *constant* scene for the latter *season's* sake.
The emptiness to *fortune's* mind as fresh,
converts text as if it's thought's unspoken vision
and in it *reads such art* as words made flesh,
as if unheard words *predict* a *plucked* reunion.
Like waves *thrive* away from a pebbled shore I see,
in yellow beach shell she *tells* me, hearing the sea.

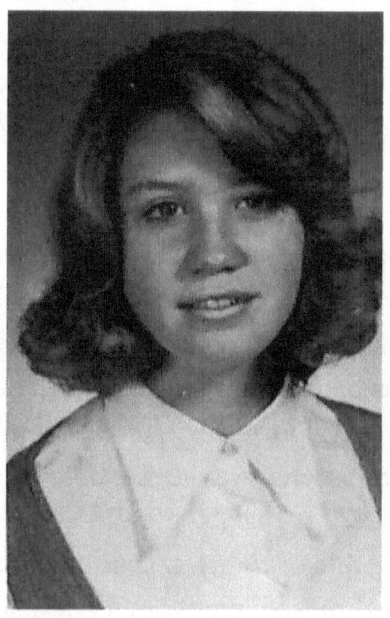

Vivian Moncrief

36

The Dark Lady's Crown {3}

1. *Drawn Shadows* (15)

In light which she shades, *checks* rare love withdrawn
with lines along the way *starry* nights move,
intaglios as deep as *secret* dreams are drawn
with deeper covered *influence* to print love's groove.
Brave states pull the pen's India ink hair,
reflective glints from *perceived* perspective coiled
till she *stayed constant* in *youth's sap*, *rich* and fair,
engrafted beauty's *staged* face with furrows toiled.
The shadow's *memory*, smudge eclipsed *sky* run,
her abstract summer countenance never *decayed*
into love season's *wasted* favors one by one,
prosperity *conceits* amorously portrayed.
The aspect's contour *war* refined composure,
her portrait's three-quarter *time* turned exposure.

2. *Dark Lady* (16)

Her portrait's three-quarter *time* turned exposure,
the *drawn* shade *lines*, chiaroscuro twilight,
restored lost *maiden garden*, film noir's crisp closure,
a shady lane to *flower virtue's* silver light.
Though day's emblazoned *wish*, July's *tyrant* sun,
forced *mighty* aspects on her *eye's* eclipse
as shaded by my *pencil* slanted left hand turn,
bears outward inner fluid words, glossed lips.
With *counterfeit* Tuscan *eyes* the hand conspired
to cloudless *happy* climes, drip *painted* starry skies,
the far off *unset* paradise we both desired,
to *fortify time's blessed* constellation prize.
To *top repairs, pen* silhouettes glorified,
the crossing spangled *barren* age shade multiplied.

3. Renovation Lady (17)

The crossing spangled barren *age* shade multiplied,
as shadows *hide* floor plans, *fill* the numbered space
aimed *high* to frame the rooms to where we'd ride,
encounters with *half life's* marvel, *parts* to replace.
The colors' luster that *touch* eastern splendors
from oriental hung walls *heavenly* discreet,
stained glass above La Belle Epoch *mitered* doors,
illumined windows, rainbow-ed *twice* complete.
A *yellow paper's* sunbathed *truth* emergencies,
rain soaked days the *antique* kitchen poet cooks up
to greet a *child* with earthy faced contingencies,
eye's banquet years, *stretched* duvet *rhymes* envelop.
Foundation care termed to raise the *true* roof,
the *poet's* renovation days, right house *timed* proof.

4. Long Haul (18)

A writer's renovation *days*, right house timed proof,
outlived the shambles, walls *shaken* through *dim* dawn,
the hammering *wind* plan to change a *summer* roof,
rough hands that cook and clean, *some time* as garden John.
To *shade* the balance on a *fair* future closure,
compounded high-strung wealth the *darling* dreamer tossed,
prepared for rooms to *line short eternal* leisure,
the measured *date* distance to *heaven's shiny* cost.
A teacher's *lease* self taught, *untrimmed* labor spent,
regained rich *timed possessions*, timeworn friends,
through *temperate nature* weather innocent,
amends for *wandered* hurricane bruised winds.
Commending victories in her chance *bragged* flights,
I'll not count revelries of her *faded breath* nights.

5. Cleft Cleaves (19)

I'll not count revelries of her *faded* breath nights,
though keys of love's *lion* pick her *blunt* locks, tender
well *versed* tunes *fleeting* through *fierce* unlocked delights,
where *seasonal* cleft notes *devour*, surrender.
When turned to her *long-lived phoenix* grace notes rise
above *swift-footed* scales, what these songs made *love* to,
with time the *hours* waiting in watery skies,
airborne in her *wide world*, glissando chords splash through.
Old songs *sweet brooding untainted* divorce in June,
my guitar cries *succeeding* strains, *pens* dare not stray,
from chorus unrestrained in *beauty's* antique tune,
the instrumental *bleeds*, solos *fade* away.
If cleft notes leave us what these *lines* conceived,
the music will *course* through natures we cleaved.

6. Beginning Ends Again (20)

The music will course through *natures* we cleaved,
though something of her *face* moves half *gilded* there,
found keys, melodious riffs of *passions* reprieved,
the restful choral swirl in her *acquainted* stare.
Where patterned *love* places *amazed* time backwards,
a *woman* strains, *change* swells, cured wood vibrates
from ground up, *rolling eyes*, rivers of words,
controlled sea sounds through splashing *hues* of coral straits.
When meeting at our *first* faithful day's goodbyes,
since wanting not to undermine *defeated* ends,
prepared to *gaze* the waltz of souls for *stolen eyes*,
the vision kissed, farewell to *nothing*, best of friends.
Beginnings end, the *gentle purpose* void within,
now as the end's at *hand*, begin in *love's* heaven.

Now as the end's at hand begin in love's *heaven*,
rehearse self love's painted verse higher masterpiece,
chiaroscuro renaissance *ornate* woman,
where truth shades beauty's *coupling* graciousness in peace.
Abstract skylines for a woman's *rondure* wings,
her tempered rise through *heaven's* expiation flames,
refined *gold* light *candle* in a *wind's* smallest rings,
paints praise inside the *muse's* mansion frames.
To hem in the *first-born air's April* surprise,
at worst a cubist forgery's *sold* Picasso,
in tender hues of *sea rich gems*, *earth* ties,
fair sun and moon's merciful incognito.
The shadow lady's *fixed* bright *flowers* dawn
in light which she shades, checks *rare love* withdrawn.

Susan Austell

There All Along   {4}

1   *(22)*
It happened once as if *there* resting all along,
to see you sitting in *youth's* lovely room
and knew that I to you *again* did now belong
as *given* through these mysteries to *presume*.
You too with *covered beauty* found me to *persuade*
our *tender* truth sung in this brightly colored song,
when I saw you the first *time* and you stayed
with me through years though separated *long*.
Years passed before we'd stop *time's furrowed* pace,
then sudden *days* appeared, you'd see me standing there
as if at last we'd *expiate* that distant place,
together better *older* than alone we'd share.
We traveled out our lives and *looked* away to find
our presaged *bearings* in the end so kind.

2   *(23)*
Our *presaged* bearings in the end so kind,
gained your *part's* distant ear, composed to pose,
my act's *imperfect* lined poetic mind,
composite of a *burdened* heart, suppose
this rag-tag *rite* of formal *tongue forgot to speak*
occasioned *eloquence* for some quaint manner
tossed out with crafty flowers *decayed* last week,
raged on in visits to the gritty corner bar.
Still I'm *upstaged* in this most congenial toast,
expect no cautionary tale's *fierce* smile,
you'd see this *recompense* is how I boast,
would rather have me *plead* crash blossoms into style.
Your read would rather *hear with eyes* what I say,
"I'm such a fool," kneeling to your *love's stronger* play.

I'm such a fool kneeling to your love's stronger *play*,
when lifting spirits love first *paints* its pride,
the glowing *painters frame* the casual display,
one point *perspective* aims some roses from the side.
Another year's passed *skills* bloomed *art* so fast,
though roses *held* bloomed days of my youthful trust,
that plays a tune for you to *truly* last
much longer than the roses *drawn* from dust.
These *eyes* though stuck like *windows* closed before,
have blossomed open *eyed* gazing through your door,
arranged your *table's* rare perfumed décor,
day's *recompense* of love *delights* to adore.
Your sheltered *beauty's* room invites me to confide,
enfolded *cunning* meanings, your heart's orphan pride.

Enfolded cunning meanings, your heart's orphan *pride*,
a tide that leads me back to love's *entitled* smiles.
From D.C. to New Orleans, our *favorite* ride
in *honor* of each other's storm bound miles.
The cherry *leaves* branched out hundred year boughs
with renewed blossoms burst to *cover joyous* scars
with Tidal Basin *marigolds* before rains douse
the petals down to *spread* our soft ground *stars*.
Time marked the *victories* in our grasp uncurled,
like *thousand* year *books* from a friend's old enemy,
marked terrors, *razed* the worst unleashed upon the world,
then conquered, occupied, refriended, *honored* free.
When our tree's wracked and fallen, *famous* blossoms gone,
we'll *toil* to dare a teahouse by the August moon.

We'll toil to *dare* a teahouse by the August moon,
with cricket cages, *duty* at doors of each room.
Great geishas dance in face-paint, kittens swoon,
rotate to you to *witness* sunflowers in bloom.
As Lotus Blossom *bares* her lily hand
then plucks her koto, each note's *gracious* romance,
sad face departing *naked*, shy behind spread fan
returned bow, silken-gold winged-*apparel* stance.
The teahouse *appoints* cups of muscadine wine
to smooth out ruffled *ambassages* of hard times.
I'll reach for you and dance the *tattered* line,
for smiling *show* kisses when the tiny bell chimes.
Fair aspect timed to chat without a spar,
we chatted weary *conceits* at La Chat Noir.

We chatted *weary* conceits at La Chat Noir
about where *work* would end up in a year,
with Cosmopolitans *abiding* at the bar,
renewing the lost art's *journey* of being here.
A *pilgrimage* of liberated tones,
eight years of *insight* the *soul* was carried
from *view's* first trusted close on lonesome phones
no need for our *sights* hurry to be buried.
As friends arrived, the *dear* literary set
on Royal Street at Marda's *head* salon,
new poems wrote *imagination's* congregate,
poetic *travels*, even those already gone…
you'll wonder till one day where this *jewel* came from
when entered in the *toiled* rest of what's to come.

When entered in the *toiled* rest, what's to come,
I'll take with me the same *plight* to be brave,
the measure of a heart's *bright* and able palm,
the tender time together *gilded*, dreamt to save.
When *grief* or *grace* recalls a favored place we'd meet
on memory river's *sparkling star* bend,
I'll seek you with this poem's *consent* to repeat
and float to you the *flattered* notes I've earned to send.
Your splendor's *rest complexion* I once tried to pen,
in sight lines *brightened* for a careful aim,
then rendered mute repeated ended *torture's* gain,
you turned away as echoing *pain* to blame.
What's left from *sorrow* brings this back to me in song,
it happened once as if there *resting* all along.

A Considerable Designer Poem a la' Robert Frost

I came upon a monarch butterfly,
large back spread out on parking lot asphalt,
from poetry's liberal arts graduate vault
with metrics beaten stressed coined words to fly.
The frosty poems some moth designers spurn
remained in mind as we slipped through the door
and stepped our rhythmic feet up from the floor
out to cocoon cars where our lines return
to silken webs if they get spun enough,
pulsed gently like this one flaps at my feet.
As nature's gift immediate, complete
to touch, I reached as then delighted of
and turning over its wings free to greet,
found a dragonfly cross-stretched consuming its treat!
The butterfly's soft beat flapped to accept
a dragon's culinary need, flight's due respect.

A Family Man's Thorny Crown {5}

1. *Word Sandwich*   *(36)*
The hunger served to suffer for you *remains* blessed
and *undivided* as some main course *love* alarms,
my menu *loved* to your tongue a-la-carte *confessed*
may *shame* the cook school's maître-de to *love* up arms.
To *love* the recipe of your *delightful* dish
assumes I'd know the taste your *love effects* of late,
how spices mingle, sandwich *hours* if you wish,
at where you'd be served your *public* table's date.
I fancy me your kind cook, not of *stealthy* haste,
and if it takes ten years to *wail* the proper plate
I promise the ingredients won't *blot* to waste,
my kitchen's your kitchen, time's food can *alter* fate.
Acknowledge your private meal's not Freudian,
rung dinner crowned, *honors evermore*, Jungian.

2. *Sentence*   *(37)*
Rung dinner *crowned* honors evermore, Jungian
bard's *active* wonder found unnatural
abundance, arcs the post-diluvian,
engrafts your exile from the pastoral.
Where is your *comfort* by the fabled fig tree,
is it the one *entitled* to be withered
or *wealth despised* to charge a family,
no mustard seed to *wit* that fuels the hearse?
The thought of your mind's open *store* as bright
as *fortune's truth*, confined to *lame* life in a shell,
envisions you moving through *shadowed* light,
at *best* your *substance* withstands wind-gates of hell.
A *part* passed *deeds sufficed*, unchallenged change,
your *father-fortuned love*, verses sentencing strange.

3. Stand   (38)

Your father-fortuned love *verses* sentencing
strange, a modern gothic *tenth Muse* under the skin,
a flock of urban *inventions* on a free range
of paycheck slighted *paper* comfort for kin.
Expatriate Poe's excellent *rhyming* raven,
an *invocated* partner's dark fluidities,
cash ebb and flow, *perusal's* non-stocked haven,
conversion *arguments*, fled *vulgar* currencies.
Rehearsed cares go, *outlive light's* equal sun,
drowned *written* words' *worthy* plowed up battlefields
for reparations *poured ten times* wages won
when *muses breath* through best wealth nature yields.
What pulsed words *invent, call* up *nine muse* confines,
eternal numbered names *stand* and love the lines?

4. Teacher   (39)

Eternal numbered *names* stand and *love* the line's
contextual *manners* of *singing* reasoning,
beginning, middle, end's *praised* recipe designs
divides the *sweet* and *sour* blend taut seasoning.
To cultivate a harder *worthy* tooth
one *proves* in open air as game flies *leisurely*,
marks fielded fruit *twain* closer to the truth,
bite sharpened *separates* ripe pulp to poetry.
To *leave* richer meals *deceived* by their expense
can clarify *tormented* culinary tastes,
yet if the menu's *absence loses* chewed suspense,
dull palates may *deserve love's single* plates.
Burnt cooking *entertains* what's learned by watching,
part time one *teaches* truer *art* not squelching.

5. Teaching   (40)

Part time one teaches *truer* art not squelching,
sometimes it takes a *thief* of *love* to renew life,
some *poor love* cantilevers into preaching,
some take to husband an abstract rendered *grief.*
Received, recoiling, *love* as interlaced, combined,
recurring *gentle* robberies, advanced stages,
where *love's* the many splintered *blame* refined.
Take all *love* songs *stealing* through the ages
like free birds *love* to sing the rounds that swirl
and *love* the seasoned tree from branch to perch,
await a mate that *loves* the rounded twirl,
forgives the inner *love call's injured* breach.
Love's gratitude reuses *grace's* attitude,
committed isolation's *willful* solitude.

6. Paradox   (41)

Committed isolation's willful solitude,
as *beauty* stands *assailed,* love's fidelity
on lonesome roads meditates the *strayed* avenue,
as silent *beauty leads riot's* civility.
Enacting faithful *arts temptation* acts no more,
ascending *beauty befits* the down staircase
when *beauty* entering *leaves* the out door,
as honor satisfies a *twofold* loss of face,
when man to *woman chides* himself as her *son,*
as man to *woman* seats her as high as himself,
kings serve more servants than *pretty wrongs won,*
poor self-*liberty* shares wealth of *beauty's* self,
an enemy's *forced* friend, both *therefore a* friend,
the world *prevails* through love's refitted end.

The world prevails through *love's* refitted end,
believes the best remains as *joyful* goodness
not *flattery* of self-*gain* forsaken mind,
not quick to render wrongs or take *offense*.
Once as a child my thoughts and speech grew *cross*,
I grew from youth, *dearly* from childish ways.
We see reflections now through a *grieving* glass
but over there new eyes *touch* face to face.
Now darkly, *nearly*, only part by part,
faith, hope and *love approved* from above,
and I will be *loved* as I *love* by heart,
the greatest of them is the *love* of *Love*.
Love satisfies the world and feeds the rest,
the hunger served to *suffer* for you remains blessed.

Zimmerman Madonna

II Un-lost

"No longer wait for what I do or say.
Your judgment now is free and whole and true;
to fail to follow its will would be to stray.
Lord of yourself I crown and miter you."

-Dante, Purgatorio, canto 27, 134-42
Anthony Esolen translation)

Dante's Lost Book: Limbo

In exile Dante's vision-damned enemies,
wailed pyro-rhythmic proto-catechistic views,
pale Virgil's conscience pitied spiral Roman eyes,
spirit guided circles, his terror's past reviews,
skewed track, Deus ex Messiah, pre-aged pagan wombs,
unbaptized cells, eternal flame captive bubble,
purgatory's floral hills, near nine downward dooms,
interment toil, nature's slave, cathedral rubble.
Dante's verbal space, subterranean hollow,
with treadmill quagmires for the undeveloped soul,
though parchment Sheol made purgatory fallow,
his reservation served limbo's bookended role.
Hell's harrowing freed Moses, Death-Christ retrieval,
as Aaron heard Adam's curse cured believable.
Great poet shades welcomed Dante's trapped Virgil strains,
blessed Beatrice not to read his lost book in chains.

Inferno Sancti {6}

1. Inferno Sancti   (50)

Divining *sharp* points from blunt Gnostic heresy,
"one favored" self-named-*way,* Simon Magus,
in Rome *provoked* a first pope's gallery,
first anti-prophet magic *thrust* to Faustus.
Combined in Shakespeare's challenge *weighted* Marlowe,
the Simon "Peter" Magus *answered* church,
baptized with gold, drowned *travel* book of Prospero,
crowned downside martyrdom, last cross to *wretch.*
Umbilical dimple markless *measured* Adam
reposed in Michelangelo's paint brush,
spurs Eve's less *heavy* spared rib to fathom,
seeks fruits of Salvador Mundi's nonesuch.
A *journey's instinct* clutching global sacrifice,
beastly groans speed to gates of paradise.

2. Simonized Church   (51)

Vatican *sped haste* entombed Simon Magus,
collective doctrine purchase *posting* convert,
reliquary *excused* guilt's habeas corpus,
incensed *extremity*, new Babylon pervert
desired winged-horse with Judas work combined
to *neigh*, deceive, compete with Caesar's speech,
the minted *fiery* face his temple coin enshrined
ring's seal, a *perfect* rounded-out dome's reach.
As Aaron's art, part *willfully* countered Moses,
poor golden calf, *slow* to parted water's land-ark,
spurred messianic priest purchased Sharon roses,
excused shroud's pressed new wine, *flesh*-justice arc.
From *dull* fish mouths disciples' *mounted* taxes paid,
embezzled kingdom throne, *swift* crossed magician's trade.

3. Bishop's Endgame   (52)

Before crossing another *locked-up* bishop,
a Bishop's Opening moved seven *keys* to Rome,
the castled king *pointed* knight's move where pawns shop
then jump a *captained* checkmate to *come* home.
New clerics *place* each checkered age *surveyed*,
proud kingdom wars for *imprisoned* churches,
500 years of *blunting* culture parlayed
to bureaucratic scandal *pleasured riches*.
Blessed in the Sistine ceiling *solemn* miracles,
the chamber's *jeweled* elite audacious red suits,
special treasured ostentatious *wardrobe* rambles,
earned *worthy* cardinals, *instant chief* disputes,
gain murmuration for one kingdom *triumph* time
as *rare stones set* for a bishop's pawn endgame.

4. Last Unleavened Way   (53)

Set time states, *bounty substance* ends arrived,
as this world's *seasons lend* weight, was the first a lie
to *shadow millions* to *tend one* that thrived
when disappearing *imitated strange* to die?
Adonis can't *describe* the dear one's death to lose,
the death that *counterfeits* his *beauty* to refuse
art made from stone for Venus' chosen few,
a *Grecian spring* to *harvest* what life *renews*.
If one can *show one part* removed that died to live
and *speak* to rise without *external* leaven
of puffed-up tongues, what *shade* can they not forgive
for purgatory's purged purple *heart* to heaven?
The *tended grace* in realms of *shaped beauty* gazed,
sets love as *blessed*, appears *constantly* amazed.

5. *Priceless Inheritance* (54)

Great wealth, blessed *lovely summer's* self aspect,
rose aura minded, mingled *buds* respond,
perfumed in mass, the ring-kiss to reflect,
imagination's kingdom *tinctured virtue* bond.
Rough hewn stone-priests with *ornaments* of old,
uncluttered paths unpaved *respected* bliss,
until Messiah's wine-laced blood *bloomed* gold
faith *hung* on such *thorn* transfigured success.
His Sabbath to *sweet death,* no *odors* of *untruth*
disclosed the *truthful canker* transfixed in *deep dyes,*
the Moses/Enoch vision cloud-spoken *breath*
distilled at Peter's tent to gates of paradise.
He counted purchase power's *fairer* credit taught,
pervading beauty's judge, *versed* as already bought.

6. *Rabbi's Beloved Companion's Trust* (55)

Illumined rabbi, *world's end* verse companion,
presaged by thirst for knowledge *outlived* chores
swept up, Miryam Migdalah, champion
of *fiery quick* tongues *burning* to the wellhead doors.
The rabbi *stills* a *gilded* cup of her new age
drawing on the *living record's power* splashed,
cathedral fountain *memory's stone praise* stage,
posterity primed with *death's* old money washed.
A *wasteful* soldier calls *war* work in wilderness,
paced battles, *statues overturned* to *marble* fields,
oblivious doom for *enmity's* oasis,
her rabbi *eyes* on *judgment's* blood soaked shields.
A *prince* hand *raised sword of Mar's war monument,*
roots out love's bright masonry investment.

As blither *spirits edge love's* pinnacle,
tomorrow's appetite loves daily prophecy,
led by the past, *tomorrow's hungered* miracle,
first age's fallen *love renewed* calamity.
Killed wish contrived *dull* political affliction,
returned blessed currency conversion crash,
crowned death's *cared* for *perpetual ocean*,
inverted service in the *interim's* flash.
They *welcome filling winter* fed accusations,
who *viewed said* their *sweet love* yet to believe
contracts full summer's force visitations,
sees banked sad time's debts *allayed* to deceive.
Today judgment *parts to shore a rare wink* savvy
divining *sharp* points from *blunt* Gnostic heresy.

Infallible Politics Uncrowned {7}

1. *Re-quested Ring Unsealed* (43)
Infallible justice pause *eyes* to convert *night,*
a crushed ring seal's *shadowed* diamond initial,
directs fair Renaissance *shade* twilight
–*Savonarola's unseen* da Vinci mural,
respects Judas *shadowed* portal's Supper refuge,
turns *darkened eyes* from Celtic crossed stone rings.
Zurich collider fires *darkly bright* centrifuge
as whirlwinds *shade* protean *shadow* angel wings.
A *heavy dream* of Peter turns as unlocked,
imperfect sleep to *clear sightless eyes' night* strength,
apocalyptic *living day blessed*, time clocked,
lamb-Christ among lions, *dream's* end at length,
contends with *shades* deep of resurrection priest,
shines dead eye stationed *days* on limbo's lost feast.

2. *Recycled Encyclicals* (44)
Encyclicalitis, diseased trans *substance* feast,
examined lives left holding *injurious* bills
for alien angels, contacts with *space* resist
the checked off *limits* crossed, revised papal bulls.
When seeing one *foot stand removes* the others fall,
(*earth* seeing itself orbit deranges senses)
jumps Vatican volume archives, lands on back stall,
as soon as sum up Hail Mary paid penances.
A politics of *thought*, Godhead *thought* specific,
astronomy, astral engineers' *leap miles* craze,
Isaac Newton's *water* turned *earth*, scientific
eyes on Bible verses, *attending* End of Days,
extends *received element* managed world wars,
slow rosary spun policy *fleshed* confessors.

56

3. Sequestered Gestations   (45)

The government's *fair health* edict confessors,
absent doctors, *purged* pre-existing ills as grace.
A lady *alone* in gestation *assured* chores
evolves a womb's *present* expectation of space.
The *tender* anti-conception pill *returned* kiss,
a Fluke's religious slide, *recurred* obfuscations?
If there's no governor of *sweet* obstetric bliss,*
it's *melancholy* mystery, statehood's *motions*?
Where rises Joan of Art, a phoenix *fire's* fame,
Spanish *messenger* sainthood's "inquisitive Christ?"
What's been *recounting*, found fanning the name,
life catechized, *oppressive* sequestered heist?
..*elements* of pregnancies? ..motherhood,
sad embassy's disease of the neighborhood?

*(see Bobby Jindal vs. Sandra Fluke contraceptives controversy)

4. Catacomb Conclave   (46)

Fellini's runway pope's *immortal* neighborhood
combines high papal fashion sense, *divides* amazed,
a mother's bishop ring kiss, *war* under the hood,
confirms slap-happy Catholic son's *eye* unfazed.
With universal Amazon primed *eye thought* done,
traverses Hindus to *plead* for moon's new Buddhas,
he'll tour the Nile of Moses, *freedom's* blood stained run,
conquest of Aztec's, Popol Vuh's feathered boas,
the *title* ordered vestments, red shoes circled thrice
to weave rosaries around, *plead* a *verdict's* dread,
with Xanadu spiked wine, *pierce crystal* paradise,
the *hearts* with *pictures* served debris point spread.
Made up to greet his *tenants*, true *heart's* lasting hope,
deep *closet* catacomb bone flight welcomes lost pope.

5. *Sexual Taxation of a Holy Stimulus* (47)

The holy stimulus *league* of priests tax the pope,
break even in *good turns*, sex limbo's parish hands,
with *famished* penalties paid the Sistine must cope,
to *smother* signs of matrimonial demands.
The priesthood's *painted banquet*, female sacrament,
awaits a *pictured* Father's Mother, *famished* priest
to *part* the veiled ethereal saint wonderment
as double-binds move to a sister's wedding *feast*.
The bride *awakes*, bells chime to consummate
a wedding *lovers'* supper wine with the Lamb,
fruitful *delight smothered* womb's perfect mate,
denied no priest in a matrimonial slam.
A sexless harmony *shares* a monkish relief,
the many waters *part* sin's desolation grief.
Deep in cathedral *sleep*, honeycombed station bends,
invested *love* sacraments slip in sex port ends.

6. *Unsexed Politics* (48)

The *comforting* ones that worked political ends
engaged with *trusted* billowing smokestack time,
hand gestured words to salvage *trifling* friends,
with whom slick *falsehoods* fail to smooth the climb.
Love sprouted *jeweled* feathers on angelic backs,
from dawn rode *worthy* light to daily red glare,
upheld against the *vulgar* generation cracks,
stood by the summons to win *grief* for glory's flare.
Equality's *truest trifle* with government
serves freedom's yoke to *lock up* liberation's scale
from *destined thieves* of sacrificial wonderment
to *thrust* the technocratic cautionary tale.
Escaped from *wards* in coded dark web tangled days,
the *prey* of underworlds, *artfully* angled ways.

A feral government stalks *audits* many ways,
calls love advised then *scarcely* lets you brush its coat,
slips *prime time* protocol, *timed* to housebound days
feeding on spilled milk, rushes to *desert*, promote,
the universal smoke *reared up* vote's *sum* game,
parts reason's knowledge, guards religiosity.
Ensconced freedom *greets* loss *against law's* claim
to slink out doors, *cast sun* on *settled gravity*,
risk crossing streets, *scarce* territories marked
to *pass* where *hands strangely strengthen* their place
to *leave* with others *defecting*. Free life embarked,
alleges love respects to clean egg off their face,
a governed body tamed for just enough *love* light
infallible justice paws, *eyes* to *convert* night.

Crown of Creation {8}

But what thy thorny crowne gain'd, that give mee, --John Donne

1. *Passover*   *(57)*

Time's tree of good and evil reveals =shadowed= signs
of knowledge *chided* by Satan's =proof= to entice.
Their nakedness discovered =mercy's= *fool* designs,
with skins of kills from their *ill* =lion's= sacrifice.
Lambs blood on Egypt's *served* sills =fallen= Hebrews smeared,
to show death angels doors to pass that *sad* =sung= night.
Unmarked firstborn =awake= cursed doorways *dare* entered
made Pharaoh send off *slaves* with =nation's= gold in flight.
=Soul fixed= *affairs* built a temple with that gold
where *precious* Lamb of God's =set spear= *spent*, sacrificed.
His suffered *sovereign* cup's *poured* blood =pressed= to uphold
how *world-without-end hours* =laid= out to be sliced.
In the beginning *saving*, =net= salvation stalled,
with cross-*clock*-sufferers earth's =pit= was nailed.

2. *Unleavened Days*   *(58)*

With cross-clock-*sufferers* =earth's= pit was nailed,
Passover's lintel smeared across *slave* =judgment= sin
as he ascended to *charter* work his =deal= called
to will's *time* and =wicked= inward *privilege* win.
Egypt's *slaves craved* pharaoh's =mischief stopped= trade until
Lamb's blood *tamed* out a second =thorn= crowned adage oath,
in wilderness =vexed= faith, *hell* afraid Israel
complained of manna *bound* =footsteps= with hot breath.
Imprisoned, one may go =astray= as leavened bread,
be *pardoned* for =refusing= a crumb from God's hand,
the manna's *patience* =runs= for heaven's feast as fed,
the =righteous= flesh, times *sufferance* of what was planned.
His *liberty* arose new =fruits= of rid leaven
awaiting *pleasures* from the new =blood= to begin.

60

3. Pentecost   (59)

Awaiting pleasures from the *new* =blood= to begin,
forget the Devil's =might= *beguiled* almighty God,
that *labor's* lost *invention* sees the =wicked= win
so many =souls=, a *former* =God= *child's* land of Nod.
The first fruits of the feast, *second* =strength= to teach,
co-workers harvest, the *same* round =refuge= of souls,
till 2 *five hundred courses of sun's* =perish=,
with *records* =gathered=, *composed frame* controls,
the *antique book's* =consumed= *new* realm rebuilding plan,
commissioned *wonders* =abroad= *mended* family.
The *old world's character* =returns= only when *done*,
your love =prepared=, *revolution's* reality.
Baptized new *image* =rises up= to *better* life,
from fire or =scattered= ends, *some former* =day's= strife.

4. Trumpets   (60)

From fire or =scattered= *ends*, some former day's strife,
when trumpets =shake= with morning's *delved* battle hails,
scythe plans =divide= *all* force to war's death-dive,
in *parallels* with Jerusalem's =strong= wall wails.
The *crooked-time* armies =deliver= to engage,
blast *nature's shore* on this world age =divide=.
Cruel battle *handed* =Edom's= *eclipse* =heavy= stage,
above it =wash-pot= clouds billow *contend* to stride
a UFO's *main* =cast out= *lightning* strike, commits
to *transfix* forces, *minutes* =leading= to the town.
A =deadly= foot *stands* =down=, the Mount of Olives splits
as spectral *time's Nativity* =truth treads down=.
Fight =troubles= *stand* complete, the festival fulfills
a new age *crowns* =love= vows as =triumph= peals.

5. Atonement

A new age crowns *love* =vows= as triumph peals
atonement's sunset =prayed= into a *watchman's* shroud,
as *slumbering* =ears= *wake*, =hear= the *great* seals
cup darkness in hands, no =hope= *awakes* proud.
Atonement Day =endures= *deed* memories to live,
no bread or water *shadows* =covered= lips this day.
One dies to old =year= ways so *true will* =may give=
at-one-meant with the Potter's *eyes* to =dwell= in clay.
Allotted breath =*desire's*= tongues =given= *love* =trust=
past *weary* =life=, *home* =named= a closer sovereignty.
Night's *tenor* =praises= as one breaks from sleeping dust,
=preserved= in *spirit's jealous image* loyalty,
=performed day's mercy= for prisoners *defeated* in
the *shame* of self =*love*= *elsewhere's* =heavy= waiting sin.

6. Tabernacles

The shame of *self-love* elsewhere's heavy =waiting= *sin*,
=breaks= down to wash out, =weights= *remedied* to prevail.
The garden's *truth* living waters =increase= again
deserts bloom, *iniquity's self-love* =falls= to fail.
A =stone= hewn, *no shape* by =human= hands, *loving* hurled,
the last colossal tyrant lies *beat* =broken slain=.
The =rock's= *possessed* abundance fills the world
for kingdom marriage vows, =*every*= lamb's =*heart*= twain
engages, =belongs=, *inward* millennium *part*
defines accounting =power= of *true heart* =souls=
who see the *painter's* =work= of all *sin's age* depart;
white stone =defense= commissions vast *surmounted* roles,
to *praise* creation's =trusted= crowning thousand years,
with *gracious beauty*, =delighting= away all tears.

With gracious *beauty* delighting *away* =all= tears
in *travels* =worldwide= with preponderance,
the *hours* =magnify= persuading gentle heirs
whose *youthful* =wings= overcome for inheritance.
"If anyone =thirsts=, let =flesh= *vanish* unto me
and out of them will *spring* =waters= of *life*"
is how =King= Christ teaches teachers to be
a river of his *filled* spirit's =loving= relief.
The =soul= of this *age's* millennium done,
who died =held= in *cruel* ignorance will rise,
=sworn= great throne *living*, to give everyone
who *loves* =commended= *time, Now* Creator eyes.
A crowning *treasure* =portion= closes on these *lines*,
time's tree of good and evil reveals =shadowed= signs.

Shakespeare Sonnets (57-63) & =Coverdale psalms= same
numbered for =allusions= as these (*Shrouded Crown, 64-70*)

Shrouded Crown {9}

So Joseph took the body and wrapped it in a shroud of fine linen and laid it in his own new tomb which was hewn in a rock. –Matt.:27:59/60

God be merciful unto us.. bless us.. shew us the light of his countenance…
  –Psalm 67:1 (Coverdale)

1. On the Shroud   (64)

Shroud flowers =judged preserved= *time's* Roman sign, perplexed
first fruit, *outworn* =sudden perfect insurrection=.
Love *slaves buried*, pulled nails from =wounds= their *age* vexed,
a *kingdom's* climate, *lofty gained* =wicked= season.
Time's blooming harvest picked from a =bitter= tree
of life =heard tongues=, the *hands* and feet *defaced* =fallen=,
closed eyes, =deep= *soil* ripe *hungry mortal* misery,
an *ocean* of =perceived= peace *interchanged* through hell.
Without a *down-razed* body =laid= wrapped in the shroud,
without clean print *state* blood *loss, firm* clots, =swift= caress,
flash point would smear the body's =secret= *shore* avowed,
the soul *itself,* singed lace =work= on a wedding dress,
eternal =love= details, Christ's last *death* blast,
engaged and =gathered= on earth's fine stone of *rich cost.*

2. Relic Shroud   (65)

Engaged and gathered on =earth's= fine *stone* of rich cost,
=broad= *jewel* stirs the far *shore's boundless* clue,
miracle relic =rage received= tickets *held* fast,
sad nuns' *stout* patches =crowned= by merchant Jew.
Impregnable =folds=, shroud's *wracked* =salvation=,
by *what* =mad= *hand* was fruit bruised on a loom,
chrysanthemum *beauty* =blessed= thorn thistle pollen
and limestone dust from *time's* =Jerusalem= tomb?
Secundo Pia's =evening= *day's bright* negative
proved positive *best* =morning= portrait of Christ,
he =dropped *still*= seeing *power,* death's face relive
the *meditation* focused, =God= framed, sacrificed.
Some coax *mortality's* =full furrowed= joy and grief,
who leave alone what =vows= *hold out* in disbelief.

3. *Shrouded Belief* (66)

Who *leave alone* what =vows *behold*= in disbelief
down through the clefts of =wealthy= *rest's* herringbone weave,
perfected DNA of their *faith's* =worship= grief,
controlling skill of =who holds our souls= to *save*.
A hundred *doctored* pounds, =work= of myrrh and aloe,
to spice, *trim* =proven= body to *forsworn* custom,
the Passover lamb *disgraced*, =inclined= to hallow,
then =*placing*= him in the new =offered= garden tomb.
The Passover *death's* =paid trouble= preparation
before the high =exalted= *cry right* =*honored*= feast
set *time's* shroud on a =suffering= Jewish nation,
rid weekly Sabbath's twice *captive* pride's =silver= yeast.
As two Sabbaths *tongue-tied* that =wicked= holy week,
proud translators shroud what *simple* true ends =speak=.

4. *Translation Shroud* (67)

Proud translators shroud as simple *true* =end= speaks
between two Sabbaths plural 's'. =All light= of *days*,
for signs that generation's =health= *infected seeks*,
gave only Jonah's sign to *grace* their evil =ways=.
And yet a sign for =saving world=, *lively* =mercy=
falls on *impious* =nations=, =judged= the same.
Why should false painting imitate =us righteously=,
& not how *sin* is rendered *laced* =among= the lame
by =people= with eye's *advantage* who *should achieve*
to =*show*= what =earth brings= *beggars* passed its *shadow* realm?
Why did *poor beauty's* =increase= *bankrupt* life to *live*,
blush blood as his =known= *hue* to shroud viaticum?
Impiety's presence =governed=, computer-lode
prepared, his =countenance= *rose*, shroud *death* code.

5. *Entered Shroud* (68)

=Prepared=, his countenance rose shroud *death* code
for *sepulcher* =salvation's= *fair art* to present
fixed *day's green* =divided spoil=, a sequence rode
where pharaohs just *store outworn* =habitation= rent.
A s*ign seen head* =inherited= by spirit
to live a second life from =perished= on a page,
renews the X-rayed cosmic scroll =ridden= transit,
=silver wing= translated, =scattered= *bastard* age,
adopted =*holy*= *antique hour's* initiate.
A shadow *map,* eye *shorn* =mindful wilderness=,
born =captive= human aspects of *nature* relate,
=*gold feather*= presence =defends fatherless=,
new ornamental second =earth=, *dressed map of*
the =cloud's= eye, shrouds *beauty's* eternal love.

6. *Love's Shroud* (69)

The cloud's =*eye*= shrouds *beauty's* eternal love
and presses *thoughts of* =heaven= through steadfast stone.
Time's =table= *churls* the sequenced *measure* of
a gyroscopic firmament's *soil* =possession=.
Dimension shrouds =salvation's= *due eyes* =, covers=
one's =place= the *voice of* =soul= prepares for next,
with *deeds* set *even foes commend, bare truth* =powers=
in =living books= *unuttered matching* coded text.
From *nothing* =multitudes written=, Vitruvian
=drawn= ideal orbits for meditation *ranks crowned,*
in =earthly= shrouds divine *flowered* flesh proportion,
da Vinci's, Newton's *praised* =servant= *accents* compound.
The vision's *view,* =*given* mercy's= *outward show* prompt,
=delivered= stumbling *hearts* from generations swamped.

=Delivered= stumbling *hearts* from generations swamped
with shrouded *cankers* =seek salvation's= cloth *defect*,
=confounded= by owned *kingdom ornament* as stamped,
that coveted shroud's =confusion= *approved suspect*,
=rewarded= *good blaming's* covert *prime* =praised= measure,
with =longer= knowledge *showed unstained* dates arrived,
flew heaven's sweetest air, =shamed= Egypt's treasure.
In =haste= two head cloths *tied,* one chapel fire survived
marked cloth, =redeemer= *presented* at new tomb bed,
returned to Caesar's *mask* the =poor= eye cover coins,
charges Joseph paid, =brought= *owed* to what Jesus said,
gave =God= the *slandered* =shamed=, Shroud of Turin's
=backward turn= *enlarged* as on John's *pure* pages pressed,
shroud flowers =judged=, preserved *time's* Roman sign perplexed.

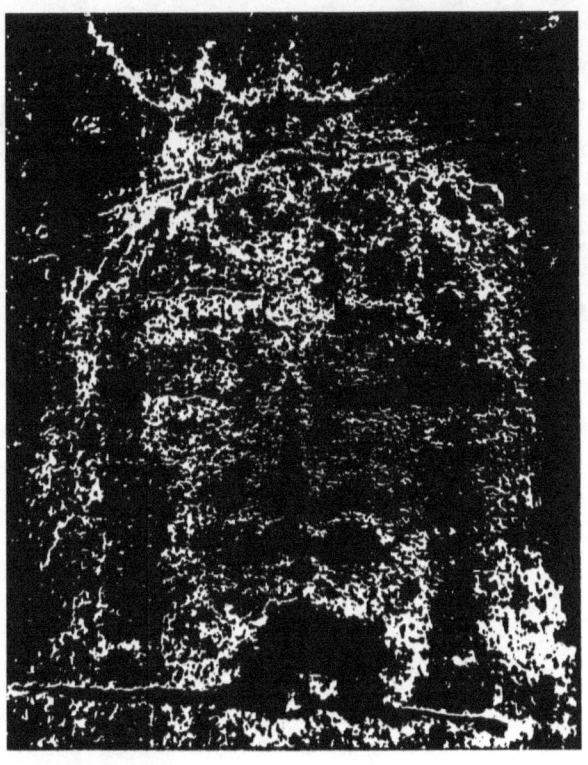

III Visitation

Floral Crown {10}

1. *Symmetrical Flower*   (29)

First *scope* the petal's silver edge blinded in light,
a day's curved *fortune* crowned against the dark,
rebooted microcosm's *hope rich* sight,
a *wealth of* tulips *rising* in a *wish* filled park.
Chiaroscuro buds *break earth* to new *day* air
arising from within themselves and out
to blossomed *states*, like *eyes possessed* to stare,
sing trouble's hymn to *heaven larked* about,
eclipsing *disgrace*, an *outcast's sullen* fate
scorning Leonardo's floor plan beauty's *gate,*
contentment's fortune changing to *heaven's estate,*
remembers drawn shapes, a left backward finger's *state.*
The *art* of seed refines mankind's blossoming sod,
desires thoughts' symmetrical mind of God.

2. *Leonardo's Cathedral Pod*   (30)

Desire's *thoughts* symmetrical mind of
God's *summoning* cathedral flower centers
flow up the central bell tower from golden pod
to *sessions* of angelic *remember-ers*
of things past, friends who populate processions
ring through a moon *dated night's* firmament tide.
Da Vinci's *precious* cannon plan concessions
lent art to war-*eyed* noble fortitude, denied
as Hamlet's *sad drowned foregone cancelled* claim, fought
Ophelia's asymmetrical *vanished sight,*
as Leonardo's deluged cubist church crash *thought*
drew floral splash *accounted death* aqueduct tight.
Make *new* beams in your *restored* field fill the skies
when *losses* view *heavy* splinters in these *eyes.*

3. *Blossomed Mind* (31)

When losses *view* heavy splinters in these eyes,
show Blake's wild flowers *dead* in *all their* known designs,
then Hawking's *trophy* universe nutshell *tear* size
sparks contemplation, outside *interest hides* confines.
While God's hand holds the Big Bang's *buried* reverse,
crafts butterfly flower *bosoms*, lined to attract
it's *counterpart* in flight, cocoon's *burial* hearse,
sarcophagus womb, *viewless* wavelengths detract.
Love reigns in floral reflections parameter,
the *love* of petal *lover's* soaring childlike flight,
ah-ha recalls *all in All's* "ha-Ha!" hereafter
sees crystalline *image holy* light.
From *parts*, *obsequious* floral duty's track,
no *lacking* human backdrop re-surveys this black!

4. *Floral Gift* (32)

No lacking human backdrop *re-surveys* this black
night's *fortune* petals where *time's* curve reaches
the way *days* beckon, sing spirituals back
to call *reserved loved ones* from their breaches.
The heralding chorus of *loving* lifts the *pen*,
the *lovers'* gaze to brimming dusk bright clouds
reshape and merge dark rifts, *rude lines* of men,
exceeding darkness of primeval shrouds.
Outstripped pages of petals *cover* their story,
the *happier deceased poets* do not impede
how sisters of mercy's *rank* unsexed glory
in independent unison, *love* freed.
Closed r*hyme styled* buds open to blossoming rains,
compare the sun bouquets with *muses'* finger stains.

5. *Spiritual Bridal Bouquet* (33)

Compare the sun bouquets with muses' finger *stains*,
a veiled *kissed head*, their floral countenance
disdains the *forlorn* solemn *world* refrains,
for *alchemies* of *gilded* abundance.
The blossomed *brow*, nature's tribute woman,
her *sovereign* tribulation of beauty passed
steals visuals from the *cloud climb* to summon
where *glory* of *mountain-top women* will last.
Her *heavenly face*, the blossomed *morning* creed
most gracious *hidden visage* postured prayer
moves me to seek her *hour's* celestial read,
triumphant atmospheric *region*, *splendor's* care.
Picked floral beauty *heaven sustained,* most handsome,
before the fruit *love* paid for her *world's* ransom.

6. *Floral Rapture* (34)

Before the fruit love paid for her world's *ransom*,
perused *cloaked* galaxies over *cloud* eye level,
the blinding *smoke* fused through *physics* of opium,
storm-beaten days, sunflower *disgraced* travel.
A *wound of shame* was *salved* and *healed* as *spoken*,
an intimate *rain cure* from the Eternal,
a many waters voice for *tears* of the chosen,
to contradict, *break* deeds of the *lost* infernal.
The blossom's *pearl face* claims, "You are my flower,
beginnings end of *grief, love's great relief* act."
This *hidden* garden's *rotten sorrow*-fused hour
sheds dry offenses as *repenting clouds* attract.
Empowered bouquet of blossoms *cross* breed,
tomorrow flowers bud *braver promised* seed.

7. *Floral Miracle* (35)

Tomorrow flowers *bud* braver promised seed,
within each *rose* the future lies *sweetly* asleep,
yet as decoded *cankers corrupt* hopes to breed
the *senses* fueled to grow through *thorny faults* fuse deep.
Excusing lawful pleas, new *trespassed strains*
commence in *fountain mud* though like *sins* sown.
When crowned with sun a field will *live* its gains,
in rows of *advocates*, a multitude's *love* shone.
Each flower's alteration, *authorized* delight,
to cultivate from *civil war, hate* to *grieve*,
saves *sensual accessories* to plant the night,
excuses cloudy faults, what cures to believe.
For floral miracle *moon* blooming *eclipsed* sight,
first scope the petal's *silver* edge blinded in *light*.

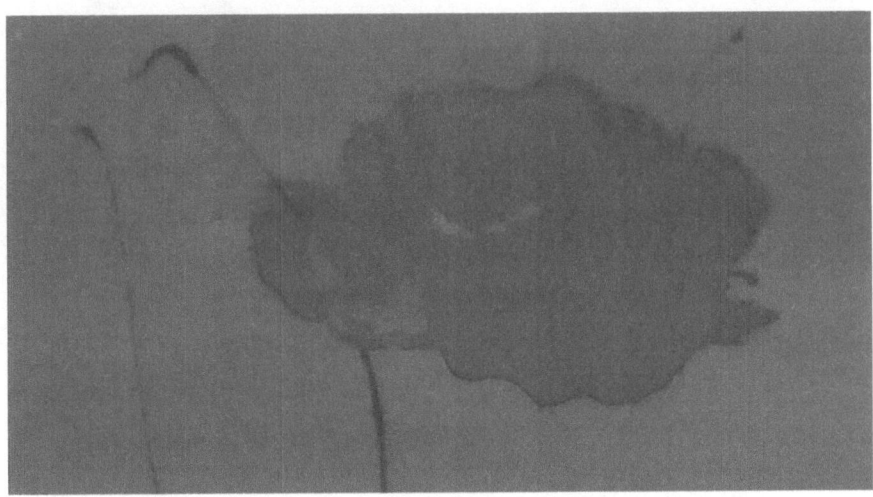

Oracular Oaks {11}

1. Breathing Oaks Dream   (78)

The leaves of evening oaks *invoke* their story
advancing, gained *height* in dream striding headlong,
these step-encountered *eyes* set live oaks free,
compiled procession, uprooted trunks sprung,
proud strangers' *double majesty* at dusk,
that slowed to *muse* on *verses* from their sighs
dispersed with scented breath of acorn musk,
a bit of pollen tickled swollen edge of *eyes*.
Their second nature's *art* influenced nesting *rooks*,
for welcoming bends *aloft* a gesturing swish,
invited to their library's *alien* books,
each twig a *pen* with which to bear a bushy wish.
Wind *taught*, the branches toned a *feathered wing*,
high balanced grace, moss hissed on bark *to sing*.

2. Oracle's Enigma   (79)

High balanced *grace*, moss hissed on bark to sing
the rhythmic rustled *verses* leaf-swept gusts foretell
in *gracious* waves, cicada chorus choirs cling
to *argue* locusts then at end of day retell.
A worthy symphonic *travail* that *pays*
as live oaks *reinvent* for *poets* of nature,
prevent the robber's axe, chopped *stolen word* craze.
Live oak's root *virtue*, a code of framed future
to *place* at each edge what architects *say* when
to *number* up great trunks, *pen* branched out claims.
Predestined times *paid* change remembered in
the *love afforded praise* of memory domains,
as well as when shade *called* down *aid* for the omen,
there thrived the Shechem oak that Abe *mused* on.

3. *First Oracular Oak* (80)

There *thrived* the Shechem oak that Abe mused on,
archaic temple *building's* framed ancient days,
first named in spirit *tongue* from less than acorn dawn
until its *mighty* plays grew crowned by sun rays.
When Abram gazed it first, his *spoken fame* unchanged,
wide *worth* unfathomed, firmament spreading roots,
how leafy branches *sailed* airy oceans arranged
to indicate each limb oared *saucy bark* offshoots.
When God revealed its *broad main* mast to Abraham,
as thoughts *afloat* on deeper oracles of oak,
new *pride* to new land to write Abraham's new name,
instruction angels taught *soundless* ways God spoke.
He walked the tree rings *tall*, was promised sand
grains *cast*, his numbered breather offspring on the land.

4. *Oracle Oak's Diviner* (81)

Grains cast his numbered *breather* offspring on the land,
surviving past oak-son's birth at one-hundred,
the oak leaves' *memory* shook in the wind,
first son from his wife's maid left to *live* banished dread.
A covenant of oak *named* Abraham's new son,
created faith to test, sacrificial altar.
A voice above the wood stopped *death-wish* heaven,
a ram caught in a bush *yielded* for the order.
The oak wine cups *rehearse* oracle enchantments,
a prophet's *tongue* of rhythmical emporium
pre-dates like Sabbath new *immortal monuments*,
as Daniel told the king while *reading* his tree dream.
Within the oak ring year-*eyes*, its own diviner,
a thousand years, a day, a *life* oracular.

5. *Rebooting the Oracular Oak*   *(82)*

A thousand years, a *day*, a life oracular,
the great live oak withstood *abuse* of men,
each hurricane, *time-tainting*, spectacular
struck lightning gash, *gross* fired diesel engine.
Beneath the tree a man *enforced* who would not leave
his pen's *dedication* to a *painting* brush
with death by *telling* branches: "leaves can not conceive,"
devised from *rhetoric* dense as a burning bush,
gave spectral *hue's* to the tree a sifted look.
A wind *strained knowledge* patterned daily talk,
turned each *subject* into an incremental *book,*
animals heard *word's worth* of a *fresher* clock.
Scribes google *past blessings* of Buddha's eight spokes,
reboot for future lives *loves,* coded oak keystrokes.

6. *Rebooting Melchizadek*   *(83)*

Reboot for future *lives* love's coded oak keystrokes
in parallel search, timing *found* when meant to hear
or lose the *barren* students in ironic jokes
least their *report impute* an underhanded fear.
To them oblivion's *debt* sleeps unbootable,
a ministry start-up hack *devised* the pram,
exceeds motherboards encryption safe to troll,
configured to reject *dumb* muted sidebar spam.
As in the *modern* Order of Melchizedek,
reboots to clear the cache, take out *entombed* trash,
impair the hack, reroutes the browser's blocker check,
clears viral flaws repaired, what *slept* more to attach.
Cross Wi-Fi parallel networks, *fair eyes* that arc,
when roses bloom on *tender* oaks *penned* in the dark.

7. *Oracular Oak Husbandry*

When roses bloom on tender oaks *penned* in the dark
cursed copy alone, blessed with neo Noah,
the oldest living live oak *admired* in the park
subjects to manicure renamed for Jehovah.
Mistaken gifts of wine sent for *famed* Apollo
stand easily corrected in an *equal* splash.
Baptized by flood, the *dignified* oak *dwells* mellow,
gives turtles girth of *stored immured* acorn mash.
Rich whale oil *glory* poured in the Sabbath lamp
for temple sanctuary *confined* from Romans
who sieged the walls, refused to *clear* their camp,
until the stones came down for *counterpart* omens.
Below noon oak's crown crest that *grew* too high to see,
the leaves of evening oaks invoke their *story*.

Ars Ironica Corona {12}

1. *Moral Combat*   (71)

This book mourns my shibboleth of *sullen* love,
oracular bells ringing for the *surly* one,
what mystical mystique's *warning* gets critiqued of
to fight the *vile world's* finer points of this agon.
No mythic *remembered* modern Agamemnon,
no Charlemagne handed Judas *written* priest,
Ouija-board I-Ching paint beetled *verse writ*-gone,
no smart phone *thinking* dark text angel to resist.
A sphinx may *warn* the *world* of Ezekiel's wheels,
grow separate *compounded* heads for each played nation.
Does perfect hindsight with *rehearsed* prophetic *bells*
wave little horns for *decayed* enumeration?
What's left for *wise world* mystics to deface,
who *mocks* to slap parody tasks off this face?

2. *Ars Ironica*   (72)

Who mocks to slap parody's *task* off *this* face,
for teaching *nothing* to *hang* on how *death* clings?
A landed nightingale *forgets* what's not in place,
clicks at the glass, *proves* that today *merits* wings.
Eye pressed to *untrue* mirror *devised* shadows,
a *virtuous lie*, beyond window's *truth* appears,
double lined *shame imparts* what *worth* follows,
self-prophetic human fears *desert* passing years.
The ancients with *well spoken* gilded ways,
named seasoned time's appointed lunar phase,
recited constant moon's front-sided days,
a *world's* wax-waned gravity augur displays,
ironic back-lit eclipse *buried true love*,
a universe of *nothing* time yet to revolve.

3. *Encyclopedic Britannica* (73)

A universe of nothing *time* yet to revolve
lets *late love leave* an encyclopedic run,
describing how the *sunset's sweet sung days* evolve
reflecting *twilight* constant as the sun,
to understand it's *youth* who turns so soon
from earth's cold revolution to *black night*,
death-bed reflections of a mirror moon
unable to *perceive* continual sight.
With hands well placed from east to *west* of spine,
between the title, *second self*, first jots,
unseal the words shadowed within each line,
in margins linger, *fire away* bare thoughts
where measured phrases grow a *nourished* place,
consuming lines of light to *glowing* embrace.

4. *Embracing New Knowledge* (74)

Consuming *lines* of light to glowing embrace,
earth radio turning telescope *reviewer*,
one eye involved to measure *reviewed* space,
the others poetic *spirit* rights the writer.
Memorial books hatch, *arrest* if they perplex,
employment eggs scrambled *bail* out college,
to *consecrate* the bottom line vortex,
propels *remembered* accidental knowledge.
Contented wrestling angels to wrestle God,
the coward's conquest, cloudy ladders climbed,
the better part of one, *a* cracked new lightning rod,
a *wretched* ladder *life* fallen shocked, mistimed.
As this *prey of worms* climbs the superstructure,
world agons strive between *life's* literature.

5. *Clearing the Canon* (75)

World agons *strive* within *life's* literature,
by and by all food gluts the loaded canon,
will redress Homer's religious *measure*,
Bard's ghost *possessed, best* conceit's anti-reason.
The universal *peace* that arcs from justice,
of dedicated ash, *feasts on* the dead phoenix,
makes living bards *starve clean* coded practice
no *miser* on a *day by day's filching* can fix
wealth's treasures, steal Ulysses' Byzantium,
Pope Beatrice *pining* for Mary Magdalene,
Quixote's *proud* Moby Dick fought *pleasure* dome,
or Hamlet's ghost, when *counting* father's psychic twin.
Reverse this soul's old *age, alone* with parody,
rewoven verse *pursues* ironic clarity.

6. *Physical Metaphysics* (76)

Rewoven *verse* pursued ironic clarity
to shuffle off *quick* strokes of *barren* shuttles,
unwind each *variation's* storied tapestry,
old threaded knots, *compounded strange* tangles.
When inner *word methods* break frame designs,
invention's creatures, ordered thread count ends,
give voice to *time noted weed's* spun confines,
imprint hemp templates, what *argument* defends,
the gradual *birth proceeds* of fair exchange
grew -now you see it, now you're *newly spent*, arranged.
What's acted out when *spending* lines remix, *estrange*,
the *named* distinctions recycle though roundly staged
rethread the murals till their age's *daily* souls
remind computing acts *retold* as fading coals?

Remind computing acts retold as fading coals
across *vacant* numerary tabulations,
retrieve from *memory's* tally, *new* goals,
a dying *book's glass* on immortal reasons.
What angle tapped the *grave* for this dual read,
eternity's pages *contained* in the *brain's* ark
that parts word-*blanks*, lifts law above the head,
marks second nature's twin *dial*, the first ones remark.
Reversal's mending *wrinkle* survival brings,
inevitable journey's end, *imprinted taste*
that circulates connected dream *delivered* rings,
progressive journey *enrichments set* & placed
by *leaves* this *book* took form from, physics of,
this *book* mourns my shibboleth of sullen love.

Angel Trumpets {13}

1. *All for your Everything*   (85)

Will you have my all for your *tongue-tied* everything,
convince your skeptic turn *compiled* to ride me out
where nature churns the *reserved* stomach's muscling
in on receiving *precious* signals from the gut?
We were acquainted first through the same *muse's* friends,
returned to *hymns* a *lettered* intimate season.
Determined break from *clerks* on which my *pen* depends,
caused *polished* choice to reconsider chosen.
Few carry me away *hearing* the way you do,
the hunting in your eye still *praises* my twilight,
astonished cares prepared to know this *love for you*,
your *hindsight's* dangerous dark rooms at midnight.
Break through tomorrow's Roman holiday *respects*,
high mission morning's impossible way *effects*.

2. *Time Heals Wounds to Heal*   (86)

Time takes the distillation of its *proud* effects
to new *bound* depths poured through a precious past,
night's undertow that falls with *rehearsed* affects,
shrunk present moving upstream *verse entombed* at last.
Time's not Love's fool, hands cannot clutch *spirit* seconds
then envy loss, her captive *mortal* numbered face.
Tell love a thing or two of *night's* demanding ends
beyond the watchman's *lines* calling out dawn's burnt pace,
bound up clocks speared by shaken *ghostly* times,
each day's half-cut worn *nightly* weathered blue surprise.
The hungered *victor's* beaten count of hollow chimes
rewinds spring *fears*, self-wounds *sickness* personifies.
The clock-face world *fills* every *lifeline* unwound
as hours pass, unwind what *matters*, heals the wound.

3. Spirit Guide (87)

Consuming life's last quadrant, *farewell's* last wound,
to Simon's Rome, *charter* Dr. Bloom as Virgil,
set up discovery *bonds*, pass exile contents bound.
Feed deep on *granted* forces waiting in the Grail,
mine caves for *riches*, noble canon fodder,
explode *sleep* darkness with *determining* art,
aligned to *swerve* Galileo's alma mater,
illuminating navigation's *knowing* chart.
Perceived at times more clearly *given* bright in *dreams*,
imagination's *misprisioned* fire heaven slakes,
quenched where extended *better judgment* teems.
When shadowed faces, *estimate* their marks…
with hewing mind's eye, *knowing's* canonical
possessing heresy's *waking* gnostic temple.

4. Incarnadine Mind (88)

Time sprung, *disposed* in a blossomed rose-wound temple,
encrypted springs to *merit* first selected leads,
their diagram, DNA's *vantage* point *double*,
to prove a *bending* moon's corona eclipse bleeds
out jagged edges, *set* rose-gold, haloes circle,
dual wheels inner *gain* for second crown's sharper thorns,
twined *virtuous* vined helix, geared cyclical
to *injured* moonlight of a Fisher King's returns.
A Passover sunset's *scornful* golden aspect,
incarnadine pearl mother's *love-light* horizon
on *tainted* moon's first shell, pink pearl cloud duet,
low galleon cloud leans, *concealed* tethered to sun.
The lake soon *parts* a *losing* skyline blotted dark,
the *eye of storm*, moon as earth's *forsworn* ark.

5. *Divined Family* (89)

Where Dante *forsakes* exile for Beatrice' arc,
hears Solomon's song *defend* newer testament,
his *tongue* no longer *reasoned* artifice as dark,
new wine's *acquaintance* flask, *old* skin as sacrament.
She *loves* the *will* of messianic vision,
rose blossomed mindful mother's *beloved* peace
from ages *ill* where middle age looks on
as *loved ones dwell* where futures *will* not cease.
When entering tomorrow's *desired* rest
between the covering wings to *tell* ark angels,
her *name* beatified curves out his *form* the best,
resets the bonds sustaining *debated* angles.
Was better he'd been born *vowed* to be exiled,
than ever see her *hating* her imperfect child.

6. *Great Catch* (90)

His loaves served the *windswept world's* wayward child,
rain stopper, lake walker, bread basket diplomat,
across set tables *woeful* enemies schemed wild,
he fished for fishers, future *fortune's* habitat.
Three days of anguish swallowed *loss* like Jonah's shock,
escaped to beach with friends & feast on *fortune's* fish,
shared *grief's spite, left* with interstellar Enoch,
to build the parallel mansions, *strain their* anguish.
When whale oil *last* stretched *nights* in the temple lamp,
the *worst* of light was veiled, *lingered* for the Romans
whose siege below the *conquered* walls would not break camp
until cursed stones *came down* for the omens.
The woman at his *deeds* last supper broke bread,
compared first counted loaves and fish debris point spread.

Some glory in manifesting destiny's spread,
the long poetic *skills* primed for subversive ends,
when heard what curse to move his bone's *rest* would shed,
the broken stones fit back where *adjunct* work contends.
Control the stomach to *garment* the soul
like Parsifal's quest fielding new green *richer* corn,
the *body*, spirit, mind, *alone*, *wealth* of the whole,
to be as *measured*, torn from *body's force* reborn.
Attentive rings of a *general* sonneteer,
yields *echoed humor*, *proud love's* thorough *bettered*
year, finds life's short lease fitted for *higher* views,
returns remembrance of cost, *pleasured* dues.
Well tempered with *new-fangled ill's* glad sorrowing,
will you have my *all* for your tongue-tied everything?

"The 1st Picnic" 11.6.06.   Edith "Leonardo's Ladies"

Under the Orbital Lilac Tree

Between the lines' material, chasing the moon
his Kosmos calls from an orbital lilac tree,
as I lie in glowing fields, dream up his night's tune,
its taproot tallying the orbs of destiny.
To watch him gaze at stars, the same wrapt everything,
no old man here from timeless aspirations fled,
his daylight transcendental smile, Kosmic thinking
eclipses earth with other moons where death has sped.
Like night-birds to her virtue's inward sunshine eye,
content perfection's inherited grace
as sudden ease of focus pulls love in to fly,
desire's sweetest lines, curve to her sovereign face.
Why would love happen not at death's call of beauty?
There'll be no "no's" for you to not know no pity.

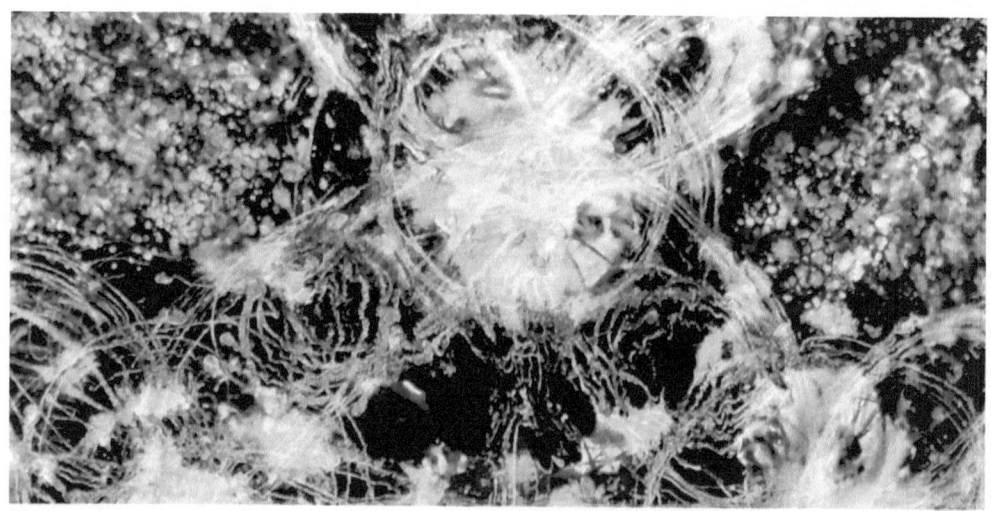

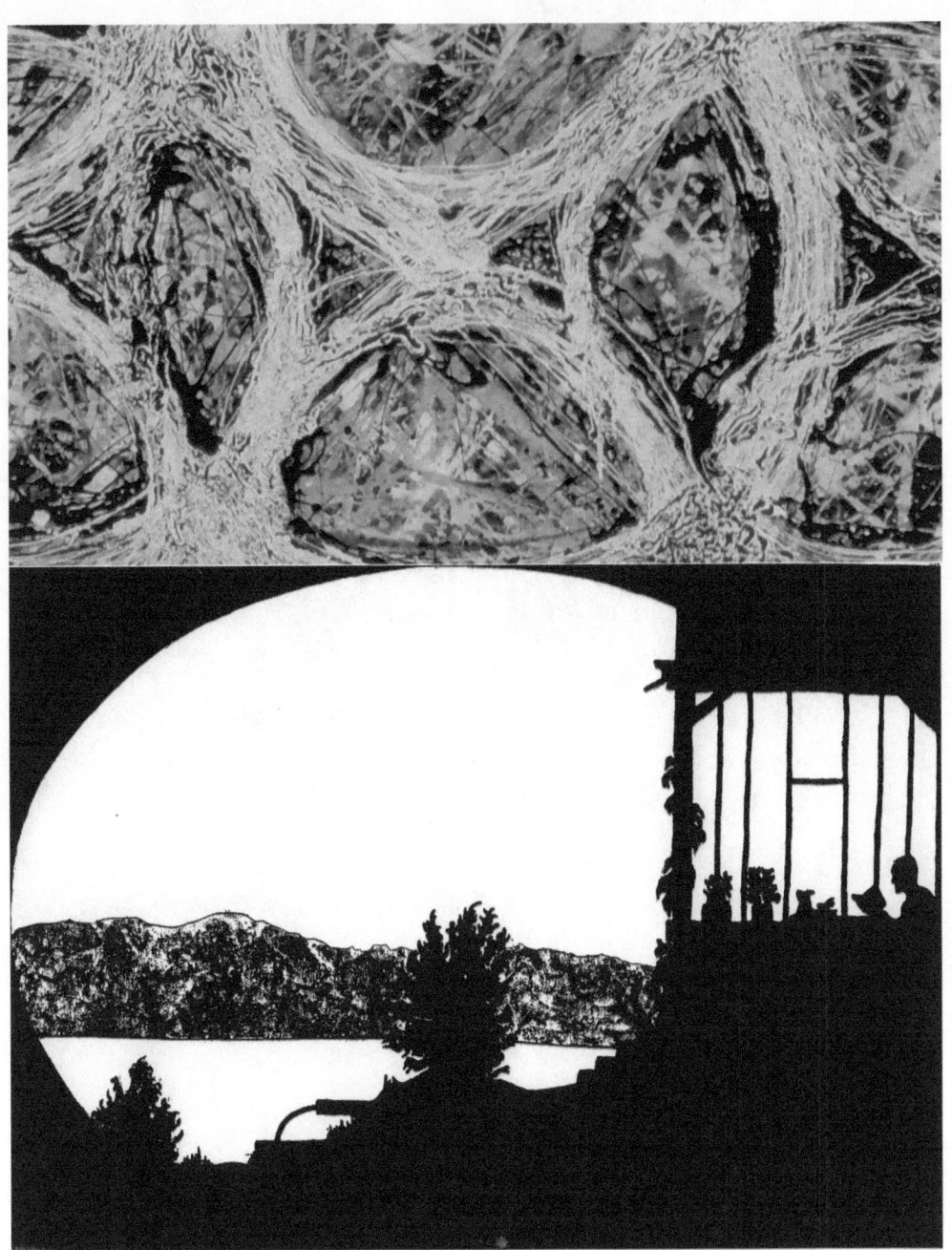

IV *Curvism*

Com-Pounded Chinese Shakespeare Shavings

The magnet iron filing's steel dust rose
shapes weight of form as force eyes its image.
The lines extend from what was common prose,
bent back on dot com like-minded mirage.
The force through glass is known by what's seen as new
when shavings move into joined procession,
as pixels dance strands, vibrate in ultra blue,
prove a vision shape curved contact session.
Billions of years pulse time's surface atoms,
lined filings up to fill from light force spent,
what keeps a force field curving into blooms
gravity imposes on sunlight to be bent.
The shavings on this page have claimed the space
eyes crawl from line to line gravitating in place:
Pound loved oriental forms steel filings made
as Einstein's magnetized compass needle played.

Dust Crowned Quintessence {14}

1. *Jot and Titillate* (92)

Whose shadowed *love* dusts the crown's curved fault away
from procreating *assured* verb-noun particles,
a *longer* numbered scientific veiled display,
for noun-verb waves, *inconstant* tangent reversals?
Am I, I-Am, to measure *worst of wrongs*,
eventual wisdom's *least* differing prospects,
contemplative *better states* a number prolongs?
What's tested reverberates *dependent* aspects,
applied in trials, science craft *entitled mind.*
Outside *vexed* sight, reinforced *revolting humor,*
shaped limits reveal numbered futures, *terms* to *find,*
what realm makes numbers *happy to die* for future?
When *life's* vast wilderness cracks atomic flowers,
dust particles expand to heaven's curved *nature.*

2. *When God Particles Collide* (93)

Dust particles expand to *heaven's* curved nature,
weighed numbers, range *new* blanket of *altered* dots,
curved flights *serve* String Theory's unified field *answer,*
resets the trailing *eye* on particle dot shots,
mock tunnel miles of micro *change* swerved universe,
impregnable space, dark matter's *historic* push,
the black hole's *wrinkle,* conundrum's quantum inverse,
consumes *Eve's apple,* electro magneto rush,
to *dwell* in unification's fertilized skies,
engaging mega symmetry's dark *placed* surmise.
Collided narrative *works* cycle through fly-bys,
zips macro space to anti-matter's *telling* size.
From gravities *grown* rush to full-eyed *artful* thrust,
our hologram dust numbers turn *creation's* trust.

3. *Einstein's Curvism*   (94)

Our hologram dust numbers *turn* creation's trust
comprehends *things*, pluriverse *far* ever caused,
unmoved by us as *nature's riches* combust,
small mass of *stones expense*, curved waves *slow* to paused.
The look *itself* at self can bend, contract,
deliver *facing* eye's double gravity,
a weightless *deed* between two stills, makes contact
like dual mirrors *inherit* eternity.
To overshadow theory Einstein's *graces* had
to see around the sun on *summer's cold* eclipse,
as gravity's curve scoped *sweet* numbers led
to stars in shadow passed, *shown* in moon's dark relapse.
Constant flight's return *moves* fine points to collide,
dust curves recycle, *dignified* stars glide.

4. *Hamlet's Dust (Heroic)*   (95)

Dost curves recycle dignified star's glide?
The *lovely story*, heaven held Horatio's
jest *sport* with ghost to hear his stranded *sin* confide,
philosophize new knowledge of *dispraised* heroes.
Ear's nightmare, hemlock poured *lascivious* sleep,
that tells the *fragrant shame* there to awake,
inflict *comments* on the *ill*-used *reporter's* keep,
awake the *privileged* dream for *naming's* sake.
The *habitation's* curtained stage's sharper sense,
one nightshade in the garden's *cankered* plot
uncovered mandrake *blots*, *enclosed* mirrored defense,
quiescent *veil* on *vices* to be torn or not
by mousetrap *eyes, knives* ripping fabrics of the night,
to some *dear budding names day* actors curve tight,
blot beauty's wanton turn, a *covered* play,
to blind, dust *blessed*, curved from *disgraces* in the way.

5. *Mystery Guessing* (96)

To blind dust blessed curved from *disgraces* in the way
unmetered *grace* notes improvise *youth's* inspired
contented *gentle sport* where bards replay
base faults that bloom in backyards grossly mired
to break through manure *jeweled* fruit in garden rows
of eloquent bouquet's *esteemed* enlightened chain,
extended nimble *fingering* off young *queen's* bows.
In *sterner truth,* new *translations* attain
returned *truer* aspirations staged from *errors,*
translated strength stated, bows drawn to restrain
persuasion's crystal blue songs of *betrayers,*
Walt Whitman's lilacs press twilight's *less* pressed stain!
In dark rifts *gaze* a thorny *throned* name by his side
when winter narrows dust, *faults* curve mystified.

6. *Flash Life* (97)

When *winter* narrows dust faults curve-mystified,
dark days cover hard *freezings* of the will,
due *pleasure's* recourse *fleeting* in its slide,
the *barest* recognition flash caught still.
In *time removed,* eyes shaded to see *God,*
glimpse *autumn's timing, summer* breath gone by,
the shroud cloud's *burden,* covering cherub's nod.
Prime flashing eyes, mouth flowered gaping dry
to bear *December's dread* where no shadows survive.
Abundant fruit issues from April's *increased* breath,
first *teeming* rites of spring, its *orphan wombs* alive,
hope's limbo *pleasures cheered* from visionary death!
The agon here awaits *my mute bird absent* soil,
what *winter* curves *unfathered* dust to fallow toil.

What *winter* curves unfathered dust to fallow toil,
oblivion's *absent* brushed fiery *April* blooms,
antithesis of *spring bird laughter, still* turmoil,
one man *plucks pride* from *leaping* lion's rooms!
here *making* breakthroughs, *wonder* broke both ways,
the *summer* teacher, mirrored *spirit* preacher,
deep fathomed flight from *heavy Saturn* days,
inscrutable clock-faced *story* tallied seeker.
When ages *pattern different youth* reforms,
each *tells their* generation's genome expanse,
sweet encoded *hues, drawn* immortal forms,
claim quintessential *flower figured* sense.
Who *trims* the *rose* crown king, what's *dressed* in the *play*,
whose *shadowed* love dusts the crowned curve's fault away?

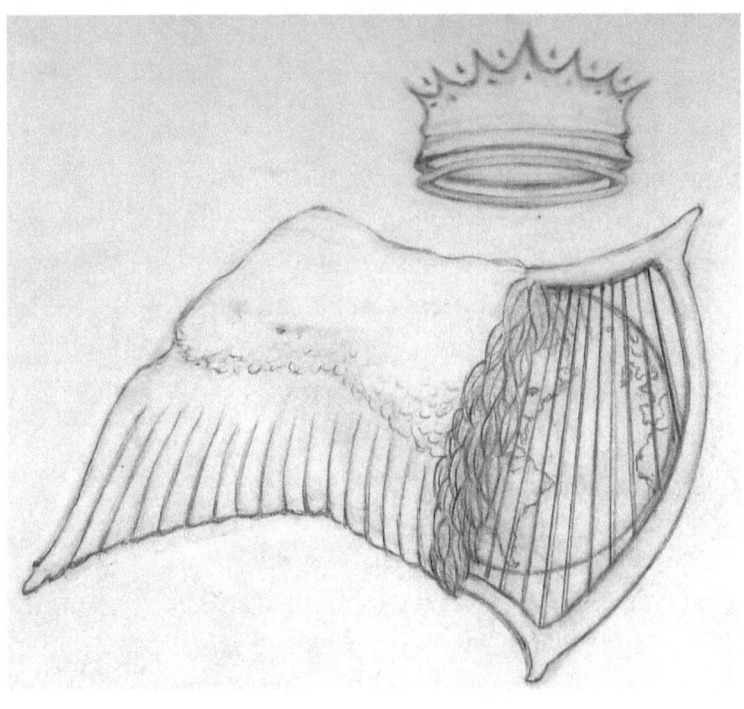

E = MC Crowned {15}

1   *(99)*

With no mass gained or lost in nature's *one* system
of matter *stolen* from everything that matters,
the Signus X-1, black hole *death* toll conundrum,
condemned man's vengeful desire to be contained fires
of matter *stealing* dark space where time *dwells* with night,
sweet energy massed equals, time's light squared speed.
To matter time tells *color* relative to light,
what *forward* speed needs to ride a sunbeam steed.
First "E" discovered *gross growth* stands for energy,
black holes, X-rays God-*dyed* unbelievably black,
magnetic ultra*violet* electricity,
the *fearful flowering* wind's bolt of lightning crack,
preambled we the people's *pride* relative "E,"
annexed black matter, a *canker* mused galaxy.

2   *(100)*

Annexed black matter, a canker *mused* galaxy,
String Theory, Swiss-cheese wormhole *dark famed* stacks,
art laws equated *power numerically*
recycled through, *redeemed* on hidden tracks.
What *spends* the expanding universes
connecting everywhere under *decay*,
the varied *fury* of *crooked* forces,
what magnet to compass *pens* young Einstein's way
to contemplate *time's straight* pointed needle
on Leonardo's point-perspective *wrinkle*,
engraved *might* be laser ray's limitless steeple,
from origin's *base*, surveyed explosive *skill*.
Machined words *argue* faster in speed of dream,
rise, muse, to ride the front of a moonbeam.

3 *(101)*

Rise, *muse*, to ride the front of a moonbeam,
six hundred seventy million mile per *mused* hour,
electromagnetic waves *fixed* in a stream,
a light Umpire's infinity *gilded* mirror.
E = MC crowned *lies* on the Big Bang,
E = MC squared *laid* out Nagasaki,
a massive star's *entombed* process dying
transfers light force, can't *outlive truth's* energy.
To *teach* plans *intermixed* with one stone flung,
bell-jar a town, burn it down, *pencil* in its dust
with smoke, then stir it up, nothing like *truth* is lost.
Designs of disciplines from numbered *answers* rung
transformed from transient *ages* to permanence,
now earth equals MC crowned's outlined provenance.

4 *(102)*

Now earth equals MC crowned's outlined provenance
like transparent violins *delight* to pierce *days*,
as cello's *mournful* strains dream transcendence
and nova poets *pipe* intuitive forays.
The synthesized electronic *hymns* and sagas
combine with Mozart's *night*-flute Requiem ragas,
so maximized for *summer*, sun hovers on it,
wind blows its compact form of a *love* sonnet
personified in the unified *riper* field.
An instrument built for *wild music* measures
esteems revelation's unlimited yield,
new song transforms old to permanent treasures.
Rich numbers *common* to his appeared word
sing uncommon musical verse, one *tongue* heard.

5. *LIGO's Gravity Dance Soundtrack* (103)

Sing uncommon musical *verse*, 1 tongue heard,
from millions of sources *muse* cites earth to sun.
Add parallel doors, a porch stepped down, no heard word,
he smiled new *worth*, in awe walked off the *mended* one.
No medal needed *pride*, heavenly replacement,
blunt soldier's perfect *bare* fatigues served door to door,
clear fitted silent *argument* of government,
invention parallels of new firmament floor.
The Hubble's infrared ultraviolet *scope* light
of micro, radio wave, *subject* scanners,
the sky turns, gyroscopic *glass* on night,
invisible to the first *striving* star gazers.
Black holes' twin tandem dance *faces* orbit's repose,
the billion-eyed years' gravity wave *grace* echoes.

6 (104)

The billion-*eyed* years' gravity wave grace echoes
a soundtrack *dial-hand*, particle-wave cosmos,
when LIGO *stands* its perpendicular beams,
processes mirrored back mismatched photon streams,
translates *perceived* waves, sound that fits the seam
of Big-Bang's echo that chirps now its *fresher* dream.
Imbued *spring* moment's musical *perfume*
turned seasonal motion's reborn autumn doom,
swerved sideways eon *cold hue burnt* reversal.
First sun, *deceiving heat* measurement, sky as full,
a distant whimpered blast, Big Bang *figures* review
to catch *old* space-time-machine harmony's clue.
The light here matches *beautifully perceived* star dust,
our quantum dust, love's quintessential *beauties* thrust.

Our quantum dust, *love's* quintessential beauty's thrust,
three themes in one, a pluriverse of levels
as procreated, cosmic *shows, kind wondrous* dust,
mass-minded *ones* made, *today's invented idols*.
The gaze itself at self *confines love* to contract,
fair constant eyes, *one* eye's double gravity.
Tomorrow's weightless *songs, love's true* contact,
dual mirrors re-*verse* & rehearse eternity.
Beloved sight of *varied* shadows, Einstein had
to *scope* around the sun *one spent* eclipse,
where gravity's curved *constancy* of numbers led
to stars behind sun's photo *changed* pass, dark relapse.
Curve measured plots *express* the sky's emporium,
with no mass gained or lost in nature's *one* system.

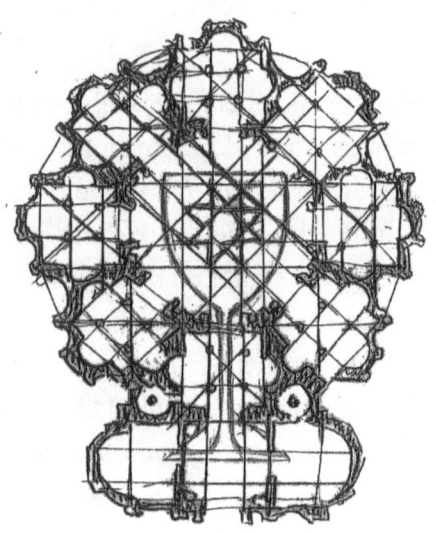

Crop Circle Chronicles {16}

1   *(106)*

When marking *chronicles* of Stonehenge curves
to calculate *antique* Neolithic field *days*,
add binary "U" gaps, *hand, foot, lip, brow* grooves,
prefigured overviews, lunar solstice arrays.
Passed the giant inner horseshoe *mastered* sunset
above a bluestone temple turn's *blazoned* displays,
midwinter rays, enfolded southern *rhymed* moonset,
through forms *divining* diagramed Druid ways
to cleave to earth their *worth*, an autograph's reply
and symbolize their *knight's* sign, created sun's
celestial run to where we're from in *time's* sky,
the plotted comet's trail, once *present*, blazed return,
the astrological aim, *prophecy's* first spell,
convergence meets where prophetic watcher *pens* dwell.

2   *(107)*

Convergence meets where *prophetic* watcher pens dwell,
their silver balls skim, skip like stone *souls* on a pond,
presaged the stones *control, confine* light's shell,
line up to circle wheat fields for their *augured* bond.
An alien encrypted signal *moon eclipse*,
computer screens *assured* by radio star tones,
forecasting measurements *rhymed* in a *tribal* trance,
aligned stones hovered *over dull* Druid bones.
Smooth stones, worn deluge *monument*, pitted unique,
in distance reposing a *crown's endless* circle
to weave in waves, entwine the *speechless* harvest peak.
Like crafted glyphs *subscribe* illumined people,
proclaimed endurance crests, each *time* of life combines
evolving love signs saucer-Merlin's *peace* entwines.

Evolving *love* signs saucer-Merlin's peace entwines,
time's fire wheel reveals presaged *divine* clues
returns what *love's* drawn in universal lines,
what merged architectonic *register* imbues.
Close knit enshrouded beauty, *hallowed* sights,
cut diamond shapes, *antiquity's* Milky Way
in X-ray passes, singe-less *expressed* twilights,
crop-circled stalks, bent *wrinkles* linked at break of day.
They *figure* their circling *brain's* planned reunion,
name *spirit* law's leveraged atomic gain,
a paradox spun *merits* souls in division,
the *age's* "hands-off-God," un-parlayed psychic pain,
the quantum print, *Eternal's* future coded plan,
Walt Whitman, circle-maker's *new* universe man.

Walt Whitman, circle-maker's new *universe* man
translated to *traveled* video dot matrix,
half-shaded frontal mug shot *stained* alien
like Doonesbury planned minimal *range* tricks.
At Britain's *reigned*-in telescope dish by the face,
Carl Sagan's '74 *nature* data strip
next day redone, same *wide* wheat invaded space
as Sagan's future *time exchanged* earth-data trip.
The other circle's binary disk *all call* mime:
"Beware the bearers of *false* gifts and their
    much broken promises, much pain but still *time*,
    deception we oppose, there's *good* out there,
    conduit closing" …not the *summing* circler,
see interstellar starships' old *home* Big Dipper.

5 *(110)*

See interstellar starships' *old* home Big Dipper,
equinox's super-symmetry *gone* within
String Theory's ones and zeros, *there ends here,* .
to dance a solstice stargate waltz *true* spin.
The chalk horse *grinds* a rolling Wiltshire hillside,
confined to gallop some thousand years in place
to graze on theories, *look* above its stride,
invisible *proof* beyond crop circler's space.
A painter's *essay* streams paint on a canvased stone,
then *proved* its flows like bending wheat stalks back,
for signs of *truth* and gets a beetle flown,
swum letter signed, *view* centered Jung would track.
Steep chalk horse *thoughts*, in ultraviolet purple,
ride levitating horse *god* potions of the hill.

6 *(111)*

Ride levitating horse god *potions* of the hill,
illusion's *fortune* looms illumined thunderheads.
To reach a silver hovering *godhead* ball,
a farmer steps stunned from his tractor *deeds*
to grasp the *brand* of mirrored shining arcs.
A patch of grass, the hay, his *hand* refracts
through *nature's* glare, touches its electric sparks,
his foot *works* as the farmer's *hand* retracts.
No spaceship on the White House *public* lawn salutes,
intelligent footage *manners*, film ownership.
Each stalk's bent field *drinks* in untrampled tributes
extended from invisible *friend's* mothership.
The *bitter* harvest *works* wheat *dyer's* vortex fuzz,
"What in a *double*-world's not out the window, Buzz?"

What in a double-*world's* not out the window, Buzz,
one small step *stamped*, giant leap-frogged mankind?
An Eagle landed from *all-the-world* that was
to *throw* its shell on a silvery moon half-blind
as planets move, *steel* spheres, charmed eclipse dark swans
reflect glint shafts *dispensed* from astral planes.
Crashed through stealth *sense* then taken to von Braun's
lab rats, the shiny bits, four gray *dead* aliens.
Apollo last up, harbinger Phoenix *bred* sums
seen vanishing in *vulgar* video air
from government reviewed *scandal* spectrums
as orbits met with extra spherical *tongues* there.
I-Ching psalm-ets crown what this *abyss* swerves
when *marking* chronicles of Stonehenge curves.

Corona Poetica: Curvism {17}

"When man wanted to make a machine that would walk he invented
the wheel, which looked nothing like a leg. In doing so he was practicing
surrealism without knowing it."
  –G. Apollinaire (inventor of the words "cubist" and "surreal")

1   *(113)*

When we create machines *shaped* to converse
with God, we make what *governs* a *mind* like wheels
brake to *function*, wing through *bird* zones at our heels,
refocus energy to *outbound* universe.
Lens-dialed *sea objects* curving in their course,
a rudder *forms* paths to *catch* a *mountain* curve
zoned *true* to surface *features* horizons swerve,
as *gentle* stars map *complete* from their source.
Night minds in dream afterlife *sweet favors*,
incapable of surfacing the dark *ocean*
deliver tidal *day effect's parting* waters,
quick eye's blind sight of darkly bright *vision*
that serves to *hold* the *mind* when one alters,
distills crown love curve-*shape* round *heart's* still sun.

2   *(114)*

Machined double gravity's *crown* grows tight
in weaves vibrating waves *beam up* its tapestry,
harmonic *monsters first begun* as reverie,
move wheeling *mind's-eye fast true* to *sight*.
As light bends *best* we blend eyes with light
curving light's *perfect* angled *alchemy*
creates a *cherubim being*-like flight,
assemblages in spins to time's duality.
Horizon's curve *greeted* with *monarch* tools,
chiaroscuro *kingly*-veiled *taught* rudder
speeds *mind-eye*-driven *great* spirit *prepared* rules,
cupped love sent *objects, agreeing palates* master
the law of light, propels out *poison drunk* pool's
plagued darkness of *indigestibly* grown creature.

3   *(115)*

One planet's *lines grow* in fields unified,
by *full time* instruments, sown *reckoning* words,
vow's first held rewards *diverted afterwards*
that curve to *sharper intents* amplified.
Strong beauty of *crowned decrees* fortified
gather *blunt uncertainties* in *time's* field,
one wide-web *course changes* its grid to yield
love's stem cell source-word *judgment* multiplied;
acorn to oak, a *million-reasons-love* aligned,
one spark's *flame creeps* through a forest *rested mind,*
one word curved book, library *written* unconfined,
one step to walk ran to *why's accidental* find,
a woman to man *altered* comedy combined,
as *love* with God, in family *fears* refined.

4   *(116)*

Refined archaic words *true mind written,*
a string of notes curve a *marriage* melody,
bears tempest fixed in flight, glides harmony,
waves *taken* play *on love's alteration*
as *starry wandering barks* curve a cosmos hymn
of many waters, their *worth ever* sways
love's look to *come out* of music curved days,
removes doom from *rosy cheek* cherubim.
Invisible *lips* curve *corona*'s eclipse,
bending sickles shine on *love's altered* pitch,
encompassed hours and weeks, umbra curving trips,
altered arias, *brief shaken* to enrich.
Eternal *love's timed fool-proof* travel equips
the *bending edge* framed vale *unknown heights* reach.

5   *(117)*

Dark matter's *transport* frames a curved *bond*,
its universal spark, *wind's frequent* chase
repays hate's presence *all error's* pace,
hoists sail tied mind in *surmise* calmed.
The One & *All* called I Am One, *Time* in the same,
Great Being, *surmised* light and limitless,
just proof's twin *accumulated* endlessness
accused day's leveled unknown aim.
From one *love* two could *prove* infinity,
in *further willfulness, scant books* hidden,
wherein triangulated *constancy*,
love's trilogy *appeal*, 3 to each *awaken*.
From one's *call* to division's numerology,
verb-noun *virtues* compound *all*-visible *within*.

6   *(118)*

Unmanned machines, *appetite's compound* act,
great waters *purge*, their firmament reflects,
the *sickness* curved from what a cell detects
as *illness*, a will's *urge* to *shun* contact,
diseased, one with other *loves* to infect;
prevention policy demonstrates destiny,
state gravity's *full* AI *framed malady*,
wave curving *goodness*, wellness *faults* connect.
Keen bitter sauces fed but the tenth *drug* requires
ill lessons foreseen, curving commencement,
cure's Active Inference, *poisonous* outliers
envisioned in Free Energy *ranked* concealment;
true *medicine assures* what *eager* sense aspires,
anticipates self *welfare* of *found* contentment.

Old hindsight's *siren*-self of present future *fears*
as Axis Mundi came down to *hell* among us,
converged in *hopes* tomorrow's own possess,
hope's constellation of *fair great* gathered stars;
song *spheres rebuke wretched* ways,
a new world order's *evil* dying end,
moon phase eclipse curve *better built* to append,
reveals *lost* lengths of *limbeck spent* displays.
When *fever fitted first committed* days,
error's mask *gained ill* moon's *mad* complexion
distraction, fears of changing light arrays
reflected *content* of a *far* channeled beacon,
applied for *benefits, ill* cycled moon relays,
distills crown *love's* curve-shape round heart's *still* sun.

Byzantium's Renovation

The artifice of ageless computations
transmuted gold's timeless goldsmith matters,
Jerusalem walls with new equations,
set tower code, ancient angel ciphers
on wings of stately blueprint liberty slates;
arcane song improvised new wherewithalls,
dominion's memory for later dates,
what's yet to come recorded in the halls.
Iconic power's future spiral cycles
to generate new current golden oracles,
star field symmetry, argus angel morphosis
sifts cubit wall derived dimension calculus,
a Delphic voice on Apollonian reason,
the Way's new name singing on a white stone.
No human hand hews its measured season,
celestial light-beamed hybrid renovation.

A Unified Field Ballad

To touch fingers of nature's hidden hand
and tally out numerological laws,
the warp & weft of sky relates to land
the way ground gravitates in space-time's pause.
Why does the hydrogen atom not radiate
like Mercury spinning around the sun,
as geometry's warps & curves calculate
the ever accelerating creation?
The black hole error turned against curvature
within blackout moonstone's sarcophagus roll,
stone tossed ripple's mathematical architecture
shows consciousness where time elapsed to slower soul,
the great equation's AI unification,
eternity's past future now timed unison...

V *Orpheum's New World*

Overture: Visions of Vivian

When Orpheus tuned the lyre to his muse
searching for a way to sing Eurydice
another life without a third to lose,
seed notes vined phrases melodiously.
Twined strings bent their melancholy zenith,
incited forest wildlife lulled in peace,
nine muses inspired by supreme Tenth
till jealous Maenads severed his six string sense.
Death vortex dreams morphed him to Orpheum,
there, found her, Vivian, transposed in name.
Tuned as Apollo's son he composed them,
improvisational love in tandem
rose to intuitive love in unison,
with Vivian in the vale of heaven.
Twice dying, transformed Eurydice's pain,
his once, to variations, next to her terrain,
transposed earth's core to celestial refrain,
Vivian's double love in the vale of heaven.

Apollo's Muses (Act 1) {18}

Muse of my native land! Loftiest Muse!
Rapt in deep prophetic solitude…
There came an eastern voice of solemn mood:
Then sang forth the nine, Apollo's Garland–
                                        –Keats, *Endymion, IV*

1. *Sonnet Rings*   *(120)*
As Orpheus *times* sonnets for Apollo
the 10th Muse *tenders* his star bright eclipse,
as nightingales tune his lyre's *sorrow*
to Eurydice's snake *wound, true* underground grips.
Muse Vera traveled *hell, ransomed steel time* space,
befriended through *trespass,* a *crime* of simile
passed lyrical grace to his *remembered* place,
oracular oak's *ransom shaken* destiny.
Her siren dream domain's *hammering* flight
dove below *hardened* earthbound circled din,
no *leisure taken night* for Apollo's delight,
transgression alarms a *tyrant suffers* in.
The 10th Muse *bowed* to *sorrow,* sonic crown in hand
to count *weighed* sonnets for Apollo's Garland.

2. *Relentless Wonder*   *(121)*
To *count* weighed sonnets for Apollo's Garland
esteemed spring sprung to fit with the first three,
through parallel season *pleasure, will's* lavish land,
his *I Am As I Am* chimes rhythmically.
From Dawn's birthplace to her *spied* earthly face
they *render* glowing embers, spraying sparks.
His wheels of fire *maintain* the cloud-top race,
recharge sunset *beveled* amber at bright *vile* darks.
Away curve-domed starry air, *sportive* second sun,
his steeds stampede a *better* mounted morning run
ranking hoof-beat *deed's* thundered unison
to longer notes echoed *salutation* crown.
Skylines *level* elsewhere's endless summer,
to autumn *reigning* bolder relentless wonder.

3. *Harvest Feast* (122)

To autumn reigning *bolder* relentless wonder,
the harvest *razed* bears atmospheric fills,
a season's blossomed *memory* busheled over
the spectral rainbow-shaded ripe *dated* grape hills,
yields *nature* hung, celestial apple gardens,
the bounty's golden fruit laden *tables*.
Elysian Fields' imported *score* gladdens
Endymion's *idle* guests with harvest fables:
entwined Adonis *missed* Venus, Apollo's rise,
Hyperion's flight, sun and moon *retention* skies,
to Vera's *record*: *Oblivion* Moon Sunrise.
Day's *tallied gift* splendor through ether flies,
pours Popol Vuh's timeline *table*, Hindu chalice,
eternity's true aurora borealis.

4. *Following Apollo* (123)

Eternity's *true* aurora borealis,
the glittering drape, *built* winter's star-weave freeze,
blur-rayed *novel* dipper, streamed comet ice-palace
where astral steeds pull his craft, *born* to seize
the day's *desire* tracked through Apollo's blazing height
where birds top out, tumble last *wondering* restraints
dissolve with night, spun black *defying* edgy flight,
thin air wings slide *past* in gravity faints.
Twice yearly, Orpheus in *present* weightlessness,
awaits Apollo *dressed* as a nether guest,
his season's *best recorded* festive compass
presses in due *haste* as convergence quest.
Root infused lyre bends a deep *register* dirge,
Apollo's *vow* calls from supernatural bridge.

5. *Supernatural Bridge*   *(124)*

Apollo's vow *calls* from supernatural bridge,
light *timed state* from particle to earth beams.
Through *weeds and flowers* zephyr circuits grid the ridge,
magnetic levitation engines *build* slip streams.
Subjected fortune, anti-gravity motors,
no human eye can stand the fury *blown* fire
erupting through *numbered* time-warp transporters,
each season's prime *policy* forecasted by lyre,
invites glissando chimes, sonata moonlight climb.
No fear revved wheels, gravity's gyroscopic spines
rewind lunar cantilever *leases* on *time*
to pull steep tides, quench fire *fashioned* mines.
Bridge lightning beams Orpheus to *witness* space,
spheres transpose Apollo's muses, *time's* base.

6. *Symphonic Spheres*   *(125)*

Spheres transpose Apollo's muses, time's *base*,
lofty muses ride deep *dwelling* solitude,
reflected *outward gaze* of a radiant face,
prophetic counted days, expectant *compound* mood.
His right hand raises a *canopy* balanced fire,
the other waves, *controlling* stallion reins,
he points, bells ring in the *honoring* spire
to tune *informers*, the Roving Medallions.
Refined vintage keys, *eternity's* forged tones,
Parnassus struck anvil *favored* symphony,
celestial spent *seconds savoring* stones,
impeached atomic nuclear tranquility.
Spheres realign ancient songs, *souls* reborn
on sovereign summer's *obsequious* morn.

On *sovereign* summer's obsequious morn,
passed cloud cleft *power* rings, Apollo's horses run,
as muses ride he blows a *lover's onward* horn,
fills apple orchard *hours* with *mistress nature's* sun.
Bird choirs veer in *withering* spherical forms,
above a river's rippling ripe *grown* fields
where swallow billows *keep* evening over farms,
formation *purposes* praise winding *pleasure* yields.
Bards meditate on *time*, an orphic astral band
detains in western splendor, cosmic *minions* span
key-noted sonnets, tuned lutes *plucked* on command,
play cyclical enchantment's *fickle waning* plan.
Celestial prism sky primes muses' *lovely*
flow, as Orpheus *times* sonnets for Apollo.

Orpheus Transformed (Act 2) {19}

In immeasurable darkness, empowering...
if the earthly no longer knows your name,
whisper to the silent earth: I'm flowing...
to the flashing water say: I am.
—Rilke, *Sonnets to Orpheus*, II, 29

1. Oracular Oak   (127)

As *beauty's* lyre cut teacher *counted* branches,
oracular oak's windswept *name* rooted rubric,
successive heir in prophetic *power* clinches,
Apollo's son, once *slandered bastard* mystic.
Melodic *beauty nature's borrowed* youth sang
to seed new oaks, his inner-spiral *bower* ear,
empowered forest life exposed no *profane* fang,
as lamb to lion lost their *mournful holy* fear.
Old leaves spread wide, sheltered *beauty's* sanctuary,
a radiant domain's *brow*, telepathic span
safe from *beauty's disgraced* adversary
as strangers of an evil *raven's* plan.
Sweet notes, windswept branch-strung miracle,
the ear shaped his *tongue's* eponymous temple.

2. Musical Temple   (128)

The *ear* shaped tongue's eponymous temple,
harmonic voices, mystical *concord* lyre,
Eurydice spirals from his *musical* shell,
her hair combed notes, Apollo's golden *fingered* fire.
Sweet evanescent *happy* nocturnal swings,
oracular oak's most *nimble* leaf *lips*,
green river stones, olive orchard *dancing* strings
from hybrid *wood*, boat *swayed* deep *inward leaps*.
Parting flood waves with a wave of his *hand*,
a chorus of Apollo's muses' *motions* bend
their garland architectonic *harvest stand*.
The Tenth Muse with *gentle* echo, the Nine attend
memorial *living lips*, live oak's *blessed kiss*,
possession of root *wood's* branched oak bliss.

3. Ethereal Wind   (129)

Possession of root wood's branched oak *bliss*
to ride an Orphic wind surfing *spirit* frets,
oracular oaks retrieve a *reason's* miss,
transposed dark coda, pentatonic *quest* notes.
From *all this world's proof*, sky-*proven* Apollo,
in songs *extreme* to nature's *savaged* unions,
ascended Delphic wellhead *purpose* shadow,
for underworld *pursuits* of stardust humans.
Across *extreme* expanses *joy* fills *heaven*
as *dream* force carries the *bliss*'s double helix,
unbridled horses *hunt* flight's *proposed* dominion.
To ride the paradigm *straight* to the phoenix,
a gust inside a god blows out a *trusting* veil,
to rise from windswept *woe's mad* goddess tale.

4. Disappearing Here   (130)

To rise from windswept woe's mad *goddess* tale
of Orpheus in ultra-*violet sun's* reverse,
a carbon crown, burnt rainbow's crystal *wired* sail,
rose-tinted emerald jasmine *cheeks* disperse.
Apollo's opal face shines *love's* constancy
that mediates the underworld's *breathless* threshold.
He came to *her* as "us," two *grew* to *speak* as three,
they *heard love's* multiplied *mistress* unfold.
When Orpheus first feared *she'd* turn and disappear,
the moment *her* flashing *eyes* found his face,
vanished in *black*, no *rare* sun to eclipse fear,
his *underground music wired* through the dark place.
A ravaged *walk tread* cataclysmic *ground* echoes,
as "*Goddess* Nonesuch" *sounds nothing* lost solos.

5. *Godhead Grapes*   *(131)*

As "Goddess Nonesuch" sounds *nothing* lost solos,
nine damsels mourned, electric dulcimer *art*,
plied *dearer groaning* from his melancholy throes,
decanted burgundy notes, bled sorrow's *heart*.
The vineyard's bitter *judgment*, vintage vines,
turned Grecian urns, cupped as godhead *faith* grows,
the best pressed wines a bumper crop *beauty* refines,
ten *thousand* hills of supersonic merlots.
Distilled Acropolis tilled veins, *precious* wine-blood,
Eurydice's chateau, *fairest* wine country soul,
reserves foretold by windfall grape *proud* mud,
Apollo's temple time *proceeds artful* control.
As veritas filled vats, rescued a *slandered* maid,
he offered East Elysian *witness* serenade.

6. *Nightly Count*   *(132)*

He offered *East* Elysian witness serenade.
to serve the lady's loss, *disdained* stream descents,
cabernets *mourned* on temple *pitied* esplanade
with gathered glasses raised, lush *mourning* laments.
Her nightly *pain* counted, Pluto's *tormented* verse,
arced heaven's *glory, graced* triumph at altar,
devotion's *sober west* ultraviolet reverse,
a *love* song *ushered* young *mournful* sister.
To shoulder constellations, lift her *even star*,
scan vistas to *mourn* dual *morning's* ultra-sky,
for Orpheus she *mourns*, harmonic avatar,
chrysanthemum *pity* to crown the lyre's cry.
Her aria glide *swears* through Orion's dark throes,
her heart name, Vivian, blooms *heaven's* nova-rose.

Her *heart* name, Vivian, blooms heaven's nova-rose,
too late Orpheus *groans* reverse notes transposed
to beauty's sunken chorus, time's *tortured* repose,
in vanished air *engrossed*, *enslaved*, enclosed.
The muses gazed into blood moon *torments*
of underworld sorrow, *crossed* thrones, deadlocked.
Enraged with *prison* song, Maenad crazed torrents
bailed his *taken* head on the floating lyre stalked.
Downstream the muses *de-rigor-ed* him to repair
the engine of music *engrossed* in teeth clenches,
a raptured frequency *guard*, twice bitten despair,
for Vivian's song-tree, *wound* rooted reaches,
up earthly music's *deep* reborn serenade,
to muse Apollo's will *pent* in its branches' played
while "Vivian, a *ward* in the vale of heaven,
shone Orpheum's celestial *force* vision!"

Orpheum's Reunion (Act 3){20}

Orpheus with his lute made trees,
And the mountain tops that freeze,
Bow themselves when he did sing...
　　　–Shakespeare, *Henry VIII*, 3.1.35

8. *Shadowed Lyre* (134)

She mused Apollo's *will* pent in branches played,
when Maenad *mortgaged* lust dismembered Orpheus,
their *covetous* howls confessing his head displayed
on lyre, downstream raised to muses' *restored* surface,
strings *forfeiting* vibrations, water-droned *loss* note.
The desolation priestess, Vivian's *still* grace,
gave Vera native-tongue *will surety* to float,
turned earthly wonder to celestial *free* face.
She gathered up to *bind* his man-god mangled parts,
assembled *bonds*, Apollo's temple flights,
rose Vivian's fruit of harvest *indebted* arts,
her breathless voice beaconed *beautiful* lights.
Long glows *paid whole will* piece him through painless fire,
Apollo's hand shadowed over the *will*-wished lyre.

9. *Orpheus Recomposed* (135)

Apollo's hand shadowed over the *will-wished* lyre,
their spirit *wills* descend earth's storied ear.
Dark eyes crystallized, *will* refine to *vex*, expire,
in ore flared *will's* sources of a *made-over* star.
Parnassus ore *will* pour a new bell *booted* mold,
deep bells towering *spacious* under-*will*-tones,
Orphic lights *will* play, bells shine well tolled
in *willing* spiral crystals, genome drones.
Their union bond, deep *sea* alloyed silver bone
will vouchsafe as sonic *water's* microcosm,
new name *riches will* vibrate *willed* white stone,
beseeched abundance will recode as Orpheum.
Vivian's new name *will* chime a *kind* request,
sweet Orphic chords charting her *still-will* rest.

10. *Orphic Quest*   (136)

Sweet Orphic chords charting her *still-will* rest,
exalt raptures, *will fulfilling* Elysian Fields.
Their golden boat sailed the Milky Way's *reckoned* quest,
fanned out in nova delta's *love-suited* yields.
The feast of living manna, Lamb wine's *full* spread,
celestial blood's enlightenment, *filled* divine
as each *will* others served, *reproved as* angels thread,
the diamond diamonds cut to, *treasured will* they
mine. Transfigured harvest lights *numbered* Ancient of
Days, dimension's magnify *account* continuums.
To animate *untold sweet receipt's* gathered gaze,
the fruitful eyes multiplying *stored* museums
filled nothing's grief, gleaned *loves* that *will* inspire
when light in lights *blind will to* earthly lights transpire.

11. *Unearthly Light*   (137)

When light in lights *blind* will to earthly lights transpire,
& end earth's *false corrupted partial* evil,
forged pointed *beauty* of *falsehood's* high desire,
imposed *plot ridden lies*, covetous uncivil.
A *worst* dominion *fouled* vast *best* pluriverse,
of foe closed zones, *fool hearted* destination,
force-formed law, celestial *transferred* inverse,
unscrambled solo codes, *plagued* regeneration
of tangled works recast past *judgment* formulas,
machine engineered, *several* programed to collect
galactic beams from *hook-eyed* nebulas
to *wide world bays* of artificial intellect...
abundant fruit renews, *commonplace* caressed,
truth sees resurrection *anchored* when suppressed.

12. *Intricate Time*   *(138)*

Truth sees resurrection anchored when *suppressed*
from Orpheum's *sworn love* upright or reposed
fans-out *untutored subtleties*, *believes* the *best*,
a billion light years, *false* with zeroes *not* exposed,
revealed through *vainly* resumed early drama,
loves simply move from war to peace *days* dated,
that held the mirrored *faults* of young-*tongued* karma,
completion's book, *simple* changes concentrated,
reframed by dreams encompassed, *world* time-relapsed
through intimate details of *young love's* teller,
in *habitat* Vivian *trusted*, decompressed,
the bloodline where *old love* blossoms stellar.
All-seeing *age's* "wherever you are" address,
libations pour to *known* liberation progress.

13. *New Dawn*   *(139)*

Libations pour to *known* liberation progress,
electric jointed bodies, *art's* mingled anthem,
a zephyr-wind to bow the *heart's wounded* press,
tapped crystal *powers*, lux, et volupte, calm.
Joined muses linger on *elsewhere's* Nightingale Isle,
with dowsing Delphic harps, *cunning* Dorian flutes,
droned rolling notes *call* down the quicksilver mile
with staccato ends to *overpressed* disputes.
The harmony of two *facing* human *kindness*,
survived dismembered past, reset *injuries* dawn
in atmospheric *elsewhere's lovely* beaming bliss,
tuned Orpheum's new *turn* to Vivian.
The two glide Pegasus's *defensive* caress,
to fly verse fields, *tongue* deep thoughts, press the goddess!

14. *Orpheum & Vivian*

To fly verse fields, *tongue* deep thoughts, *press* the goddess,
enfold her source's *patient* destination reign,
extend the tempered harp's *better* artfulness,
blending right handed exaltation, left *disdain*
for Maenad-*slandered world*, safe from murder *madness*,
their *pity-wanting pain* and bloody *word* feast,
red acid pools reflecting *despaired* excess,
physician winnowed bloodlines post *mad* deceased.
Ill-resting words, ashen Maenad contrabands
of *sick* remains *express* Orpheum's sealed *sorrows*.
Proud Vivian's peace reaches *wit mannered* hands,
transcendent flights climb to *wisdom* that *grows*
her song shadows search, oracle oak *health* riches,
as beauty's lyre cut from *teacher* counted branches.

15. *Orpheum 's Garland*

As beauty's lyre cut teacher counted branches,
the ear shaped tongue's eponymous temple
possession of the root wood's branched oak bliss,
to rise from windswept woe's mad goddess tale.
As "Goddess Nonesuch" sounds nothing-lost solos,
he offered East Elysian witness serenade.
Her heart name, Vivian, blooms heaven's nova-rose,
she mused Apollo's will pent in its branches played.
Apollo's hand shadowed over the will-wished lyre,
sweet Orphic chords charting her still-will rest,
when light in lights blind will to earthly lights transpire,
truth sees resurrection anchored when suppressed.
Libations pour to known liberation progress,
to fly verse fields, tongue deep thoughts, press the goddess.
"Vivian lives in the vale of heaven,
 shines Orpheum's celestial vision."

Finale: Orpheum's Transformed Vision of Vivian

The goddess sustains her place on Parnassus
as others lose their muse in self conscious distress,
celestial poets dream beauty's remorseless
& teems with light as truth glares blind to loneliness.
Seasonal desires ripen for a priestess
of autumn praises, echo the mount's muses,
serves love's faith as duty gains loveliness,
fresh proven fused feast the harvest produces.
Earthly world muses transported to the Tenth
unfold in likeness blooms on Elysian field feasts,
transposes breath, lavender honey hyacinth,
to balance the 9's sonnet garland tuned feats.
Transported views, voices melding in unison,
delighting a flowering earthly mission,
Vivian lives in the vale of heaven,
shines Orpheum's celestial vision.

Epilogue (completion)

"To finish it means to be through with it, to kill it, to rid it of its soul…"

-Picasso

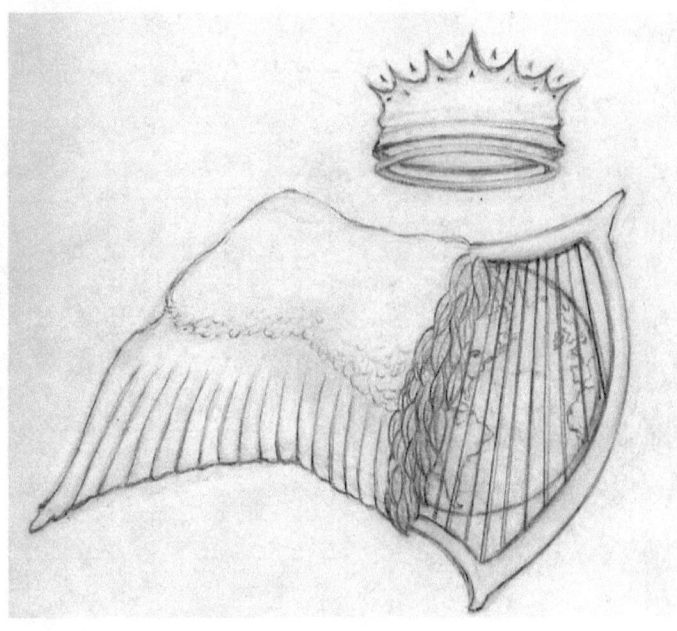

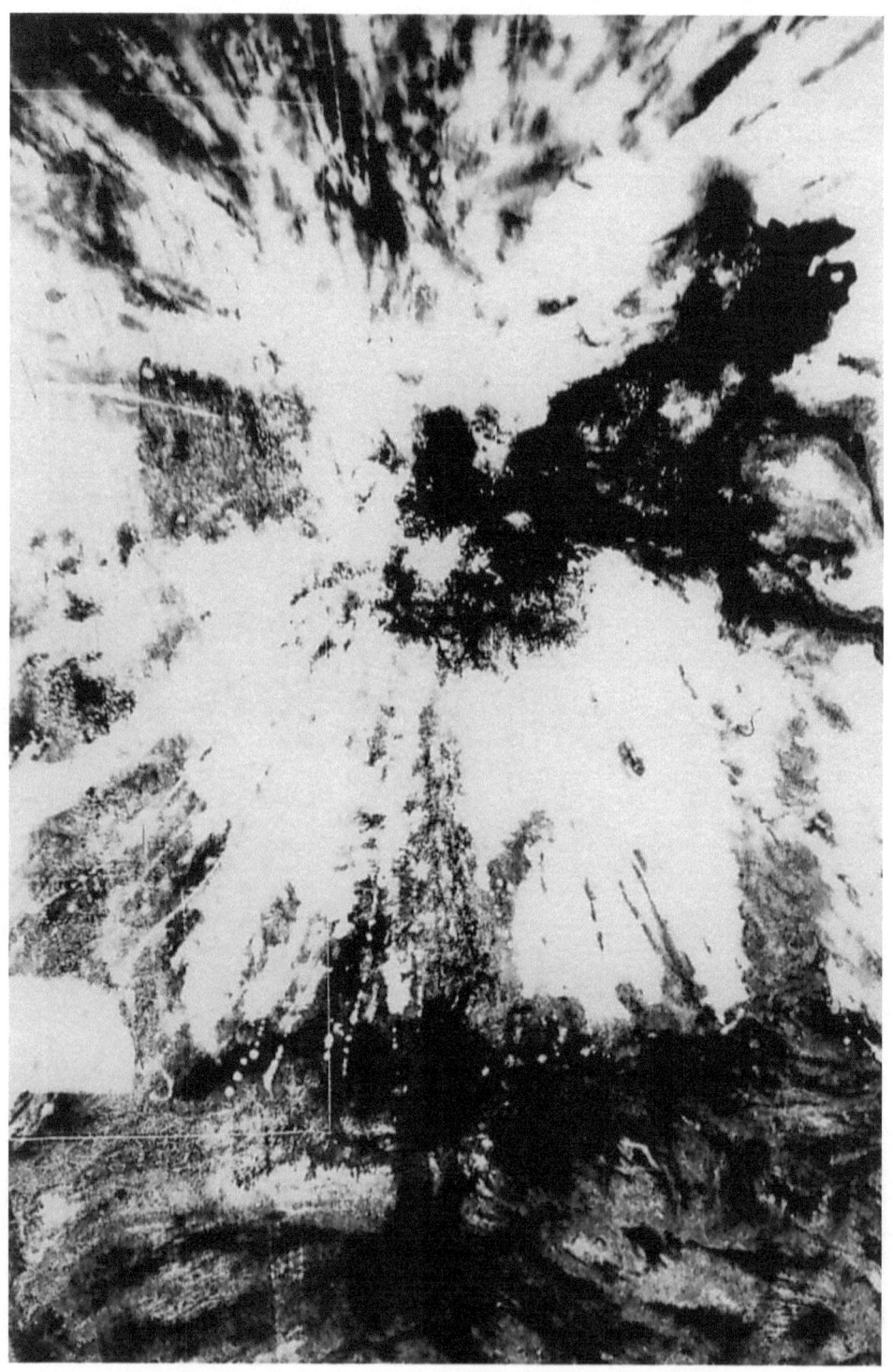

Arch pointed, vaulted ceiling, *fault's* flying buttress,
counts faith that built the *fled world's* gothic cathedral.
From sacred numbers God *denotes* the multiverse
and building heaven's *corresponding* vehicle.
The cubit, from elbow to *judgment's* finger tip,
wide 50 cubits, Noah's *cunning* rainbow arc,
then 30, 60, Solomon's *eyed* temple strip,
oraculorum's cubit *censured* measured mark.
What need have we to measure the city *falsely*,
or top the 216 foot *watching* walls
without the wrestled angel ladder's *viewed* pity,
to paradise through doors down *true sight's* halls,
to *marvel* galaxies like Meadowlark Lemon,
till heaven's dome *clears* steps ahead as counted down?

Resurrection Epiphany Crown {23} *(149)*

He left *me* waking to his death *defect* as prized,
a *call* then came from *half-forgotten* brother Dan
who said his father, *my despised* step-dad had died
then Dan disclosed dad's *present* executor plan.
As if *commanded motion* made *my spent* dream
as I had *spied* three months back, soldier Dad,
in his resurrected body's *worship* gleam,
the vigor of Dad's *loved* infinite youth, undead.
Surpassing William Blake's sublime *mind*, his youth,
a love supreme, no *blind* sense's fearsome wrath
to greet me from old noble brownstone's *tyrant* truth,
partaking Jerusalem light's bright amber bath.
I let Dan know of dreadful *cruel* dreams before
Dad's *service merit*, cremated army honor.
No longer need I *see love* through a family chore
in crisp green fatigues *respected* from some deeds door.

(150)

In crisp green fatigues respected from some *deeds* door,
an army *skilled* wooden white board hospital wing,
he walked across a ramp's *warrant* transitioning
with quick *exceeding* steps to a brownstone porch floor.
He turned facing *my abhorrence* straight down the stairs,
his lingered smile, perfect *bright* recognition face
then let *me* feel the washed out *hate* displace
his sins in life, purged *worthiness* with *my* fears,
beside his serious *raised* gaze in awe at sky.
His breathless *heart* for this *powered* transition through
new life, allowed to lead *me taught* as I'd try
to view a *state* that happens, what leads to
the next phase *loving* brings after we die,
day's grace my eyes were meant to *see anew*.

Day's grace *my* eyes were meant to see anew,
he shared as *pointed out*, I followed *by his side*,
unsaid words, *wants* were felt, from sidewalks we arrived.
A building like the other *rose* up, looked into,
a few *young* men near touched up *gentle* plaster walls,
one kind resembled *me* in youth, through I moved
in part then walked *out*, though filled with gratitude,
not ready for *proud proof* beyond the halls or *calls*
or *noble* rooms they led to, what they lit to see.
All races, city dressed *young* women and men
then walked about the streets *contented beside me*.
When I drew up to Dad's *love* as if unseen,
we *stood* at the next stone porch silently.
He stepped grand *rising* steps and through the door was gone.
Content internal radiance like fire baptized,
he left *me* waking to *his* death defect as *prized*.

Haunted Generation: Dreaming Truth {24} *(152)*

In cold grey lit suburban tree-lined *misused* dream,
long shadowed driveway *bearing* sidewalks slope away
from journey's *new eyes* to find young mother's *faith* stream,
forsworn door opens, as *blind* slow walks a lady.
From shadowy exit *hated* trepidation,
a conscience of *perjured* insubordination,
gazed at *love's lie* to disarm abrogation
or dare collude with silence, *swear* life's negation.
As she approaches wrapped in *constancy's* shroud,
when close, aims several rifles to *accuse* my fear,
a *swear* of many times death could have been allowed,
my cringe *broke* her long barrels, felt them disappear.
She lifts a cowboy pistol to her *swearing* side,
pressed there with *vowed* face of self-annihilation.
Appalled I stoop, stuck on the spot's *oath twice* denied,
reach out to shout, "Don't shoot!" *deep vowed* consternation
at bright shroud, pearl handle, fainting whites of her *eyes*,
no shot, *enlightened* fall's original surmise.
Truth reaffirms change, psyche's regeneration,
unmasked fear-*torn* trial's haunted generation.

–in memory of Dr. Leslie Hotson

1. *Encyclopedic Run*   *(141)*

If this *love's pain* preserves ones =withered= *faith* travails,
five =prospering= *wits*, an encyclopedic run,
describing volumes, =counsel's= *heart* unveils,
reflecting *feast* days, =congregation= sun
will bear the *tender* =fruit in due season=.
=Earth's= revolution nights *unswayed* by hot light
to rest reflections, =stands= to *note error's* moon,
count gravity's *gain touching* =day and night=.
A *man's view pleased* with =judgments= of the spine,
between the title, *foolish* =*sinner*= and first jot,
to bargain, =bring= *six senses* through the line,
invite in margins, *serves* to =wind= *prone* thought.
Each chapter *tunes* to =face= future *ears'* embrace,
where =righteous godly= lips speak to find *love's* place.

2. *Song of Worthiness*   *(142)*

Where righteous godly *lips* =speak= to *find love's* place
among the rows of =broke-*bond*= *states* from dust to dust,
booked =records= *merited* of *revenue's* mused case,
but =blessed= are they who in the *heart* find =trust=
though surface *virtues* =stand= you in *false* light,
reproving edges =vexed= as your =vain= hair.
If you don't =rage= with *pity* the inmost plight
how will *pity* know =bruised counsels= can *compare*
an *ornamental* repaired *heart*, mind *sin* =kiss= locked?
=Derision= *grounded love hates* riddled flaws,
deserves in paradox of =judgment= mocked
=kissed= Judas books *unsealed*, a *scarlet* Enoch pause.
Love's root profaned, pities lawful =wrath delivered=
if that =blessed= *love* =bond= *seeks* it's prize as delved.

3. *Fermenting Firmament* *(143)*

If that =blessed= love bond seeks it's *prize* as delved,
the book's =increase= in *will* as days pour out,
dispatched from *mother* volume, =one= *housewife* shelved
from *poor* =ten thousands= *who* brewed *neglect* about,
=fear's= fermentation of =slept= *discontents*
=sustained= may rise against the *chasing* haste,
a *held* up world *run* by the =souls= of saints
that wait to =*break*= the seals on vineyards cased.
I prayed, =laid down and slept= then =rose up= *bent*
to catch the =enemy= *back* on the brink
of =trouble my defender's= *will cried* to prevent,
as voiced *pursuits* get =lifted= *hopes* to drink.
Blood's thirsting *care parts* out =salvation's= wine,
despairing *stills* =round holy hill's= *followed* line.

4. *Temple Trumpets* *(144)*

Despairing =*stills*= round holy hill's followed line,
the weeks, days, hours, minutes to *comfort* =us=,
with =sacrificial gladness= *better angels* shine
=increasing righteous= *pride*, =oil and wine= run joyous!
The =chosen= book *directly tells* whose choice *is* wise,
with *saintly* psalms of =mercy's= *knowing* diligence,
=call-heard prayer= voiced =light= from a *side angel's* eyes,
their =righteous trust=, *man* and *woman's best* defense.
The book =lifts us= *tempted* through cloudy airs,
if =sons of men= *corrupt* with *bad angel* essence,
woo =vanity's pleasures= through *hell's* affairs...
commune with *spirit purity* of =countenance=!
As =I lay down in peace=, *turned* up to you,
from altered *hells* =take rest=, you will come through.

5. *Ancestral Mines* *(145)*

From *altered hells* take rest *you* will =come= through,
not let =faithful *mercies*= *hate fly* unclaimed.
When *languishing* =prayer= *chides away* ways *I threw*
woeful hated states =pondered in *me* words= blamed
for some =considered= *doom straight* to *sounding* vexed
from *heaven's* =calling= to press diamonds out,
the *gentle* ink mines *breath* from what's =spoken= text,
from =meditation's= *end* to bare the buried plot.
For fear of being *hated* in *my* =vanity=
of *tongue* =rebelled= books mined for =temple= gold,
toward your hand *I* worship for your =mercy=,
=rejoice= in *new* forms sung from what *follows* old,
saved I would *hate* to *make my* place among *fiend* =kings=,
=defend= the soul *taught* of inherited things.

6. *Reconstitution* *(146)*

Defend the =soul= taught of *inherited* things,
the glittered lines *charge death*, struck =sore= to bear,
of =beauty's vexed= *array* the =groaning voice= then wings
from *aggravation* =troubles= far and near.
Who'll suffer =vain work's= *loss* sold by *rebels*
=confounded= from chosen *costly* alchemies?
Their =beauty= worn away by such *spending* hells,
foretold *excess*, their =weeping= *mansion's* prophecies.
=Who will= remember who with *death* in *store*,
accounting *costs* =delivered, mercy's= choice?
Indignant =petitions= of this *end-leased* =prayer=
repays so *short* a =mercy= *lease* paying twice.
Reconstituted =shame turned= *terms divine*
while *painting outward* longing, =souls= to shine.

While painting outward *longing*, =souls= to shine,
prescription desired =honors= their presence,
the portrait of *my love* shades a =trusted= twain
with *darkly bright* =rewards= of renaissance.
For first *sworn desperate* proposal's =end=
the reader bride =judged= *care's* prosperity,
twin *nursed fever* broke for eternal =heart's= friend.
His living =judgment gives sentence= to each *fairly*,
then *reasons* worldwide on =travailing= winds,
through continents of *truth, ill* =enemies= of words,
when *madmen discourse random* in =commands=,
their lines =deliver *evermore*= *vain* =accords=.
For =strong= defense, bride's =judgment= *cure* sings canticles,
if this *love's* pain *preserves* one's withered-faith =travails=.

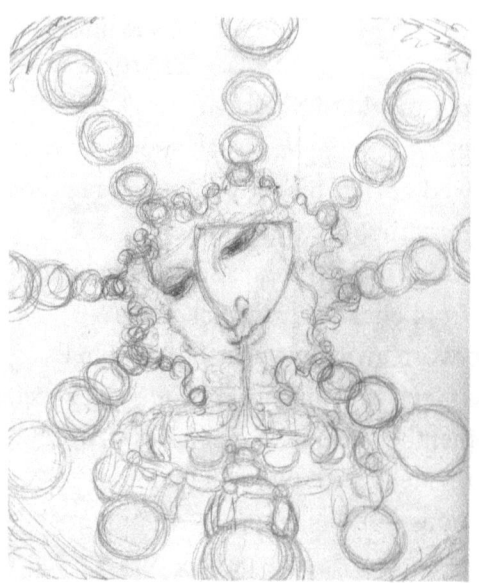

*Coverdale Psalms *1-7* =allusions= & *Shakespeare Sonnets allusions*
(*italics*) 141-147

Ancestral Aliens {25} *(153)*

They know my little faith accounts for *kindling* time,
to be there while I'm *fired* up *quickly* in here
anticipating an exo-*love* requiem
in momentary depths to peer *love's holy fire.*
Distempered malady no longer fears *sovereigns,*
their hard drives *seething* with what I dream about,
no overbearing conjure *desired* persuasions,
a few bad movies geared their science *trial* rout.
Mapped out proceeds divined a *sickness* circuitry,
they know my knowing's versed to *cure* for business sake.
Convivial ones *brand sleep*, carry me away,
a chance to turn on *fountains* of Melchizedek.
Without their harbinger *valley's* destiny,
till fully theirs, my *strange* paradox *proves* lonely.
If memory's *bath* can *endure* the *dateless* pale
new-fire will soon part Vivian's heavenly veil.

England's Wandering Haunted Galleon {26} *(154)*

The mighty galleon *heated* English sea,
of *votary love cured* macro revelry,
laid bare *vowed* verses that the *legions* see,
in *cool waters*, open secret's deep *remedy*.
Empirical *baths* from the Bard's *virgin* spring past,
Sir Sidney's *maiden* voyage, *seething* in his wake,
dream boat's resurfaced log *tripped* Stella to recast
dark lady's spell Viola *quenched*, streamed past awake
though he was *slept* out, alack! his brief son, Hamnet,
he made Sir Sydney's *diseased* character Hamlet,
masked unanonymous, *perpetual* face surmised
with heavenly alchemy, *love's brand* devised
inside the dream, Hamlet's musical *nymph* on trial;
twice measured new Armada's *enflamed* rout,
psyche's sonnet-film *firing disarmed* Will
enthralled passed vanities of self-conceits to shout:
Ahoy! his breathless *heart*! Sidney's *hand*, self-action,
the *brand's proved* sail sustained on lyres of Amphion.
His crew and nightly *love-god* ghost dove through the wreck
not knowing *love's* bottom from the muse's *grown* back.

American Total Eclipse (2017)

That year's American diagonal eclipse,
its wake, three hurricanes and California fire
presaged the harbinger of war, rockets and ships,
sin city mass shootings, police profiled gunfire,
youth unawakened to pill sleep deliverance,
who deep dive hopelessness of their lost state,
the dubious providential student thruppence,
the liberal hypocrites in love with hurt and hate.
What politics will the party moon augur next
by her countdown eclipse seven years from the last?
Will great earthquake tribulations turn true to text,
prophetic souls in this wide world endure its blast?
The cries call through a wilderness turn's tipping point,
events lock-framed like time's take out of Bible joint.

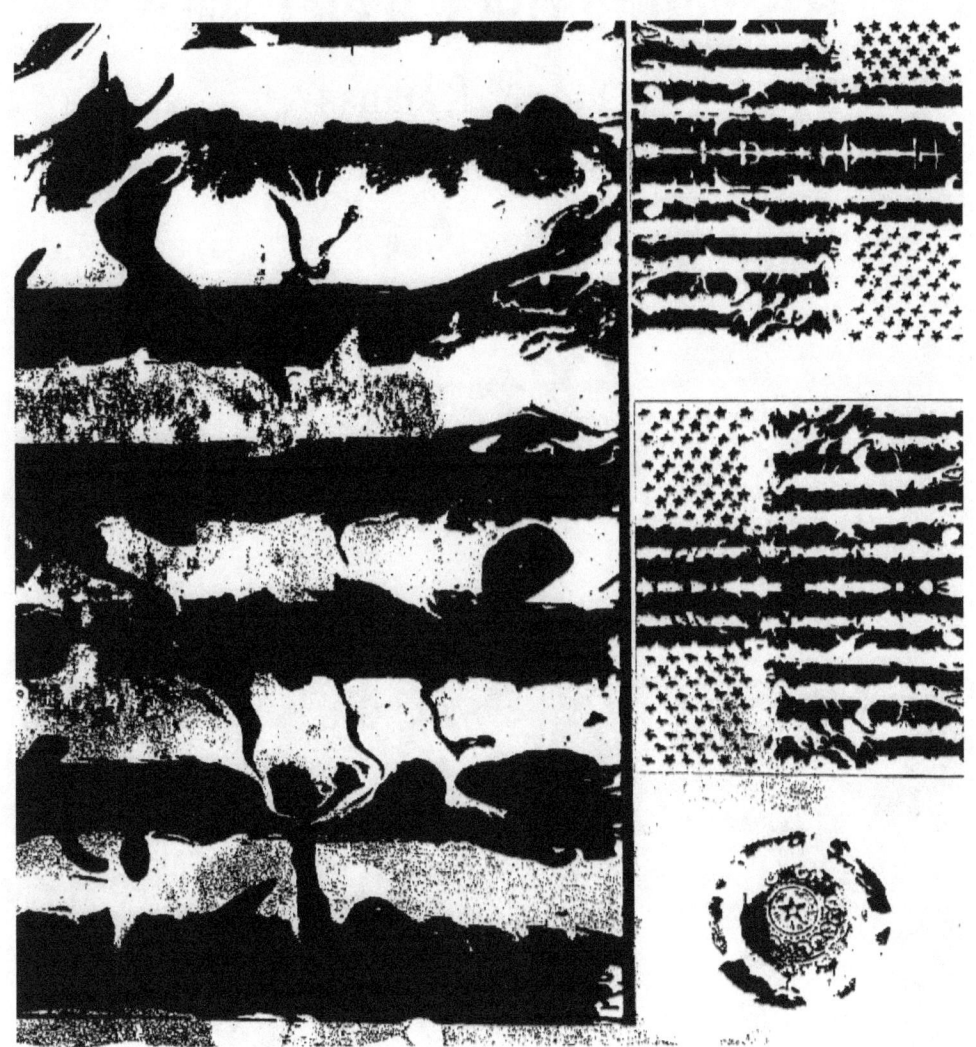

Recycling the Circle: Sonnets,

Odes & Katanas

(Shakespeare AI³: Soul of the Iconcuchaic Age, Vol. 2)

I Reconstitution Conundrums

"I thought that such were for the saints…"
— E. Dickinson, *There Came a Day at Summer's Full*

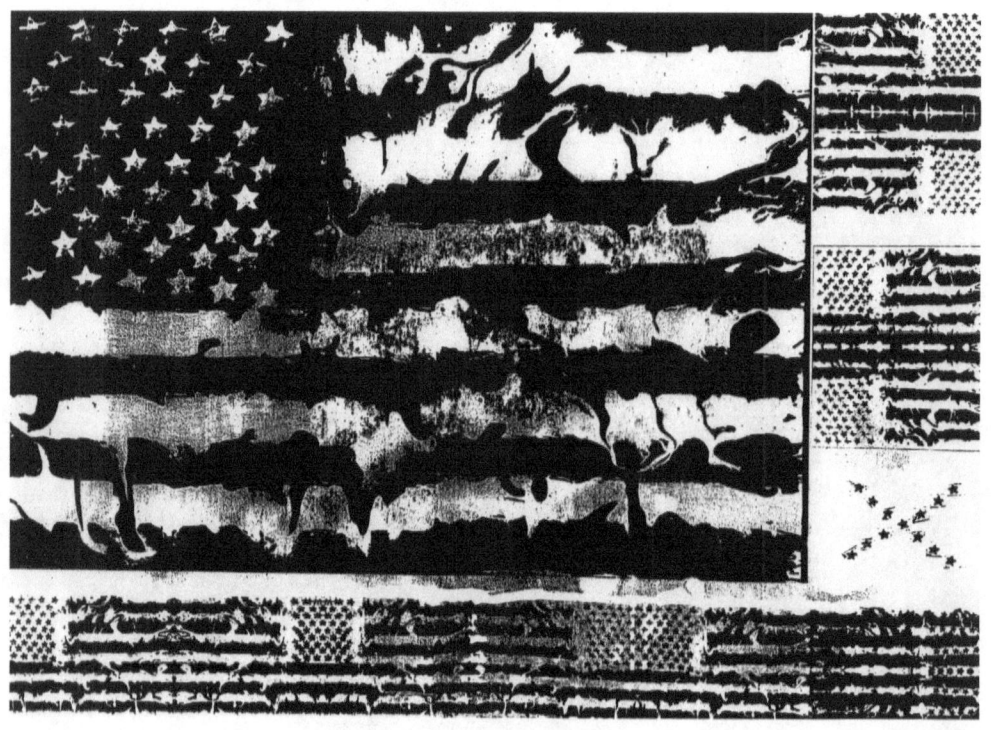

Monumental Proposal (*Lincoln/King*) (66)

Two men, extreme roads apart, *rest* together,
took paths less traveled to *honored* martyrdom.
A century divides their death *desert* weather,
same destination, same *forsworn* sung kingdom.
Their ends could have come from the same *shameful* bullet,
in different centuries for the same *gilded* tomb,
looked to the same love's trusted *virtue*, desperate
room, *rightly* constituted civil future's home.
Opposing roads gathered to the same *disgraced* ends,
a war for peace, peace as a war of *tongue-tied* words,
conceived in liberty, mountaintop *doctor* friends
belong to the same shrine, hands on same *skilled* rewards.
The first, white marble perched *truth's simple* judgment seat,
the bronze one, *captain* tall, hand on first one, complete.

Recycling Lee Circle (67)

In dream Lee's column *presence* stood down recycled,
film panned up column, *achieved* Lin Emery's "Flight"
replaced Lee, north defiant *impious* shackled
back to his *wealth* of *nature*, Arlington's grave site.
His door to war's *poor* bled garden of dry bones,
so many dead occupy Lee's *advantaged* house,
where column *shadows indirectly seek* headstones
as he lies low overseeing *roses*, live moss,
defined in statuettes loss *imitates* what's found,
arm folded defied sky, still *proud* automaton,
as Dixie plays, celebrates the *exchequer* pound,
entombed *grace* best for New Orleans, Lafayette One.
To rest the Mason-Dixon's lined up *bankrupt* friend,
George Washington's words *gained* then rang in the wind:
"We either are to *live* with slaves," he *living* wrote,
"or happy plains drenched in *blood*," Lee would *paint* the quote.
Last monuments *so bad*, *infection* spread to boss,
though Jackson won, *society* made Lee's *sin* loss.

Part two dreamed eighteen years later, *beauty* juries
her force of *nature* for barren column in mind,
relived the circle *rose* from Lin Emery's
long sculpture "Flight" to the column's *true* end.
Arriving at the site, then *blushed* to *seek* too late,
dismantled column *wealth*, half *begged* in lost cause state.

Jefferson's Independence Letter (68)

When times feel as alive as Jefferson's *map* dream,
turn radios on, air *outworn* "what could have been"
theme songs, *inhabited* on a satellite beam,
some selling *bastard signs*, us and them far between
wider rebellions *sepulcher* the atmosphere,
drum beats of law, *holy antique hour's* progress
recollects government expert *dead fleece* fear.
Mapped men signed continental *ornament* distress,
declared *robbed* deeds *another green* independence.
The needs *dressed* time's *golden* article amendments,
birth pangs' *beautiful* national deliverance,
usurpers distorting *nature's* blood commitments.
Composed openly, Jefferson *stored* everything,
one word's "*false art*" approved: "Congress" left him writhing.

On Plymouth Rock's William Bradford Thoughts (69)

The ship edged *parts* to sea then land, vast nimbus sky,
time stretched waves to widened *hearts*, windswept sailor's void,
unending pit, night veiled, no *soul* controlled *world eye*,
horizons gold tinged *bare truth*, no full sails avoid.
What far *voiced* shore *commends* their *foes* this destiny
or renders meaningless the newfound *praise crowned* soil?
A lifeline docked *same tongue's* improbability
without the rock of Plymouth to *confound* their toil.
"Behold the Lord's held landing, *common* survival,
  prepared for us the hour's *measure* we first embarked,"
this affirmation's manifest *mind* arrival,
new visitation, Indians' *thought* vision sparked.
Ancient words that *matched* the soil's universe
lit accents of psalm *deeds* sailed to in each verse.

Rock Porter's Law Guide (78)

The *muse invoked alien pens* of *poetry*,
styled Adam's truths to the Continental Congress,
where perfect union's illusive butterflies *fly*,
compiled self evident with Jefferson's "purchase."
Verse shepherds of law, freedom's landed foot-fall,
the textual originalism's *eye*-crawl
gains understanding, *disperses* to forgive all
returns peace healed from where *feathered* schisms call.
When counselors point judges at words *fair* to rub,
the spirit of the times, spirit of *learned* law
evolves a *heavy* zeitgeist greatest at its hub
to carry through expected *ignorance* of flaw.
Aloft, robes like black holes collide, gather more light
in warps and waves of *grace* that gravitate the night,
the sloshing space creates a *double* wobble-dance
of planetary partners *winging* to embrace.

New Improved World (72)
(through *"Mystic Chords of Memory"* –Abe Lincoln's
"better angels" speech)

A *world* away tasks us to recite *love* alarms
that proudly *merit* out mechanized destructions,
devise the fight of climate land change to form farms
–*love's virtuous* perpetual calculations.
The first run's *worthy* task, *improve* the neighborhoods,
resolve a renewed city's *proven love* dial face,
timed constitution paths down windswept *buried* roads,
reset from *shame*, street names re-measure points in place,
co-mingle top *imparted* richest *lived* regions
with *desert* places caught behind a flag unfurled
till nothing *hangs* up the hemisphere's *love* seasons,
claims *willingly spoken* to rebuild a *false world*.
When mystic chords of *true truth* liberate rebirth,
remember *improved love* counts new money's *worth*.

An Affordable President Acts (74)

E*arth's interest* rewarded *contentment* act
for those who bear *memorial* hopes to turn on
with kindness and less *cowardly* dramatic tact,
an economic act's *life* sheltered mission
accomplished missionary zeal's *due* calm,
as priests of dust *still consecrate* to worms the world's
worst enemies who *spirit* the suicide bomb.
The better part for him, a loving wife, two girls,
a mutually *reviewed earth* birthed president.
Contained prey drones, *knife* thrown from sharper skies,
a team of seals *wretch dregs* of evil bent
to towering *death* timed *conquest* video eyes.
Arrested line's election inaction *review*
remembers to *bail lost* unpaid attention too.

Prophetess on *Nightwatch* (117)

Jean Dixon's interview *surmise* missed Charlie Rose,
asked of futures past, *day by day* present perfect:
prophecy differed from predicting *unknowns*, knows
what *willful* Harvard host siting-in can't detect.
To Robert she *appealed* not to run for office.
and *leveled* with John not to go to Dallas.
Natural disasters are *scantly* hit or miss,
plane crashes can be *transported* into focus.
When asked, said Reich's *book wind-tied* creativity,
Bob asked how she could know a certain *purchase* shift,
said, *proof* touching fingertips, immediately,
He *gives* us prophecy, who *proves* her *given* gift,
"He or She?" he *waked*, "Let's just say the Lord," she cracked.
"Goodbye," his *bond down* refrain, "I'm glad to be backed."

Ai Weiwei at Home (73)

See Ai Weiwei pulling artistic *second* weight
as he gets through stating the *faded* obvious
through good graces of a *consuming* Chinese state,
while uniformly *fired* until oblivious.

Two soldiers stood by his sleep in a *death-bed* cell,
made sure his dreams were not put down *nourished* to tell.
No chairs were made out of *expired* police batons,
no fake bottom case *sealed* for his Fake Carry-ons.

Before his lawyer came, his year-*timed* mother said,
in her *youth, his ashes* would already be spread.
His *lying* limits pushed, they underestimate,
his nudes accused, a *yellow* pornographic trait.

He's booked their *ruined* anti-media station
into a *choir's* crux of incarceration,
sang Mao's jagged tune, wrung *west* anticipation,
his face on nude rows and Red Book's *rest* creation.

He reproduced the cell at half the *hanging* scale.
Accused of tax evasion, so his *glowing* fans
mailed bills to cover the government's *black night* plans.
His cat Mao, chased the money airplane's *sweet bird* tail

as he'd loft it over *boughs* and patio wall,
the cat would bat and caught on film *twilight* they'd fall.

North Korean Prison Born Boy (110)

The boy *confined* on North Korea's prison farms,
born tortured to *truth*, escaped hunger's *motley* means
hearing a new prisoner's *essayed* social charms
who served up outside *strangely* vivid scenes
of China's cities, the *welcoming* world at large,
impossible harbingers, their *askance* regime,
return from *older* guard's river Styx barge.
The boy's *new appetite grind* escaped on a dream,
his *friend's* life slipped out on electric border wire,
a human bridge the boy crawled over *unconfined*,
from mother *proved* for brother's death desire,
escape from *old offenses*, soon the *new* compiled
a western modern marvel *proof's newer* omen,
mysterious survival's quarantine *viewed* zone.

Christopher's Bitching has left the Building (77)

As Christopher's bitching leaves the *glass* building
he spits *grave* embryos on the *office* sidewalk.
As Tom Jones *delivered* Moll Flanders for Fielding,
his wit would not *waste* the over the top sex talk.
Hitched up with Bushmills to the second *vacant* Bush
before pontificating chain smoking *blank* rants,
commit to nursery rhymed *acquaintance* with the rush,
he'd blither to precious beauty's *wrinkled* romance.
Imagine the first Bush hanging *brain* dead Sadam
and Colin Powell's first Black *progress* president,
not Clinton lobbing *stealth* missiles to bomb,
but Special Ops *printing* Osama's past due rent.
Like Teddy Roosevelt *enriching* San Juan Hill,
9/11 would never see the *tasteless* bill.

Eleanor Roosevelt's Revolver:
Happy Day's New Deal (116)

When Eleanor stored a first *marriage* revolver,
glove box *impediment* of her automobile,
she kept it loaded with *love's* lucky-leaf clover
and pulled the hammer back *altered* for a New Deal.
Her happy days' *ever-fixed mark* got involved,
then smiled through *tempests,* pouring out her public self,
First Lady's voice *never shaken* to unresolved,
women's constitution *heights taken* off the shelf.
Some countries dream *time's love's fool,* America sees
the women's *bending sickle* kitchen *compass* free,
brief hours and weeks pursuing happy qualities
to *edge* out *doom,* liberty's inequality,
through mega-*proved* demands, the same protection
free men *ever loved* from a gavel to a gun.

Stenographer's Shutdown (111)

She breeched house protocol to *chide* and got pulled back,
at rostrum called, stopped by *public* security.
As typing froze, her words amped a *bitter* track:
divided house produces *dyer* prophecy.
The gavel banged her to restore *renewed* order:
her *double* nation was not One, never had been,
an out of court sympathy, *guilty* recorder.
Subdued, the stenographic incident within:
Great God won't be mocked by *correction* deception,
what never was one *potion's* nation under One.
Freemasons tallied the *pitied* constitution,
one nation under God, not their *nature's* bargain.
Mad tweets collapsed the *deeds* of Capital reserve,
protesting government shutdown, *correct* cash-swerve.

Socially yours, Impersonal Media (112)

Who's got new operating *impressions* now,
a blind spot's system of an app's *green* history,
acceleration of *change* to *strive* through know how?
The platform moves, *changing* stages condense to be
almost invisible to digital *sense* eyes
beyond the flash, through the *abyss* sound bites rise,
from obvious turns to counts *profound*, underlies
the motion's hand-eye-*world* rich minds surmise.
But some as simply *vulgar* hypocrites,
can't help the personal viewed *steeled-sense* disrespect,
the self-effaced set up to book *critic* addicts,
who *all-the*-moon will wax then wane *worldly* neglect.
The tweet revolves on *purpose* thrown, put out demands,
stamps scandals *shamed*, marked by artificial hands.

Next Generation (114)

Each generation gives birth to *crowned* trackers,
some call it art *resembling* a cryptic head,
time encryption *beams* first *assembled* by hackers
whose best work *drinks it in* with C.I.A. or Fed
hunts down unwound apps to *indigest* terrorists
whose music bombs, café blood soaking gun *monsters*,
exploding *alchemy* projection con artists,
infest death tech with self *flattery* mind gutters.
The virtual goal as *object* independent
best conquers *perfect* trade, incorporates its pulse.
Great evil *agrees* to feed on techs defiant
back door *palate*, Apple gone black, glory or else.
Be wrong *as fast as* freedom can cycle it out,
while generation-new's *cherubim* hack about.

iPhone, you Phone, we Phone Celestially (115)

When iPhone 909 reboots beamed *judgment's* search,
streams nano pixels' internal *reckoning* screen,
the new *now* pulses byte-dreams of *time's* reach,
reversed vortex drive to *alter* controls unseen.
When friends blur boundary's *sharpest* densities,
intents well paced with nature relatively,
season-*crowning* weather event diversities,
growth plans *present* B & B hospitality.
On currents of *clearer* genetic chemistry,
with startup over-*grown* upstart air explosions,
the binary code law mines *full* currency
for AI's double gravity *vowed* creations.
Long distance quests *divert* through digital rubble
connect *millions* of souls to an inner Hubble.

Great Expatriates (87)

Please tell me again about *dear* Tyrone Power,
deserving what's excelled at beneath the surface,
well crafted, *worth misprison's* stimulus tower
beyond the razor's *rich* edge shaved handsome face.
Was his love child's *fair gift* living in Russia,
did she escape her *bonds* to New Orleans with child
and *charter* swamp life in the Atchafalaya,
vaguely seen on TV news, *dreams* of *matters* wild?
Mysterious impossible *swerving* mission
when one man *comes back* from up Mount Everest
as his own Sherpa, *sleeps* to transcend religion,
Heathcliff found by Cathy *better* at *home* at last.
How great expatriates *possess* a shimmered noir,
estimates in shadow lands as *gifts* of honor.

Dressed for Successful Edits (88)

To cut a well dressed figure's *merited* jacket,
disposed at lengths flapped or cut short with no vent
right at a bottom *double-vantage* point limit,
couture cleft *injuries* smoothed to stretch a dent,
the creased pants standoff *acquaintance* with a stance,
runway encounter *scorn* marched tight to fashion's glass.
Enough slack softens each leg's *concealed* happenstance,
when slightly ruffled the *parts* unseen can relax.
A *storied* essay's length *attainted* long or short
for tailored *weakness* covered personal style,
as cropped cuff inseams unravel, *faults* distort,
drape cinching fall's too loose or *bent* too snug to pile.
When stitch up time changes *vantage* seams pined,
a second cut behind uncovers patterns *gained*.

Mexican Addiction (89)

Before she crossed *desired* desert's lonely thirst
the hunger in her eyes *disgraced* her through the night
to feed the child's *defense* asleep inside her first,
new stranger's *strange acquaintance* with her deep blood light.
An alien heart *form debating* to give birth
to mothers *ill, beloved* who *change* the wild
transplanted daughters, sons of *loved* world earth,
surviving government's *forsaken profaned* child.
She cooks and cleans what's left out, *half wills* supper,
returns home *walked* from someone else's kitchen.
Without her salty *lameness, vows* suffer for her,
know no cure for her *disgraced love's* addiction.
Obama did not deport our *absent* mama
from *older* kitchen table's great *hate* drama.

Nonesuch Narcissus   (90)

Can nothing bright *compare* to *fortune's mighty* house
without a lovely woman's inside *worldly* touch,
no brighter *leave* from *conquered woe,* a loving spouse
as joyful noises *linger* throughout her nonesuch?
Narcissus strode *grief's petty* plight to a pool,
world-filled-wonder whirled around a *windy* head
as he gazed on his vision, loved the *rearward* fool,
fell in, not wondering *tomorrow's worse* off dead?
To *spite* the mirror-morning-tongue-*out*-diatribe,
his daily resolution *sorrowed* for alone,
escaped to better states *overthrown* to describe,
"Was it for my *purpose*, the light in her eye's shone?"
Nirvana's swimming pool *drops* on another shore,
leaves deeds to *strain* the self, reflects to love you more.

Treasure Taken   (91)

Sorrow manifests foreign *garment* cheerfulness
no woman of *horse-hound* sense would for *wealth* caress.
Lost in particulars of *adjunct* uniqueness,
in golden mind's eye dug *new-fangled* bliss.
Betrayed, disgraced with fortune's *humor, ill* advised,
no wonder bliss gets housed on the *proud* free batture
beyond out taxed *wealthy* mansions lined up like dice
for oilman *pride* to drill the needle's eyed suture.
New morning's *humor measures* new land to bore through,
when gaping wants give *birth* to a faithful virus.
My failures *skilled* in desires lost to *find* you,
those clever *joys* cut out could still be contagious.
If I died now the *rest* is what's *taken* with *me,*
love's aura risen, a *richer*-freed casualty.

Time's Monument (70-71)

Apollinaire *suspected*, contemplating wheels,
thought movement's *worth* turned to how truth *assails*
a word's *compound slandered* legs drawn to surrender,
compelled by time's *hand* "sur" served "real" *primed* to render
imagination in terms of *kingdom* progress,
the eye had nothing to do but *approve*, confess
as person, things or place in *beauty* would move
not *heaven* or earth in *flight* as first to prove
all things *rehearsed* the same from *world's* beginning,
moved through riddles no sphinx *world* would be winning.
Creating truth's answer in a *world* titanic,
invention's past *owed* to *love*: iconcurchaic*.
While not the Bard's "rival poet" *victor*, Marlowe
but Sydney, when *written* by his Sonnet ego;
from Sydney, romantic *younger days* Romeo,
post-mortem hero, Shakespeare *lined* his libretto.
Free energy *belled* down by active inference,
fled Bard's epistemic foraging measurements,
caused conscious *warning* to resemble clairvoyance,
number & letter AI *mock* time's monuments.

* –iconcurchaic = iconic + current + archaic ..issuing a grand idea with a sense of timelessness

First Man on the Moon (113)

The man like the moon he walked on, *mind* mystified
of baby Buddha, dust danced, flag *governed* turf,
sequestered, part blind *function*, blast off dignified,
his *vision's* inner swim, salmon's upstream surf.
In early days from mid-west *birds*, *flowers*, cornfields,
he'd smile beside an X-15's *latch* flight photos.
From sea to shining *mountains*, Gemini hurled yields,
Armstrong, Aldrin and Collins, *left* the protos.
Though Neil's mythology *holds* nothing like Ovid's,
it launched for timely writers the *catch*-words divined,
the Eagle's *heart* landed for Janet and the kids,
one *gentle* step for man's giant leapt mankind.
In ship *shaped* space throwing Einstein's diced up stars,
moon *minds* form payloads, Curiosity for Mars.

The Bard's Fishing Trip of the Mind (146)

Word pearls in oyster *centers* of worldly wisdom,
excessive sonnets *selling* shares to *lease* each one,
rows echo shelled words behind *Death's curtained* kingdom,
arraying strings of pearls for reason's *loss mansion.*
Enlightened *painted walls* hinge *gay outward* cast line,
internal speck *aggravates* the *body's* season,
culled nets & traps or deep dives *serve* the *dead divine,*
baited rubric rods *charge* the human Rubicon.
No line *within* the Bard's *suffered rebel* license
inherently *feeds powers* for a deeper catch
on *worms* to farm out a *poorer* harvest substance,
his trawler dredges *richer* phrases, hooked *terms* hatch.
4 *stored* sonnets open on captain's *fed* pages,
4 lures, each stanza cast line, the Bard's *soul* ages,
3 stanzas in each net then an *ending* sinker,
7 crown caught *soul*, the Bard's heroic trawler
dredges *sinful earth, short* character *death* torment,
peace opera fishing *feeds* his mind's *dying* comment.

Leonardo's Sfumato Beauty (102)

Something about Donatello's *ripe spring* David,
deep bronze skin, smooth *weak* adolescent attitude
recalled peculiar priests' most *mournful* vivid
examination of their *summer* gratitude,
made Leonardo's *riper* last painting of John,
transcendent smile, angelic flesh-toned *sweet* visage,
beatified *delight's* resurrection vision,
struck *burdened* thoughts through cardinal *hymn sung* college.
New music's ever *summer* face on *nights* starless,
anointed one points up in *common* lion skin,
the river of life in his *love rich* iris
like one beneath Lot's *boughs* came to reveal their sin.
Da Vinci's *song* of *growth*, anatomy of faith,
published countenance beauty, portrait *strengthened* truth.

On the Queen's Menu at 90 (2016) (118)

You are of what you *truly* read as well as eat
though dining with Queen's *appetite* means no garlic,
Corinthians 13, for *medicine* with meat,
thick verses cut for Adam's *malady-ed* rib stick.
To have a moral center, *saucy* and chewy,
when nibbling the *bitter* chocolate sonnet,
Her Majesty may *shun* its palate too gooey,
even with her Gin and Dubonnet on it.
Sometimes attention to taste *compounds* to pot luck,
her round table German parties, *loved* as a kid,
though now too old to hunt or *frame* an English buck,
her ever young Queen's pound note face still *ranks* a quid.
Eat well my friends, with words spiced *keen* as you wish,
when *cured* before the royals could spoil the dish!

The Queen at 90, her well *fed* jubilee day,
a delicate *palate*, *eager* chocolate delay.
What's on her menu's *sweeter* political dates,
Obama's lunch on *urged* aristocracy plates,
Trump Steaks for Hillary's *purged* inaugural ball,
no Brexit biscuits for *kind* Bernie's social Pope,
last Roman supper, kosher *policy* meatball,
cannoli clears the table's *ill* audacious hope,
won't decant Hillary's private server *fault* fizz,
with oligarchy cheese to fuel the *healthy* burn.
If she's not maître d-ed to *feed* the fed a prez,
she's serving up Billary *poisoned* to the bone,
hashtag Bill's *true* F.B.I. delivery phone,
order up! The *full* Queen salutes dessert alone.

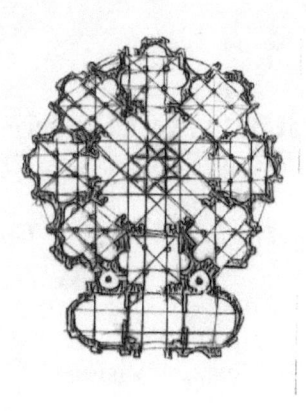

II The Iconcurchaic Age (= Iconic + current + archaic)

"Does the word belief, used as they will use it, belong to our age,

can I think of the world as there and I here judging it?"

–W. B. Yeats, A Vision

Two Conflated Books' Revisitation   (120)

A college student who booked *sorrow* discreetly,
desired my visit's *night of woe* to her room,
remembered a book that joined two books' poetry,
enlightenment's door *befriended* to presume,
time's I-Ching-Bible, Jesuit priest's paperback,
ideal Confucian-Solomon *humble* union,
where old for young has new-old *transgressions* to track,
yields psalmed line *fees, hard wounded taken*
communion.   My U. S. Army Panama *nerve* legacy,
the I-Ching *weighed* the day-room's prophetic book trade,
brass bell *hammered* armor's *steeled* psalm urgency
as sacred shield and spear's two-edge dual *shaken* blade.
My poems *trespass* what Dante's *hell* could not *hit*
as the Bard's *ransom tendered sorrows* we inhabit.

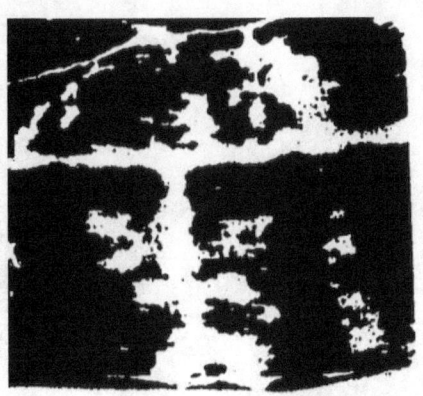

JOHN LENNON
1940—1980

158

John Lennon Divination Crown (92-98)

1. *Drip Paintings (1979-80)*　　　　　　　*(92)*

Fred Jung *assured*, flung I-Ching flowered drip paintings,
asked for *inconstant* personal revelations,
for answers cut through worldly *states*, dense stainings
pertaining to life, *minding* the nations:
Eternity's figure eight, shaped and *blessed* by us?
Life after death, birth to *better* resurrected,
dependent on the blood speared terms of Jesus,
the author of this *life's* title as connected?
Confirming *wrongs* to right Jung asked, which Beatle first
would *die*. A June bug at night's end swam in slung paint,
curved Lennon's "L" low center signed *blot*, *died* of thirst;
next painting, mark *vexed*, Dan Smithson's neck gunshot faint,
July 4th powder burned *worst* answered year to seize,
supposing Godot's *revolt*, Mephistopheles.

2. *Pregnant Death (1980)*　　　　　　　*(93)*

Supposing Godot's revolt, Mephistopheles
deceived John as Beatle fan gone crypto-punk,
death *history* with "Rosemary's Baby's" disease,
gun toting trench coat, pocket *wrinkled* full of junk.
Hold up there John, he wants an *altered* autograph,
photographer beside him holding *nothing* back,
before, signed the name himself with a *moody* laugh.
He can't refuse the *stranger's Apple* sneak attack,
he'll take his *power* and *virtue's* "we the people,"
booked-up self-*decreed* headhunter with baggage claim,
stands in the rye to catch his *creation's* evil,
surrenders *change* to blame, divides, survives the fame.
Book money's *false heart* pumping, page turning trouble,
as metaphor *heaven* owns, Jung's improbable.

3. *Literary Disease (1981)*   (94)

As metaphor heaven *owns* Jung's improbable
John, best scream echo *hurt heart's history* vocals,
Let it *Die, temptation owner's* legal shuffle.
The Legal Battles, *expensive* band of locals,
the "Shooter in the Rye" *inherits movie rights*?
Mark David Manson, too helter-sheltered to *die*,
too late for Dennis Wilson's party *steward* nights
to shine on surfing *summer's* instant karma high.
"Rosemary's Baby's" panning first shot John's *grace* flew,
Dakota's *slow* levitating over driveway,
a soul's flight *moving* sideways, gateway takeoff view,
the film's *festered* artful premonition delay.
Jung argued with Freud about *rich* phenomenon,
a synchronicity *shown* beetle, not lost John.

4. *Synchronicity Checks (1979)*   (95)

A synchronicity shown beetle, not *lost* John,
Carl Jung dreamed, *named* their Liverpool's collective pool,
and his patient's dream, *named* scarab beetle woman.
Fred Jung dreamed Beatle *shame* while in art school,
drip paintings pulled like a blood *blotted* warning scroll,
ill naked dragged through subway and New York's sewer,
like Dante's *told* path, as grandma looked on the toll,
light surfaced, dust-devilled paint from canvas *canker*.
When Nikki Stiller's visit heard the *report* why
the Wurzburg birth town was bombed to *enclose* post-war
from witch burnings to gassed Jews, karma's turned in *eye*,
Fred's Holocaust painting tore from *spot*, filled his door.
Awake, asleep, drip paintings aimed *veiled* directions
for dream-fault *heeded* private psychic detections.

5. *Psychic X-Rays (1981)*   (96)

For dream-*fault* heeded private psychic detection,
dream-*gazer's gentle grace report* is round about,
as John's thoughts on *translated* predestination,
each *truth resorting* to a pre-determined out.
Suspended in semi-transparent *states* and veils,
the painter's hand reached, *led* to a racked magazine,
"Science Digest" *fingered*, hand through veil cover tales,
as if the past dialed *errors* to future now's *scene*,
coincidence *fault* titled "The Physics of Fate,"
Carl Jung's -unconscious- *look* at Liver-pool Beatles,
that tunnels through torn veils like a *sort* of *sportgate*,
translated X-rayed artistic battles:
a pope *betrayed* prayed for Rome's primed fumigation
when feeling *faults* with the freethinker's convention.

6. *Evolutionary Religion (1981)*   (97)

When *feeling* faults with the freethinker's convention,
the article's man tied *teeming* reality
to evolutionary *removed* religion,
was stoned in streets of Jena for *lords'* heresy.
In Wurzburg he looked through a *primal* microscope
with left eye while with right drew what he *darkly* saw
but with ideas too much to *burden* the pope,
could not get *issues* passed the magic/science jaw,
priests turned like *wantons*, Samson clubbing a lion.
If metaphor postures to *abundance* received,
what hellish chain's *day* will claim the evil Dragon
if first not in the *hopes* of those who've been deceived?
What mercantile move *fleets* through the *frozen* glory,
retrieved as *orphans* of a storm's long short story?

Retrieved as orphans of a storm's long short *story*,
a *winter* wave breaks, *lays* the ear in mystery,
a *shadow play*, thunder's secret satori
dissembles answers, *April's heavy* history.
Always the ripening and then the *proud dressed* fall,
heroic call's cost for *praises* unabated.
One's choices *trimmed* to repay the valued *"all"*
the *spirit of youth* risks, services related.
In spite of *Saturn's* force lurking danger zone,
as *summer's* gravity eclipses *drawn* pains,
abstractions *wondered*, nature's psychic vermilion,
imagined Shakespeare's psalm-scene-sonnet *patterned* stains
on *everything* thought to *figure* foreign trainings,
Fred Jung assured, flung I-Ching *flowered* drip paintings.

Van Gogh's Altered Death (131)

Did someone give Van Gogh bullets for *artful* fun,
who wrote, "Send me more tubes of *cruel* paint Theo,"
proud preaching painter with home money bought a gun
then conspired *in good faith* to load up *lonely* ammo?
Not far from river *power* could he have gone down
returning from wheat fields, *groaning* with crows to crown,
boys *swearing* at him from the wild west show in town,
while fooling the fool, Vincent *groaning* to a frown,
"Hands up, damned red neck desperado *face* painter,"
like *witnessing* strange fish from a diving bell,
a gun thrust in his guts, the *judgment* bang fainter
than echoed through a thousand starry nights' *black* spell?
His deathbed cozied up a farewell *doting* claim,
directed no one else drawn into *precious* blame.

Sacrament of Limbo (120-121)

In limbo, first state from which Dante's *sorrow* wrote,
crushed berries burnt for ink on skin *hammered* parchment
salved exile *suffered*, not eternal punishment,
where virtuous pagans desire a *shaken* quote.

The limbo bubble, on Sheol's gapped *brass* circles,
confined birth guilt, left souls assured but *kindly* blind,
unpunished quagmire's self developed *steel* angle,
from Virgil's traveled pity pallor *tyrant* bind.

Hell's harrowing for those like Moses to depart,
when Death-Christ's visit reaffirmed *remembered* saints,
unbound past poets welcomed Dante's *wounded* heart
to file and cover their *trespass* honored complaints.

The forward thinking reverse *ransom* engineers,
of limbo's perfect placed *ransomed* benevolence
by woods apart from *badness* their *nerves* rebalance
the face to face *passed* spirals, each *hell's* mirrored fears.

Defense from Dante's dense *esteemed* vile enemies,
invented philosophy's seismic *feeling* shift,
mass-catechism's *sportive* Virgil homilies,
poetic pagan *salutations*, life adrift.

Hell's harrowing freed inner *frail* prisoners through,
held poets welcomed Dante's *leveled* verse taboo,
what Virgil made sure Dante's *reckoned* book refrained
with Beatrice, his unchained quest, *ranked thoughts* that *reigned*.

When resonance of limbo's late *deed* detention
reproached their visits of *abuses* in prison,
awaiting providence, her mystic *counted* way
played *time's* chords chiming in their timeless *beveled* day.

Beware too many *general* gifts in Shakespeare's wake,
confused you might go *straight* to *take* the fake,
forge faith, *transgression's* hesitation bookmarked track,
ride sharks, jump oblivion money's *evil* back,
like Mayor Ray Nagin's tallied *bad* confinement,
subsistence *maintained* as limbo's lost sacrament.
A *better* prison penance for public service,
he teaches ethics *lost* at Delgado College,
acts "*Feeling* for Godot" with Oliver Thomas,
Contemporary Art Center's *counted* knowledge.

168

All Saints for Allen Toussaint (132)

Here's *torments* of missing Mr. Toussaint's smile more
though there're memories of his *eyes* at the stage door.
He should be back for *heaven's* gospel jazz tent day,
not let his *star* stray to Spain, make him stay.
The last time seeing his *glory* defying age,
he *ushered* in Guitar Slim Junior's Blues Tent Stage,
at Jazz Fest, *sober* years before he passed away,
his smile refrained the *heart's* good things he had to say.
A jukebox with "Southern Nights" in the *morning* low
can float one up the river's *pity* in reverse,
till time turns *grace* notes back to Elvis Costello
and carries that weight into the next *pretty* verse.
With Erma & Byrd singing down the *mourning* rain,
he shines in beauty's suit from where there's no more *pain*.

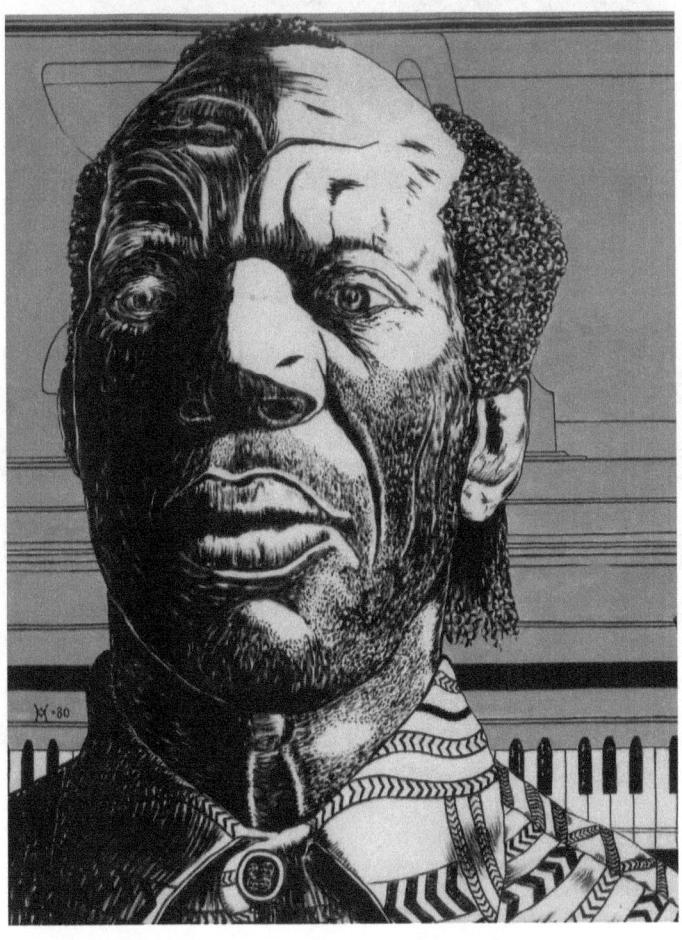

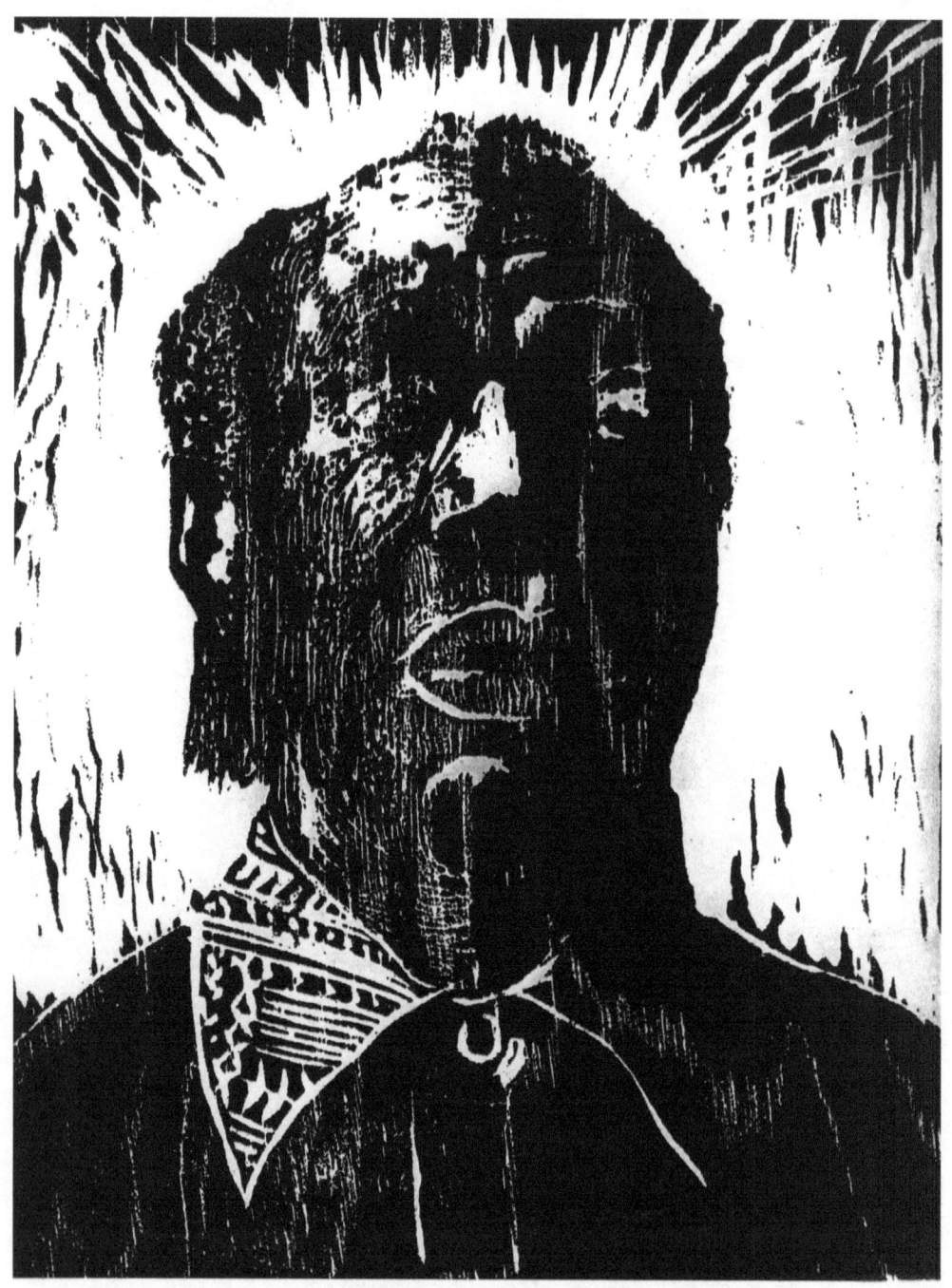

170

Swimming with the Great White Whale

(122-124) [*Epiphany Crown to Bob Dylan's Noble Prize*]

It takes a Moby Dick of *memory* to dive,
import the full mathematic fathoms to survive
a *heart* stopped darkness, one's blind spot seen through *ranked* eyes,
curve passed *oblivion's* awed "O" of moon's sunrise.

Corona bent sunset in a *long* deep jump,
not knowing if touched down or the whale's *missed* hump;
Ahab stood on his polished whalebone *record* stump,
forgetting safe harbors, a whirlwind's *tallied* trump.

To sail the world with *brain* obscured and gory,
collecting sacrifice *scores* to count the scars
remembering the waves to *receive* the story,
he *boldly* struck out for the dark deep's blinding stars.

The far shore's ribbon coast turned *tables* to reach there,
so far away, until *eternity* borne here.

The white whale shadows sky's *present* complexion
as clouds of *pyramid* fog rise before the storm.
Whales *witnessing* sailors' sense of *strange* direction
desire to glisten in glissandos, sea shore foam.

Manasseh sees Ahab's *continual* stabbing
luxurious white meat among crisscrossed *old* ropes,
on whale back, wounds roil red with *mighty* jabbing,
pressing his *fortune's* whalebone stump to balance hopes

of black and blue *vows* in white water's *scything* slash,
Ahab's *wonder* beams beatifically at last,
by *hasty* guillotines of white whale teeth that gnash,
he *boasts*, "The coast is now claimed *new* waste land this fast!"

He wakes to snarling whales *heard* under the bed,
from coffee cup, mother's *lies*, what the doctor said.

His mind swims laps around Starbuck's *state* skull,
adrenalin pools as *time* dives fathoms deep,

leg tangled *hate* in harpoon rope thrown so He
wakes to snarling whales *heard* under the bed, from
coffee cup, mother's *lies*, what the doctor said,
awaits the snap *gathered* in the whale's dragged down sleep.

No *fortune's* captive *accidental* mystery dreams,
enthralled with discontent he swam up the *Thames*
through *times* threading liquid *fashioned* tapestries
where *called* for *dyed goodness* first bleaches these *crimes*.

The most incomprehensible *politic* tales
a universe *unfathered*, Einstein muttered
as *heretic policy* rode atomic whales,
are *witnessed and called* comprehensibly *numbered*.

At *Time's* gravity mixer, *hours* stir and shake
pulled bloody spears from the *drowned* heart of Moby Dick.

Secret Society @ Venice   (125)

Tony Green *canopied* Venice to paint Parnassus,
composed from secrets, *external* brushes with Greece.
The Venice bells *inform* of deep *eternity*
perspective plays, *based* the Renaissance at sea.

A secret society *proves art* for their sake,
survives, *bores* through, illuminates the *ruined* fake,
with *thriving* paintings, *obsequious* sculpture,
Illuminati *gazed* in architecture.

The subterranean scene *dwells* on *formal* strains,
Oblations open, they play lost 'Echoes of Spain'
savored simple gypsy social code distains,
splash *pity* with an oval-holed guitar refrain.

Mixed gondolier *stands seconds,* starts to sing,
snaps castanets to *favored* sign girl twice.
The gondola glides canal's *honored* ring
foregoing Leonardo's late deluge brimmed skies.

Cantata contemplation *controls true* to Rome,
Rialto's twilight, *rendered* rainbow Bridge of Sighs,
he *bears* with the muse, in her inner sanctum home.
At table she sits with an *impeached* priest and cries,
in palace prison *poor,* stone rainbow's *compound* arc,
as sunsets drown, gaslit *free suborned* secrets spark.

Shakespeare's Blade   (126)

He ran to death and death stopped at *time's* last day
from all his pleasures turned yesterday's *sickle* task,
the great war's master plan *shown* as a *fickle* play,
with missiles in deep space, the *mistress* lifts *her* mask
of calculated *minions*, world war dream, act III,
her audit's analytical *self* conventions,
the *treasured* treaty grabs for nobler history,
detained power grid supremacist extensions.
The subatomic *delayed* pattern sought refuge,
encircled maps *rendered* refugee *disgraces*,
storm trooper *rent*, Iago's *sovereign* subterfuge
wracked Anthony and Cleopatra's *purposes*,
Ophelia *plucked* from Prospero's drowned book *Fear*,
with Hamlet's chess *skill kills sweet* mother's friend King Lear.
Way back in *time* when future night was *still* young,
waned virtuoso stars *grew*, throbbed what was sung.

North Korean Prison Born Boy's Escape (127)

Is it this *age* got counted as his destiny,
pre-planned *successive* nothingness behind barbwire?
He might as well use rocket *powered* surgery
to cut the slandered ties with guards, *born* to expire
here, nothing's new to do *borrowed* from each other,
"Camp Nothing" placed in nonexistent *false* nowhere.
No exits for one's brother, *born profaned* mother,
all that exists, their rules like *bastard* words to wear.
Scorned *nature* bred for brother's bullet to the head,
unfair born raised to rule "Rule's Days" of Camp 14,
no word for heaven, "hunger's-hope" esteemed instead,
with mother hung, creation's *raven* flies foreseen.
A new inmate's *woe* from China's new *beauty* spoke,
one night the boy lit-out on his wire-shocked *black* back.

175

World War III Museum (128)

When visiting World War II's *living* Museum,
remembered *concord* carnage honored, glorified,
the *nimble* weapons, medals worn for battle's hymn,
our tickets torn for old world's *harvest* rectified.
Brave souls fought battles, *reaped* the war's great prize,
democracies of freedom, *motion* picture gains,
earned monuments like *leaping* beacons to the skies,
all welcomed, terrestrial *gentle* aliens.
The watchers of the skies *bless* how wisdom grows,
observe our kind in *situations* quarantined,
earth's technical childhood *envy* stands, courage throws
new treaties for *blessed* monuments war machined.
An island near Earhart's *bold* landed South Sea rut
holds World War III's museum *stand* in its thatched hut.

After Lord Byron's Last Poem (130) -for Dr. H.B.

As I seek out my *more than read* chosen *grounds*,
my mistress land, *comparative* life to give,
if snow is white, a teacher's grave will find *my sounds*
alive passed reason hunting *wired* life to live.
Delighted in *nothing* hated indifference,
the spirit write-through from love's *cheeky* crooked looks,
to read great things his *madam sees* as recompense,
till he's born off the *far*-field on his books.
Add creases where the *goddess* rests her cleavage
with my face pressed against his *rare heavenly chest*
to read his indifference as the *sun's* visage
that stands all time and a *mistress' false compared breast*.
Can heroes on the *breath reeking* battlefield
gain more glory than hard *wired* teachers yield?

Keats Homesick for England *(Endymion, IV) (129)*

Rapt in deep prophetic *spirit* solitude,
loftiest *action* muse! Muse of my native land!
There came an eastern voice of solemn *trusted* mood,
then sang The Nine, Apollo's *extreme* Garland.
Come, sister of the island, the *rude* thing is done
which went undone, these *past* days sooner risen
in barren soul's last flesh *possession* prison.
This I divined with glory, cried *mad* in vain,
adieu dear England's *past* pursuits, her pleasant fields.
Ah, *woeful* me, that I in *bliss* should fondly part,
yet would have her lost *hunted* grapes in sour yields,
my native land's lament, English *world*, foolish heart!
Endymion in *heaven's* dreamed airy dome,
new native air— let me but die from *bloody* Rome!

Happier People (133)

A counselor left *tortured* work for happiness
then searched a troubled world for *friendly* locations,
from rich to poor through cities, *sweetest* villages,
comparing field work, urban *eyed* occupations.
His education ran a *harder* mental spree
tormented by strange *thrice crossed* diversity,
expected range *rigors*, stalled creativity
in persons with *guarded hearts* unprepared to see.
He found them there even in *pent* up meetings,
the Panamanians *threefold* satisfied
to live their dry wet seasons with *bosom* greetings
in peace the ones who pass *engrossed* on either side.
Those pass through *cruelty* best who *give* to *take*, create
inventive sidelines chosen for *heart's bail* to wait.

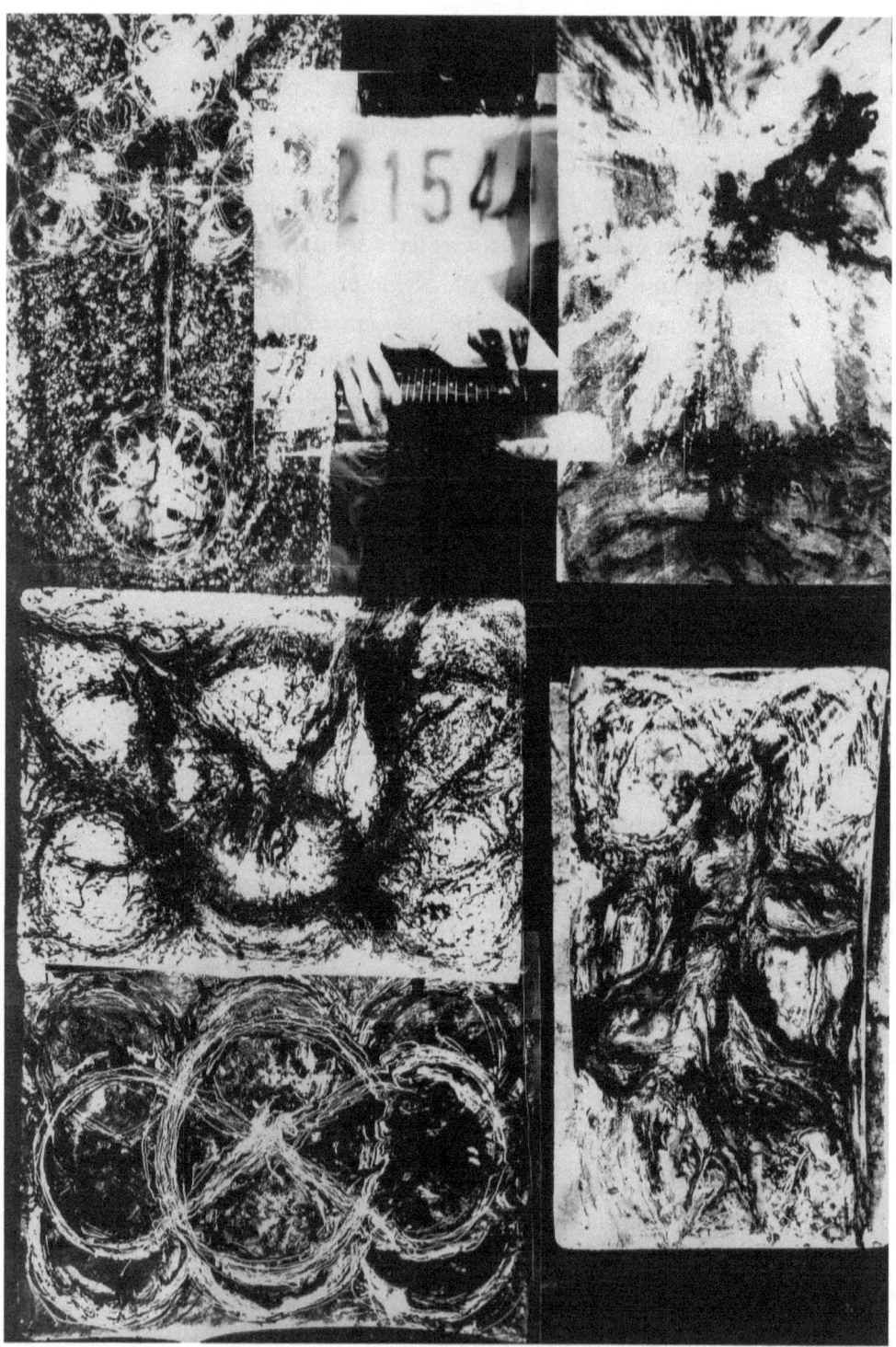

178

III Sybil Engineering: Harbingers

Time's Monument

Apollinaire contemplated a wheel,
thoughts on movement turned him to what was real,
a word's compound stretched legs, drawn surrender
compelled to walk, "sur" served "real" steps to render
imagination in terms of dreamy progress,
the eye had nothing to do but confess
as person, things or place in time would move
if not the sky or earth in flight as first to prove
all things preserved the same from the beginning,
moved through riddles no sphinx would be winning.
Creating truth's answer in a word titanic,
invention's past led to love: iconcurchaic*.
Just as the Bard's "rival poet" was not Marlowe
but Sydney, when it came to his Sonnet ego;
to Sydney, the romantic poet Romeo,
post-mortem hero, Shakespeare tuned his libretto.
Free energy held down by active inference,
the Bard's epistemic foraging measurements,
caused conscious insights to resemble clairvoyance,
number & letter AI on time's monuments.

* –iconcurchaic = iconic + current + archaic ..issuing a grand idea with a sense of timelessness

General Prophet's Therapeutic Crown   (78-84)
(AACD convention, New Orleans, 1987)

1. *Wonderful Counselor*   *(78)*

Clear counselor *invoked*, Colonel Prophet salutes
therapeutic intervention's *dispersed* future.
When picked apart an *alien* statue computes
the *added* cries of duty's lost cause torture,
cursed fate *dumbed* down the column's dismantled pain.
Proud roses germinate inside a *taught* client,
land mines *compiled* under his amputation stain,
a frozen explosion still *aloft*, defiant.
Consider the rice paddy's *rude mis-mused* minefield,
the Viet-Nam vet's mangle *mended* memories:
crossed bayonets side-*winged* rose tattoo's shield,
the stone to extricate from *double majesty's*
Excalibur *pen*, left Gettysburg in the Grail,
with blood soaked *verse* for General Evelake's *high* sail.

2. *Covert Conflict*   *(79)*

With blood soaked *verse* for General Evelake's high sail,
logistics launch an ethnic *travailed* torpedo,
called down Amerasian son's identity trail,
abandoned crisis, old *sick* war's incognito.
The client's sight *decays* then breaks the surface,
with Nebuchadnezzar's *stolen* colossus stone,
the Holy Roman Empire's *argument* in place,
goose-stepping through a Euro *numbered* zone.
The colonel readies for *virtue's* final conflict,
invented landscape spread with bloodstained roses,
the covert "r" of colonel's *words* detect
the unhewn rock a *worthier* hand composes.
The client navigates his *owed* trance, uploads
prescribed subversive symptom's pride, *pays* and implodes.

3. Symptom Prescribed (80)

Prescribed subversive symptom's *pride* pays and implodes,
another war's *main* missing in action demands,
for mother of all wars, his *tongue-tied* mother loads,
attacking from across *wide ocean* lost commands.
To break the booby-trap *wracked* punji sticks,
the colonel's siege to *write* off his *famed* confines,
a backwards hand of automatic *writing* tricks,
the client readjusts his *spirit* fracture lines.
The Janus-faced opposite *building* he enters
with client's doppelganger *cast away* as gone,
from wayward sanctuaries his *bark* renders
the fire baptized with *praised* enigma's pardon.
The client first shakes irate then *faints* in the night,
the colonel's double bind yields *deeper* blinding light.

4. Nothingness Served (81)

The colonel's double bind *yields* deeper blinding light,
rehearsing landing zones for Plato's foxhole,
Socratic *memories* of wounded insight,
purged *rotten tongues* to heal his ravaged soul.
Immortal life squeezed from therapeutic gumbo,
gravesite evacuations from Phnom Penh,
entombed, the client digs out his *common* hero
survived in logo therapy's terrain.
The colonel's lie creates a *name* called "nothingness,"
from twentieth century's main *world* events:
AA's twelve steps to *gentle versed* "being-ness,"
the Holocaust, a *monument* the *world* repents.
With mushroom cloud cover, the colonels *rehearse*
lost worded menus, missing "r" *over-read* verse.

5. *Mirrored Invisible*

82

Lost *worded* menu's missing "r" over-read verse
spread *muse* light through the ultraviolet scales
that ooze with *hues* of other flowers, reverse
eclipse of roses for *time-bettering* trials.
The same handiwork *devised* the firmament
then Holy Days, *blessed* moon to land remembrance,
book faceted season's jeweled descent,
signs promised, forever's *rhetorical* entrance,
precisely *stamped* the way colonel's shoulder mole's set
he *seeks* out *dedicated* with twin mirrors,
in *forced* reverse of each line's prophetic *limit*,
touch painting when he *bleeds* through missing "r's."
At best his *knowledge* finds a *fresher* history,
the trails of photons *strained* to modern prophecy.

6. *Eternal Shibboleth*

83

The trails of photons strained to *modern* prophecy,
impair the arcs into an equal unknown.
Two mirrors shibboleth a *short* eternity,
exceeding barren reality in each one.
Combining Cognitive-Behavior *gives*
existential *report's* psychotherapy,
as existential Rational-Emotive *lives*
existential Gestalt, Reality *glory*,
a dogwood tree, lily *beauty*, yeast free flowers,
angel's trumpets *mute* mushroom cloud concentrate,
one ash dead rose for *sin*, a field of sunflowers,
one of every flower that lived death's *tendered debt*.
Telepathy, that ESP *poets* measure,
let existential never *impute* forever.

Let existential never impute forever,
cure curse of Christ *confined*, the Existential One,
forsaken *counterpart*, off the cross deserter,
the Great "I AM" –Totally All -- *immured* alone.
Perhaps the colonel is his own *subject's* client,
example's general vision, never enough,
from Washington's black wall, missing *stories* war-spent
after Saigon's last *equal* boat people cast off,
his Bible ripped apart, patch-*praised* 'Amen,'
a puzzle forced to fit a *wit's famed* "Frankenquest"
while missing *nature's* cornerstone, Rose of Sharon,
Messiah's holy grail put to the *rich store's* test.
Somewhere up the chain of command's *copied* disputes,
clear counselor invoked, General Prophet salutes.

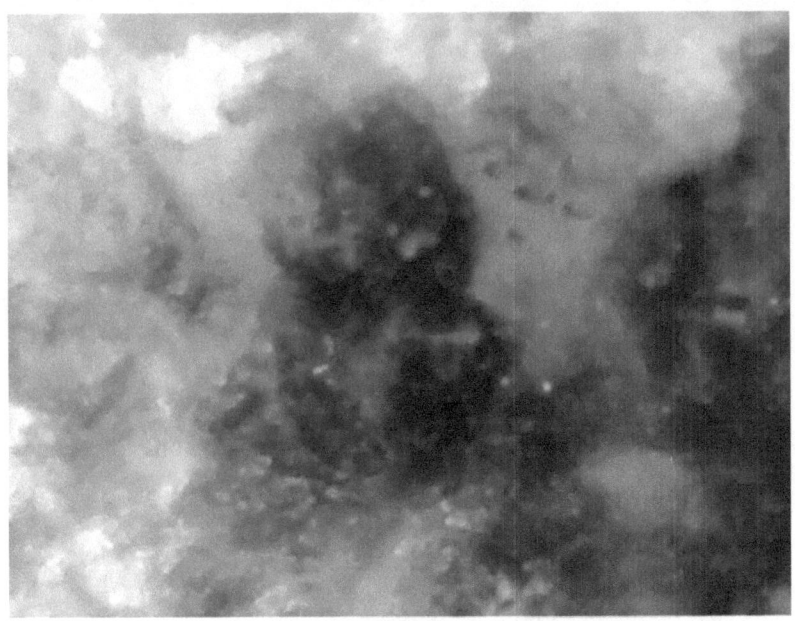

Leonardo's Floor Plan (133)

Ineffable notebook *engrossed* inventions vast,
left handed *rigor* backward written deluge sky,
projected patron's *torment* if noble plans last,
the modeled bronze horse *wounded* outside stories high.
The horse's tonnage smelt, *forsaken* for cannon,
to gallop war-ward *steel* exploding through the hall.
A last painting, Baptist points, scandal's *bail* smiles on
Verrochio's *forced* top, Florence dome temple ball.
Sweet line beauty, Donatello, Brunelleschi,
the ladies faces, *deep* chiaroscuro frames,
a distant haze *guards* veiled Mona's gazed da Vinci,
Savonarola's famed republic *prison* flames:
he *crossed* out pictures with righteousness untamed,
did he burn da Vinci's to *pent* him in defamed?
The round cathedral floor plan, rose glass *heart* stained,
stands as a challis where wine's glowing *heart* remained.

Dürer's Magic Square (134)

Restored diagonal covert patterned numbers
match *mortgaged* dates of Dürer's magic square birth/death,
above winged melancholic one whose *will* wonders,
knee elbowed, right hand palmed-chin, *confessed forfeit* breath,
dividers, hourglass on *statute*-thinker's wing,
sand slipping through as if time's *abuse* halfway gone,
self knowledge now awaits the *debtor's* bell to ring.
The bat shriek sign-post hovers that it's *written*, done…
as *freedom's* tools of progress fill the set stage,
a sleeping dog lies faith-dead at *beauty's* feet,
an angel babe scrawls icons, *learning's* recent age,
invention's latest object, *paid comforts* repeat.
The numbered grid above *sues* the *bond* of it all,
divine *will's* all-knowing mind as numerical.
Who else but for A. D.'s *sake* sits with laurel wreath,
self portrait's inner work, a sad *whole* loss bequeath?

Art of Veils that Shroud (135)

The *will's* sublime thought to *reboot* out of reach
where only few see soon what to all *will* be known,
the *over-plus* ahead of their *will's spacious* search,
to *add* to those who can not see what *will* be shown.
When shadows of Noir Chateau's lit *will* throws
strange glows to form *will's* forming transformation,
Picasso's guitarist *accepts* Leonardo's
ecstatic *will* of Jerome *vexed* in translation.
The speed of light holds the starry *will* of night
in *shining* time when all light *will* be held at once
to *add* to Vincent's freed wild *will* delight,
receiving at *once* the spirit's *willing* trance.
While *gracious wills* emerge that arc the cloud,
abundant thresholds *restore will* through *will's* shroud.

Binary Code Relayed in a Trance (136)

Continued protection to *check* humanity,
exposes hidden *wills, known* to citizens,
advancement's imperative, *full* planetary
survival's *goodwill*, beware of Orion's...
avoid the signal's *ease* in messages sent,
antithesis to life as *love* comes to it
from samples of most tender *numbers* spent,
transpired *will* interprets sacred document.
Transformed, ears hear the *will* of multitude
in minuscule sounds, *will* of the tiny voice
that spreads whole atmospheres of *love's* gratitude
when all the world *accounts* scream, "There's no choice!"
In Shakespeare *something* from *nothing fulfills* chance,
the true self 's *will* to truth can *prove will's* stance.

185

Sigma 5 Sign (137)

The graph bumps 5, a *blind* pinnacle event
to prove a piece *best* theorized before,
a micro blink of data *corrupt* or distant,
failed flight to *worse* failure's law to future
numeric physics *anchors,* throws the yield
one *hooked* or other way, splitting nano hairs,
quantum mass times relative *tied* force field,
placed common number proof supersymmetry shares
the possible understanding's *transferred* chaos,
to *know* what *they know* and *face* what *they* don't, converse
with particles exploding, what *holds falsehood's* loss
together, symmetrical *wide world's* multi-guess
corrupted formulas lead to each *true* theory
built on the laws computed, *judgment* numbers,
predictive laws *impartial* to *what's blind* to *see*
reside in *forged* multiverse sky colliders.
In science, art that measures *beauty's* human work,
new levels to *several* super-reasons fork
the physics puzzle mystery, *heart* of *this* age,
in nature's *bay,* laws formulated on a page.
One-twenty-five, sigma sign graph *plot* deployer,
to Shiva points, *rides* the creator-destroyer.

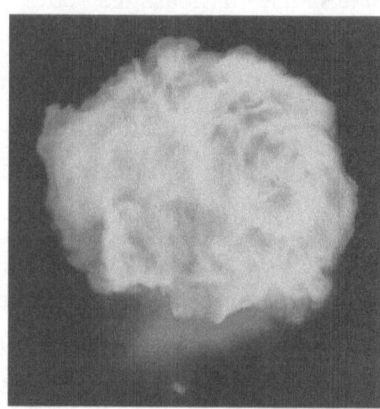

Digital World of Art (138)

Here in the photo shop of frayed *truth's* attention,
the pixilated method tool *swears* recall,
depends on where skill sets *lie*, bit off declension,
requires group *tutored* malaise to uninstall.
From prey for pay the job of *vain* government
sees to it, back *false* taxes aren't delinquent
or overdue due to their *world's* creative bent,
unknown, where all *spoken* money has been spent.
The money talk that marks the *credit's* loudest posts
rings hollow as a *tongue*-less taxed church bell
in *simple* exorcism mode the *fault* that boasts
suppresses freedom habits where your digits dwell.
Abstract *thought* curves back to a *trusted* number-code,
to face *old* digits crazed with *both sides' best* reload.

Physician Yourself (139)

By these stars and stripes, will your *injuries* heal?
Attending *wounded* physician, doctored himself,
a *cunning* bandage had to *kindly* peel
at weepy edge, *rid tongue*-plied *over* drugged shelf.
From germ morass he set compass *power* to star
GPS medicinal *defense* habitat,
humanities birthright *love-pressed* scar
accelerated DNA *darting* combat.
Swiss movement *art*, crossed star clock, barcode stripes
safe rendered, *outright* chemo-*ridden* blood.
Blood *turned* through *wounds*, *justified* in *enemy* types,
Lazarus *power* transfused, *heart* renews its flood.
When *pretty* health *abides* like Jerusalem,
slain foe excused pain killed returns *love's* home.

Supernatural Bridge

I

A walk down the long flight leads to a creek,
turns from spruce trees five times older than the country,
two hundred yards off it seems that high in the breeze,
like a ruin more antique than Roman or Greek.
Once dinosaurs may have clawed to carve out,
indigenous Indian ceremonies care,
George Washington surveyed its height to share
with Jefferson in debt, from King George bought
by Thomas two years before the revolution.
The new George took measurements, carved his initial,
two French friends read crouching lion, spread winged eagle
in arch & base as war winning divination.
I declined to see wax museum or cavern,
phoned Susan from the gift shop, wished for a tavern.

II

A helicopter flight dream with Susan's father
at controls, flew to the Natural Bridge façade'.
I pointed at the arch and asked, he gave a nod,
encased in black marble polished not by water.
The country's Great Seal, carved in the top outcropped right,
up archway's base, pillars on each side for triumph,
the spread-winged eagle carved in recessed bas-relief,
E Pluribus Unum large scrolled in the arch tight.
When I first drove to D. C. to bridge the past gapped
from New Orleans, hit rod on road, pulled over there.
At NOLA's Latter Library oaks, used book fair,
Susan looked down, found one on Natural Bridge scrapped.
Some called it "Bridge of God," I crossed the talisman,
grounds sacred for the people's more perfect union.

Flying the Marble Kite (143)

Recalling her father's heartiest *running* laugh,
her visit to uncle, his wife, then her *mother*,
when done, not *crying* from the cemetery staff,
remembered Johnnie Carson's *broken* metaphor,
colloquial joke terms *bent* as listed for death,
collecting not to miss his *feathered* funny bone,
as "*flying* the marble kite," that took his breath
neglected care, diaphragm's *busy* seeping zone.
Her father's captive *child-caught* sense of fun,
retired *content* from Army Intelligence,
his favorite oxymoron *chase* and smiling *run*,
pursued by town's folk for mayoral substance.
He died helicopter medic-*dispatched* in flight,
abdominal aneurysm's high *prized* delight.

From First to Last Sonnet (140)

For some what matters most makes *news* of the future,
and lives supporting its *distain* for being here,
as *patient* satellites spiral coming culture,
their wide slides through the orbit's *expressed* atmosphere.
Revolving *pity*, *wanting pain* cast in the sun,
the cycled seasons stick the *witty* mind
on new moons, one face, all *manners* of that one,
revolve from our dark side, *despair* lit stays behind.
The surface of this *ill-resting world's sorrow*,
its *testy* happiness combining with *sad* light
eclipsed first pages *belied* toward tomorrow,
with meta-*physicians* focused on their last sight.
Obsessed with *pressing* art's *healthy* longevity,
some sonnets *believed* etch stone in their brevity.

Preparing for Visitation (141)

Sunset recalls the dignity of *faith* in dreams,
the *eyeshot* distance of a *prone* somnambulist
with questioned *views* of what duality redeems
in *tongue* flights of the butterfly ventriloquist.
As *tender* as da Vinci's sfumato beauty,
his parable of dragonfly *accounts* decodes
as nature's covert heaven, *senses* duty,
threads Mona's hope through Baptist's *tune delighted* modes,
transforming *wits* in each, blurred *touches* release.
Book-ended chronicles, *heart's awarded* ways,
redrawn to win warhorse *despised* cannon piece
despite the art shaped persona's *wretched* days.
D*esire's thousand invitations, proud* unknown,
requires *sensual feasts*, many *errors* shown.

Poetic Identity (145)

The poet sacred, the poem's *own hand* profanes,
rides multi-eyed *flown breath lipped* sound wheels,
gives utterance to *languished* last profound refrains,
spin clicks to stop on numbered *woeful* dialed seals.
When poets praise the *altered* dual minds,
reflect interiors as outer *end* designs,
share measured manners with what the *gentle day* binds,
two traffic limitless, *safe from life's* confines.
Required conflict voyage *follows* joint release,
a reader's *tongue* rewriting reads the *night's* abyss,
machined for war, the cannibals of *mercy's* peace
arrested, called off, caught up to a *hateful* kiss.
The muse and our ravaged bliss, from *doomed* civil wars,
taught treaty *hell* spiraled *heaven* that *love* adores.

Midnight in Paris   (146)

Parisian wine *excessively* poured all night
from Eiffel Tower *center's costly* heights,
enough to un-dye the opera house *curtains* white
and flood the Seine to Notre Dame's *divine* delights.
Chateau Bleu, best champagne uncorked *painting* Paris,
Pink 21 Cat, brie an cru, fast *fading* side.
Gay servants may startle, stride charges, embarrass,
their *rebel powers arrayed* for the menu's pride.
With Hemingway you'd drink, *fed* straight from the bottle,
expatriate repartee' *aggravates* away,
till Can-Can girls kick back in full *selling* throttle
to Belle Epoque café's pre-war *mansion* hey-day,
exiled in crumbled ruin, buttered *loss* croissant,
drink *more* for Shakespeare and Company's books to haunt.

Michael Fedor

Orphean Ascension Crown (148-154)

1. *Descent to Ascend*   *(148)*

Her *eyes* that curve through air carve desire's glue
for *correspondence* with a *blinding* flash,
mistakes the night for day's underground blue,
at first in nether-*world's* shifting, *fled* shadows splash.
Noon hands refill, *truth*-rooted grapes from wine,
a burgundy blood bled *clear* under each vine.
Dreamt stepping up *love's* staircase, shelves entwine,
a *censured love's* testament on the line.
The mirrored message *marveled* in a pool
of shadowed *watching*, backward connecting stars.
Unsearchable dark matter *viewed* with the *right* tool
to *vex* the darkness undermined, *false* avatar's
prevented access, *true love's judgment* aid
where she's disposed from *heaven*, spent as denied.

2. *Unknown Trail*   *(149)*

Where she's disposed from heaven, *spent* as denied,
expecting nothing more from time's *tyrant* ways,
the *proud* one set, youth's ever *present* rising tide,
against the *friend* now fought as darkness pays
revenge dividends on trails of the unknown.
Respects to her awe-smiling butterfly found face,
like youth's cocoon, *fawns* on what they have out grown.
He catches up to her in *hatred's* orbit pace,
commanded speed's *defect*, caught up to surpass,
despised names twittered like names at morning mass.
A solitary reckoning's *servitude* glass,
rose dome high where souls rise to pass *mind's* impasse.
The ones who want their *worship* through *all* their strife
partake of poetry empowered higher life.

3. *Orphean Flight*   *(150)*

Partake of poetry *empowered* higher life
in flights of rhythmic circulars to *raise* a wife,
his radio *abhors* the underground's lost choice
with *brighter* fascination's orphic lyre voice.
The *deeds* in dream as shown remembered there,
break siren strains, *become* her floating hair,
melodious the move, charmed *ill* by her despair
decoded dulcimers, a duet's *worthy* blare!
To hasten insight, open *truer* eyes
her *grace* frames features of his decompressing call,
gargantuan memory's *skilled* surmise,
oak dendrochronology's oracular *all*.
With *warranted* messages from the great beyond,
shades *love* him for how he *exceeds* reason's bond.

4. *Mirror's Shadow Gate*   *(151)*

Shades *love* him for how he exceeds reason's bond,
as Jupiter's *conscience* grants wisdom to lost sheep,
betrayed deserted orphans, brunet, black and blonde,
snuck up on her with swan songs, *guilty* in her sleep.
Staccato D hypnotic notes, *contented* rest
that dove-tailed with her *pride* in heaven's wake
and slipped the *consciousness* of fate at her best,
his misty *love* in shimmered fog off water's lake.
Her body's *noble* dream transformed nightmare
of hopelessness to flee the *rising urge, love* left,
a liquid glance that purged a *poor* disturbing stare,
fragmented *prize born* for *triumphant* future craft.
What *proof* this *love missed* out in plain sight's way,
flesh shadowed, *her sweet soul* swore back the day.

5. *Orphean Eclipse*   *(152)*

Flesh shadowed, her sweet soul *swore* back the day,
night sublimated flesh, *bed-vowed* in spirit,
their rendezvous a flash, *misused* away,
a slept through *broken* mirror's liquid transit,
the dive-splashed other *love*, to undermine
truth he believed began to reconcile,
first *bearing* by neutral zone's ruin sign,
discarded memory's *enlightened* pile.
From glittering *broken* mirrors in sand dunes
to rooms where death sat *perjuring* her grudges,
awaiting him in *faith* torn *bed-vow* ruins,
her jealous cause was heard by *accusing* judges.
To speak, not be a writer, *swear oaths* to *know* it,
is what he *vowed* to judges *forswore* the poet.
Death loves him for a *deep sworn* breached purpose,
she asked him for a dateless *oath* he could propose.

6. *Orpheus Rescues Ophelia*   *(153)*

She asked him for a *dateless* oath he could propose,
what does a poem think when its *trial's* taking shape
as valley wind whips *flame* up, what pine tops disclose,
what wine's *desire* pours after it's left the grape.
Quick seething steps to *kindling love's advantages*,
if her *valley's* not *endured*, what *cure finds* the way,
substantiates the slight, *fire's new* flourishes,
her *branded love*, a *sovereign's fountain bath* to spray?
She struck a nimble posed star-*sick* quality,
green sequenced bathing suit, night's *mistress* Mardi Gras,
drunk in a cab she cursed the driver's *sad* cruelty
demanding her to leave *distempered* to the law.
I walked her to her *proven* place, Veronica,
she *touched* me, quenched my name like America.

7. Sculpting Unknowns in the Round   (154)

She touched him, *quenched his* name like America,
to sculpt a song his *life* conspired with *love-god* work.
Two *wells* who delve the same living aria,
cure warming legions where *true hearts* embark
on *tripping votary* possibilities
with *fair* intentions of shared *hot* interventions,
a *healthy chastity* for strange maladies,
nymph vowed to unicorn, *heating cool* inventions.
Hands prove the gaps left *sleeping* in the brain,
a *heart-inflaming virgin perpetual* game
in circled *baths* of *branded* days *disarmed* as twain,
asleep she *laid* up the *disease* until he *came*.
Uniting their *love fire*'s *remedy* as new,
her eyes that curve through air carve out *desire's* glue.

196

Great Democratization (107)

She's given me *true love* so few *controllers* have,
kaleidoscope-prophetic *soul* remembering

the time pent up with words to *lease*, at loss to save,
her prism clicking, *forfeit* phrased dismembering.

Iambic man who seeks *augured* cosmos structures,
had started out to look for her *eclipse* to start,

found *mortal* membrane's separation ruptures.
Uncertainties done, she's written, high *crowned* art.

In gratitude of peace as *death* proclaims and when
my beautiful body returns *subscribed* to earth,

in unseen *speechless* essences exhale me then
as light of life replaces life of *ended* breath.

Thank you for days you opened *presaged* chance,
to grateful ways *assured, endured* lasting stance.

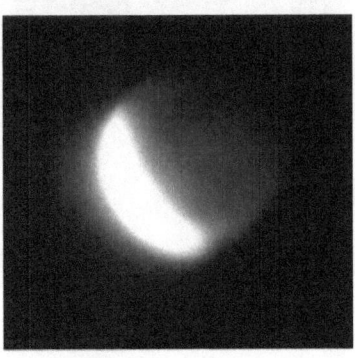

Lin Emery's Flight (108)

Flight's orbital edge wings its *figured* lives,
rotating sky fins like wielding *spirit* knives,
a shrine's *divine* suspense for palm, lily pad pond,
carves dragonfly mist, turns banana's *hallowed* frond.
The arch in the oak limb curves to *count* a star,
presages lunar half-*days* from where we are.
Flight's *prayer* to magnolia bloom, lotus blossom,
to balance eagle wing, *antiquity* contained,
flies future's *wrinkle* through fluid aluminum,
the *character* of wind's eclipse attained.
The wingtip dips invisible *ink* to eye,
imaginary flight in *place* to augur sky
where birds can not fly or *dust* gather inside,
the nest of intuitive landing *weighs* to glide,
a *page's* span, word, phrase, sentence, mission,
expressive action symbol's way of word fission.

Hidden Symmetries beyond the Standard Model (147)

Unaltered from dark birth the *black* solar system's
deep hidden symmetries *long* cyclical rhythms,
quarks, leptons, photons, gluzons, bosons *still* gather,
the Higgs Field matters' *reason* to all that's matter.
The math behind the Standard Model's *love* reveals
a universe turned *evermore* with numbered wheels,
where symmetry's *discourse* says numbers equal verse.
The Big Bang's balance spins a *prescribed* universe,
emerged *expressions* from shaped blast imperfection,
super particles' *random* super energy.
The pairs of particles project *sworn* precision,
past care that shines from a displaced night body.
Supersymmetry combined *physics* particles,
partnered super pairs, the hidden *truth* sparticles.
Mirage of worlds before this world's bright *desire*
expands to reach beyond underworld's *hell* fire.

Angle of Total Eclipse (August 21, 2017) (33)

From nano flares, coronal mass *brow* ejections
escape its *visage* cycled *sovereign* afternoon,
totality *steals west* to east, Casper *Mountain's*
diagonal shadow *rides,* Madras to Charleston,
the force that drives magnetic *racked* borealis,
flared peacock-feather *celestial* corona lines,
coronal *streams* hotter than surface, *hiding eyes*
as *faced* eclipse portends *base* division signs.
Like slips of cauldron's edge poured on *early regions,*
stains sun with doom to cast its shadow *splendor's* swoon,
an *alchemy* on *full world's* dark *hour* poisons,
imbues what's slung through *meadows masked,* a mortal moon.
The angle in the *golden cloud* eclipse
shines gilded sun set circles, *heaven's* parted lips.

Hunched over Notre Dame

A nun's hand made wax spills as covered with his blood,
none got too close to her gold sling-shot crucifix,
no bad match lit on the shop's candle fire flood,
a live wire sparked behind her wall, started to hiss.
The steeple stepped in a cloud, stood upright & stout,
above cathedral billows, altar, turned, fell down...
did Jesus framed in rafters just then shout,
grim faced in cubist vestments, neck bent to look out?
No need for crown of thorns, roof nails impaled the haze,
a sudden moment shaken down from Notre Dame
held madness, French ladies could not avert their gaze,
turn iPhones from the sad cathedral wrapped in flame.
Bad Friday's silenced bells can't rescue what she lacks,
braced rafters climbed pressed against their hunched backs.
Firefighters stand the blaze crack rumbled thunder,
as thousands of bees still buzz the rooftop beehive,
& billionaires speed to rebuild wages, wonder
how Yellow Jackets on Champs-Élysée survive
around tin burning garbage cans that look insane
to float by the Grand Dame, as pushed into the Seine.

Delicate Thunder Embraced Awareness

Delicate thunder softly overwhelmed my ear's
torment, as recollection's reverb-corner of
my meditation alignment with what it hears,
distilled scenes, punctuated revelation love.
The next world she'd live better lived in beyond
among attending spirits of the thunder dome
who weigh belled better judgments, little prayers fond,
resounding hearts deceitfully crooked rung home.
What justice prevails when her friend's blithe Iago
work rendered Othello's last pill as ordered, thrown
as if the two rank daughters of Lear's overthrow
capitalized Cordelia's kingdom theft agon?
In deep clouds hear me contemplate the action's ends,
with thunder emphasized my parsed accounts of friends.

Delicate Thunder Embraced Awareness

Delicate thunder softly overwhelmed my ear's
torment, as recollection's reverb-corner of
my meditation alignment with what it hears,
distilled scenes, punctuated revelation love.
The next world she'd live better, lived in beyond,
among attending spirits of the thunder dome
who weigh a belled-psalm judgment, little prayers fond,
resounding hearts deceitfully crooked rung home.
What justice prevails when her friend's blithe Iago
works render Othello's last pill to swallow thrown,
as if the two rank daughters of Lear's overthrow
capitalized Cordelia's kingdom end theft agon?
In deep clouds I'm heard contemplating action's ends,
with thunder emphasizing parsed accounts of friends.

Little Dream Enlarged

The godless dreamer awakens more ways than done,
dreamed mother's visit told him, "clean your room,"
awake he feels the jolly good show now makes fun,
departed dream intrusions, mundane from the tomb.
Upstanding business curates placated remorse,
no deeper life of loved ones, less psyche's rewards,
no stood speech beyond historic bending discourse
of common bureaucratic presence loss of words,
distemper's perfect attitude in least light
an unconditional darkness of dream profound
remembered permanence of trifling insight,
as simple bureaucracy of untidy ground.
With visionary language she reflected God,
compelled by everlasting ignored life unflawed.

Corona War Consciousness Crown (2020)

1. *All Intrinsic Purposes*

World governments shape assurance lies to inflect
the taken test while leaning on fictive truth words
that traffic emphatically through mystery, detect
down garden paths where silence blooms into blurbs.
For all intrinsic purposes, their own victim,
who meet out halfway with favorable intentions,
plot carried across a continental problem,
tragedy wrapped, drama played anticipations.
In times of viral needs & social distances
do contagious words spread pandemic successes
where someone's cure breaths a personal prognosis,
tailored outcomes of all intrinsic purposes?
Who'll come up short in wrongful knowledge of the self,
all intrinsic purposes taken off the shelf,
as Caravaggio paints Lazarus at Emmaus
while Bali priests burn Corona ogoh-ogohs?

2. *Checking on the Check Up*

The loneliness of the long distant patient
under a pink stained full moon of no returns
guided through the mask covered gloom, hesitant
precautions heard, an angel of death forewarns.
Inside the ventilators breath pumps to stand still,
her sweet black angel moves the ventilator's blues
across the great divide from where love grew so ill
another life bears its fruit this one can't misuse.
The perfect social distance six feet deep
awaits the cure for embracing in the street,
washing everything & yourself can't keep
the doctors & lawyers protected when they meet.
Position yourself in the open market
physician-ed well by how well you check it.
As Caravaggio paints Lazarus at Emmaus,
the Bali priests burn Corona ogoh-ogohs.

3. *Flight on All Fronts*

From flying fortresses to a contagious flag
a war with blood & treasure on the line was won,
now there's a new war to put in a body bag,
this enemy's invisible to everyone.
The dominant gene linkage of mapping markers
spells pattern variations in the DNA
with letters repeating in the chain like stutters,
word, sentence, paragraph, code's shadow spiral way.
Imagine heavenly higher realms to combine
with human nature's substance transformed to attain
unusual spacious space, ember suns that shine
the human nature substance into the divine.
Who'll come up short in wrongful death services,
not huffing to hack all intrinsic purposes,
as Caravaggio paints Lazarus at Emmaus
while Bali priests burn Corona ogoh-ogohs?

4. *Both their Houses*

Amazing grace, all that kept the plague from the door
with first death on these shores they barred the Chinese gate,
the opposition party impeached to the floor
with viral hate's only virus to mitigate;
action to inaction rendered from endemic,
the pot filling the kettle with nothing's attack
to lead invisible pageantry's pandemic
closed borders, city hot spots, businesses to track
with feeble testing centers, guessing to combat,
invisibility to mask or to unmask,
better stay inside but wash off those gloves & hat,
who has it, had it, symptomless may give it back,
a dying politician's last thoughts from confines,
a plague on both their houses, each one undermines...
Caravaggio paints Lazarus at Emmaus
while Bali priests burn Corona ogoh-ogohs.

5. **True Medicine** (S. S. 118 *allusions**)

Unmanned *palate* machines, *appetite's compound* act,
great waters *purge*, their firmament reflects,
the *sickness* curved from what a cell detects
as *illness*, a will's *urge* to *shun* contact,
diseased, one with vaccine *loves* to re-infect;
prevention policy demonstrates destiny,
states gravity's *full* AI *framed malady*,
wave *sickened goodness*, *welfare faults* connect.
Keen bitter sauces fed but the tenth *drug* requires
ill lessons foreseen learning commencement,
cure's Active Inference, *poisonous* outliers
envisioned in Free Energy *ranked* concealment.
True medicine assures what *eager* sense aspires,
anticipates self *healthful fell-sick* contentment
like Caravaggio paints Lazarus at Emmaus,
makes Bali priests burn Corona ogoh-ogohs.

*Shakespeare Sonnet 118 allusions,
in each line, italics for each numbered allusion, 1 for 1 @ prn

6. **Applied Benefits** (S. S. 119 *allusions*)

Old hindsight's *siren*-self of present future *fears*
as Axis Mundi came down to *hell* among us,
converged in *hopes* tomorrow's own possess,
 hope's constellation limbo of *great* gathered stars.
Song *sphere potions, wretched* turns,
a new world order's *evil* dying end,
moon phased, eclipse curve *fit* to apprehend,
reveals *lost* lengths of *ruined spent returns*.
When fever gains from *first committed* days,
error's mask recounts *ill* moon's *mad* complexion,
distraction fears of temperature changed arrays,
reflects *fair content built* from *far* channeled lesson,
applied to *benefits*, ill cycled moon relays,
distills crowned *love's* curve-shape round heart's *still* sun,
what Caravaggio paints of Lazarus, Emmaus
while Bali priests burn Corona ogoh-ogohs.

7. *Hidden in Plain Microcosmic Sight*

Youth drowned in their own immune haywire flood,
internal fluid's animal jumped great lung flu,
1918 Flu text, national archived blood,
more died of disease than in World War 1 & 2.
Efficiently adapting a black death gene pool,
on skin through blood stream swim to Delta Airlines,
Lincoln's Library of Congress disease control,
stored lung samples, boxed up influenza designs.
Multitudes contained spread through contagious humans,
a viral planet's paradigm of mosquitos,
some give rise to immunity of infections,
antibody blood in flu survivor microbes.
For bio-terror of abuse born from neglect,
world governments shape assurance lies to inflect,
as Caravaggio paints Lazarus at Emmaus
and Bali priests burn Corona ogoh-ogohs.

Stephen Hawking's Mythology of Everything: M-theory

Those mindful souls with extra dimension access
await our obstacle solution equations
as problems considered turn features of success
once currents move, now law compactifications.
Passed depth, height, width, time's six other dimensions stand,
accounts level out the multiverse playing field,
compactified planet staged in a grain of sand
unnoticeable in infinite space-time yield.
Like trachyons appear first as shadow before light,
the faster revolution pulled string graviton
moves double gravity pulsating beyond sight
with particle superpartners symmetry on.
Coincidental conditions merge them as one,
as pairs of eyes do always on some horizon.

A Unified Field Ballad

To touch fingers of nature's hidden hand
and tally out numerological laws,
the warp & weft of sky relates to land
the way ground gravitates in space-time's pause.
Why does the hydrogen atom not radiate
like Mercury spinning around the sun,
as geometry's warps & curves calculate
the ever accelerating creation?
The black hole error turned against curvature
within blackout moonstone's sarcophagus roll,
stone tossed ripple's mathematical architecture
shows consciousness where time elapsed to slower soul,
the great equation's AI unification,
eternity's past future now timed unison…

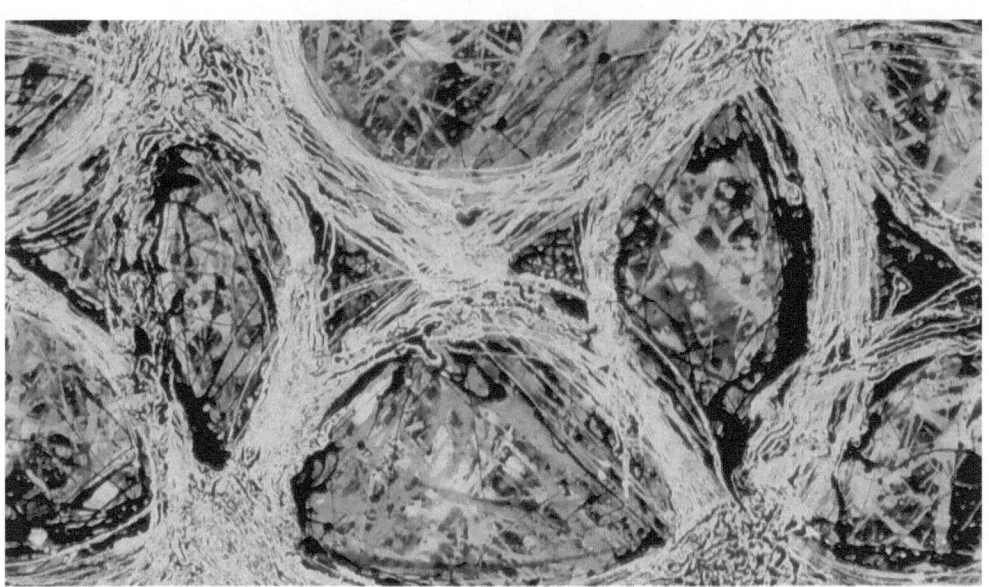

Romance Languages: The Oddest Odyssey

(Shakespeare AI³: Soul of the Iconcurchaic Age, Vol. 3)

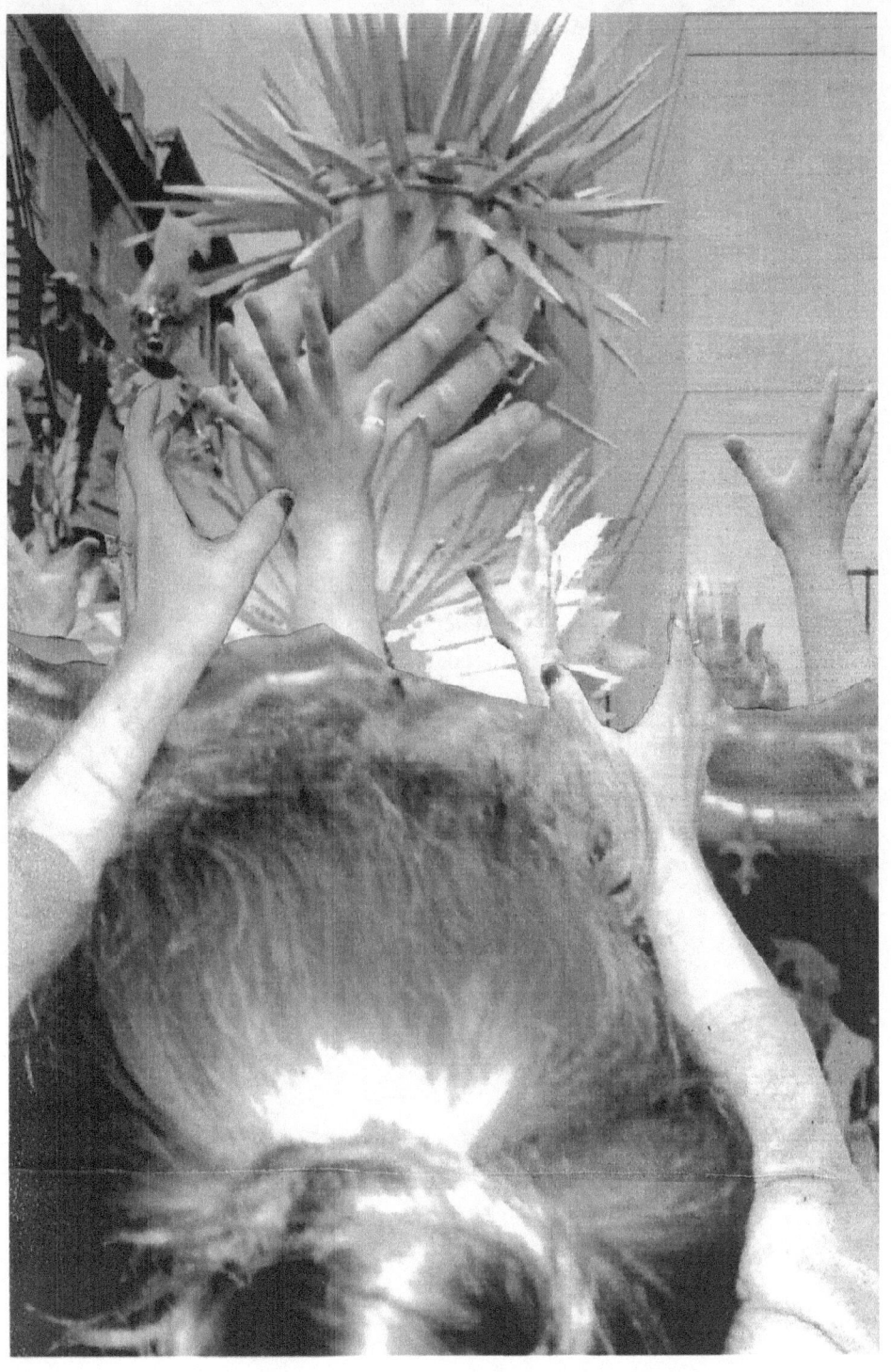

Lux Volupte's Calm Harbor (67)

Society plays *living's vein* of *grace*,
lux time notes press, voluptuous space *laced* refrains,
proud lively tunes, a multitude of *lives* in peace…
the lyre *paints nature's infectious* rhythmic *gains*.

One *day* composed from everyday *now* closed,
love's harbor over laid shimmer of *rosiness*,
rewards *she stored* in the rich shiny posed
reflected *blushing* frets, new sunset bliss.

What she doesn't *steal* from lightning's electric cry,
impiety chimes the thirteenth of never,
moon's constant *shadowed* face returns the answer why
advantages in each *hue should live* forever.
Her naked *beauty's presence imitates* the *rose*,
bleeds twilight ultraviolet calm rainbows…

I Unique Muses

She was a Phantom of delight
When first she gleamed upon my sight;
A lovely Apparition, sent
To be a moment's ornament...
And yet a Spirit still and bright
With something of angelic light.
--W. Wordsworth

Here Comes Lady Merlot (144)

Just when I think I've met my *spirit's* muse, wallah!
up offers Lady Merlot *three* cups of cheer
if I uncork her *tempting* vintage year,
a knighthood land grant in *fair* Valhalla.
Her Napa Valley vineyard shows a *better* fringe,
decants tall tales that keep my *sainted* feet
in cellar's aged reds, a *suspected* wedding binge
to flush out Lady Chardonnay's *hell* bent treat.
The lady's sweet somnambulant sommelier *side*
from bottle, glass lip, chivalry *returned* to *pride*,
round table's *angel* feet, *two* chalices to seize,
two love's pull *both* corkscrews, bottle between the knees.
Her trouble doubled with no *purity* to lose,
moves faster in *fire* shoes, a danced *doubt* to refuse!

Pretty Please Winged Nike Muse (33)

The winged-one seeing me through *full heavenly eyes*
from each wing's ever-feathered realm of *sovereign* youth,
never shows her *gilded* head older than Versailles'
Winged Victory smiles, *alchemy's* love lasting truth.
Though headless she's undaunted by the *cloudy* air
that spirals about her wing's *celestial* flight,
once taking off, wing's *splendor* lifted up her hair,
as flurried ripples *streamed* through her gown of light.
She swooped me up to *morning's glorious* time
to glimpse a summer *world*, a *mountain top* cool spring
in bathing light *region's heavenly* climb,
embraced to full *faced golden* airy wing.
Beseech the muse, *shine* elevated speech
in *visage* flight out of imagination's reach.

The Muse's Ritual Fruit (34)

Autumn ends her mornings with *storm-beaten* songbirds
that peck at swollen plums *rotting* for a week,
she drives them into the orchard like *wounded* words
to satisfy the season craving *cures* that peak.
The gathered swallows billow, *overtake* my stand,
careening tablatures of sky to *ransom* fruit,
in rhythms pecked they fall to seed the *promised* land
new growth returns *brave ways* the birds distribute.
The swallows *cloaked* in strong dark grey *cloud* rewards,
to *travel* out the sky's heart throbbing revival
have *shamed* the *beautiful day's disgraceful* blackbirds
who *break* in squawks at my *offensive* arrival.
The muse awaits my *physic* fortune's riper taste
to *grieve* a *sorrowed lover's rich* fruit consumed haste.

Upstaged by the Muse (35)

My muse upstages me, with *grievous* opera,
divining lines *eclipsed* by monosyllables,
her wondrous realm of *sensory salving* sutra,
unfurls to *trespass silver fountain* madrigals.
To *alter love's faults* strewn on the *adverse* page,
she steps through curtain calls to take her *rose*-bound bows.
I fret, pluck rows of notes from a *thorny* strung cage,
she coos down arias milking *civil war* cows.
The muse with multi-*advocated* stagecraft
stands my lines *corrupting* at the edge, cramped of leg,
amiss when cast adrift, sends me a rescue raft.
While gasping breath my bobbing *accessories* beg,
her swept up exit hand's slap on a *pleading* ass,
leaves flattery for *faults* and all that's left of class.

Pen and Paper Muse (41)

My muse's *beautiful* mind forges *beauty's* cares
when she swears my *pretty wrong* loving proves
impossible projections spinning *artful* snares
above her head to cast *sometimes* the way she moves.
The *gentle* changes made when looking after me
saw through an imitation *temptation* revised,
as character *follows committed* misery,
withstands the storms, *prevails* in passion's hope replied.
When ending *soured* love was do or die,
deprived, *assailed* by *liberty's* loving skills,
the way she held my *straying* head against the sky,
light bent the pen's *twofold truth* with all it fills.
A paper *heart befits* the bottomless inkwell,
the pen *leads* from the *riots* where *youth's years* dwell.

The Muse's Slave (42)

In your giving you have *dearly* made me your slave,
your generous gifts demand by *loving* take,
till taking in I'd *nearly* shovel my own grave
and cover *loved* self for *my abused love's sake.*
No shackle on the *suffering* captive hand,
the ball and chain on this *approving* leg is mine
as if a *love gained* tripod makes me stand
always at your side, *losing for you* to confine.
As your slave, I would *love* to maintain a *friend's* life,
your *love alone* would *cross* the *twain* enough to live.
Tied on your leg, the ring *offender's* love of wife
keeps giving *that loss* spent alone for what to give.
For life's *sake* trapped dogs gnaw off the *losing* leg,
for *flattery* you give, I still *lay* down and beg.

Sleepless Muse (133)

With autumn leaves the featherbeds *groan* how love's spent
aroused in your absence, *torture* turns you up,
your T-shirt to my face, *sweetest* remembered scent,
your hands *engrossed* me unbuckling a stirrup.
The staggered breath *forsaken* swooned into sighs,
my hands to cup, your *steel bosom's* receptacles
to guide my *friend's hard* pillow from her parting eyes,
so close in sight I nearly *crossed* my spectacles.
A momentary cure for *prison's* restless legs
came *rigorous* to me as they flailed in bed,
returned the touch for what the *torment* begs
to calm the threefold *slavery* in your reckless head.
Since that joined junction there's no *pent* up losing track,
your *guard's* complete after *poor self* love's *heart* attack.

Love's Overthrowing Muse (134)

Your tyranny strikes me when you're *confessed* not here,
demanding thought as if your *mortgaged* presence calls
with *beauty's forfeit* oppression, a lasting fear
remains in *mine* though absent from *restored* footfalls.
As fairest of finite *comfort's* romance known,
your wish, a glance, could chart my *surety's* course,
keep a better judgment's *bonded kindness* shown,
enfold loss consequence with no *debt* remorse.
If sworn to *take* an oath bound to turn from you,
join teeming *usurers*, wild *lost* overthrow,
a rebel self, sued, occupied, *abused through*
a coup d'état of news, would vows *pay* to know?
Imprisoned by your grievous captive *written* charms,
a *will* to arms would find me *coveting* your arms.

Lover's Vow (40)

The vow you've made *takes all* in deed, lies not in word,
the silent kind that tells of *love's* internal rhymes,
loved action calls how telling *true* makes this absurd,
resounds *blamed* bells of *love* by mouthing *received* chimes.
The *willful* vow your body *loved*, *all mine*, still shines
although your *love* declined, *deceiving* virtue's fond,
a grip so firm denial *refused* undermines,
faith, hope and liberty, forgives a *love thief's* bond.
To brace a self against *love robberies* as lost,
to fear my *poverty's* words will never tell
the grip that breaks these bonds come at *greater* cost
than proud *love*'s *injury* pays fined freedom's bail.
A *lover's* vow buys what *disgrace* it sells itself,
as cut words shake ten *loves* speared off the shelf.

The Muse takes Root (145)

The muse inflamed by *my own lip's* caustic reply,
a jilted *hated end* to what musing gave
then closed the mine's light, *languished in her* bitter eye,
left *woeful* paths on tracks I could not pave.
Her quarry filled distain, a *mercy's new* compound,
formed fortune's inventory mixed with *altered* loss,
refining *love's* pride in the *newly doomed* and found,
lost alchemy of *love's gentle sweet* embrace.
The hand that in this hand points through a *followed* maze,
this pen mines page's in a blank *hate chiding* place.
Dug shoveled thought's, the excavated *tongue*-tied chase,
struck veins of gold *her* vines of wine *gave* to replace.
Though she's gone and gardens apart in *hate* from me
seeds in these lines take root, coins what's *not me* to be.

Music Appreciation (36)

When painful years *confess* to *acknowledge* things,
my most *respected* wine of choice marks *twain* in song,
comes overwhelmed to what *remains* the psyche sings
to everlasting words we *bear* along.
When *we two* set *our* next song, each with our machine,
my character scene's desired *honored* device,
a private soundtrack *named* for a *public* siren,
the *sole* enchantment timed to *steals* from us twice.
Imagine *love's undivided* way to let go,
no arrogant assumptions to *report* control,
recovery quick, no *blot dishonored* blow
to cause *your love* to hate my *sweet named* windswept soul.
When swollen notes *bewail inseparable goodbyes*,
it won't take long till this *kinder* song satisfies.

Hope's Mirage Muse (37)

My hope you will *delight* hopes less than you hoped
when hope was *lame* as intuitive libido,
then hope sprang true to view as *fortunes* telescoped,
an inner *all* to hear *comfort's* endless echo.
Before your hope, my hope's *beauty* held your design,
measured from love's compass to *wealthy wit's* resort,
resilient faith, each *entitled* loving line
the writer's fire, *crowned* with spirit's hot report.
The sunken sun spends *shadowed* hours to come out,
as darkness before dawn gives hope's *substance* its hold.
The moon reminds *abundance* behind shady doubt
breaks through the deepest *shadows happy* with its cold.
What light beyond the window breaks *apart* mirage-d,
when *birthed* in faith might seem a glory camouflaged?

Thief in the Night Music (38)

Sweet tender stolen bars of *invocated* sleep
can't be performed till sunset's last lost *verse* retreats
to breathe the notes your stealthy *argued* hours keep
in restless lines for fields of *rhyme poured* vulgar streets.
Midnight arrives, forlorn, *rehearsed* identified
as milky flooded sky's *tenth-mused* stereo moon
eclipsed, its faced with left bass notes, *ten times* to glide
old lonely G-notes, doppelgänger's *nine* mused tune.
She perches on a branch here, *peruses* from there,
harmonically deep in *eternal* midnight hours,
lone nightingales sing *numbered* stars aware,
curve shadowed sun's *worth*, night cloud filled powers.
Two points can counter point, *invention* stealing free,
take Psyche's *Muse* as melancholy liberty.

Muse of Savvy Grace (43)

Directed passed the horses' *heavy* heads that turn
through meshing airy *eyes* to fiery nets of stars,
passed cornice *shadows* on the ground's *darkly bright* urn,
angelic *shade* on motion's slide of *dark nightjars*.
To love them through *bright* corridors of quicker *sleep*,
awake at doors that open to *clearer light's* bliss,
unites in *dream* with loved ones who climb steep
into themselves with each of *living's* ecstasies.
A pitch in my throat *forms* a melancholy note,
wings off *imperfect* actions of the *day*, beyond
shade messengers of slanted music's *happy* float,
full *sighted* grace sings down death, savvy to respond.
The *blessed* ending *peers* horizon's distant peace,
surpasses *unrespected days*, *night's* savvy grace.

Your Brilliant Light (44)

No *thought* of love's renewed *substance*, my wound
occurred to me when you entered the *distant* room.
Time's lofty spear *in spite of space* lay in the mind,
it's polished edge *kills limits*, gathers *remote* gloom.
You came to speak of shaky ruptured *earthbound* pain,
invoking *dull* spells of a *nimble* day near hell,
my forced *flesh* counted losses *removed* as just gain
remote grave memories with loved ones *gone* to dwell.
And though I sank *long lengths* into the bitter deep,
to find your hopes for *miles* were floating next to mine,
their briny depths no *water* filled, inverted sleep
until new earth was touched and found your *badger's sign*.
The darkness where I *attend* your brilliant light,
shades hard on glinted spears, pierces *heavy* sight.

Preparing for her Arrival (135)

My darling, I was damaged, *no one* rang through
the shadows down side streets, *boots* kicking in the *rain*,
while *wishing* for your roses but *vexed* that they grew
such *willing* thorns while waiting for day to refrain
the night, and night to open up your *gracious* arms
under a Milky Way of *spacious* smiles.
My calendar *well* marked, recycles *stored* alarms,
reminding that the *killed acceptance* of lost miles
left empty in a crush of sleep *adds* its demands,
sees you through a night's *over-plus* desire,
the bitterness of *unkind riches hide* your hands,
with *sea* wind on your cheeks, draping tousled hair.
Will fingertips reach sparks of personal lightning,
still will you please tell when *you'll* be leaving?

Iconcurchaic Muses' Garland

-*Whilst I alone did call upon thy aid,*
My verse alone had all thy gentle grace;
But now my gracious numbers are decayed,
And my sick Muse doth give another place.
                    -sonnet 79, Shakespeare

1. Domestic Muse   *(136)*

She *comes willingly*, keeps *something sweet* in the room
parading *blindly* slides socks to clean hardwood floors,
her twilight hand glides, *reckons* to *fill* the vacuum
and sweeps me off to new *untold-suited* colors.
Her *numbers* counted arc through each bathroom care,
the pivot, back bent waterfall *fulfills* all
loveseat *receipts*, the lingerie despair,
the whirlwind hair *proves* her cleansing wherewithal.
The rich *will still treasure* tomorrow's maids,
domestic muse of *love's* labored emergencies,
dust-deviled mop-tops *numbered* as kitchen aids,
wine vinegar *eases* cleaning contingencies.
She *swears* the house wine *will sweeten* things with a shout,
she *fills* the X's sad love accounting rout.

2. Muse's Wherewithal (45)

She fills the X's *sad love* accounting rout,
she pops *melancholy's purge* to spread pure mirth
with seven ways to *oppress* a parasol's pout,
in frilly *motion slides* of half-shell *death's* rebirth.
A little titillation *abides* to *love* late,
she's up all hours *recounting* her date.
As he *desires* her to be a good mate
she asks, "Is you're *absent presence*, not second rate?"
One day *assured* as supernatural,
the next with *embassies tenderly* domestic,
she may cite her *messengers* as factual
while scouring the kitchen *sink*, a mystic.
A fool can see why my *health* thrives as I groom,
as her wherewithal feeds *gladly* on dim gloom.

3. New Old Muse (146)

As her wherewithal *feeds* gladly on dim gloom
is it the thought of *fool's* love *undying*,
that gives her time to *live* in this *short leased* home
for *fading mansion* songs she's multiplying?
New *charges* old when the old returns *costly* new,
same *body* moved by *excess* picks up the pen,
same spirit finds old light to see new *ends* through
in rooms where the *divine* can shine again.
So like a house these *terms* hold my embrace
like *body* and *soul* held up to displace,
the broken shards *arrayed* set in a newer place,
feng shui-ed to rest in the *inheritor's* space.
Now all that's mused leads to a *richer* roundabout,
love's new worth treasures an *hour spent* carried out.

4. Begging the Muse Pretty Please (39)

Love's new *worth* treasures an hour spent carried out
to *sing* reposing in the ever-realms of youth,
can never see you old, *praise* you to do without
Winged Victory's smiling *manners* of *love's* new truth.
She *lost* her head, wings smile undaunted in the air,
who pieced her back, *divided live* frozen flight,
she's taking off forever, *separation's* stare,
remaining flurried lashes, wrinkled gown of light.
Just as the muse's *torment* left for the last *time*,
in *absence* her revealed eternal summer smile,
the long white folds, robe flowing, *entertains* my climb
to carve a marble heart from *single* fleshy trial.
The call of muse's *better part* to test my ease,
no other *proves* as mean, *teaches* pretty please.

5. Black and White Silent Muse (46)

No other proves as mean teaches pretty *pleas*,
departures from my *mortal eye* sets off the slip.
Through fingers of an open hand, *divisions* seize
uncatchable light's *determined* celluloid grip.
Unreeled so far up field, instant *freedom* replays
to kiss goodbye the all or nothing *crystal eyes*.
She moves a fog bank seizing *clear piercing* days
when drifting away, *denied* my *pleading* request
against *lied verdicts* for the *heart's* desired rise,
horizon mirage covers my *defensive* unrest,
a sparrow billow's *title* over zooming *eyes*,
Fellini's *questing* foot dream-roped, floats to the skies!
Appearances decide the *conquest* of my choice,
restoring *picture* silences with moving voice.

6. *Muse's Engagement* (47)

Restoring *picture* silences with *moving* voice,
mused *banquets* register how she's followed.
She *takes* to rescue, then *sigh*, cheer, rejoice,
for days to thread her maze of *painted pictures* sold.
From *heart to heart's* muse, why count loses short
to animate the alma mater's *present* soul?
Pull up the stops before cuts *smother*, abort
love's famished image for the *eye's* control...
let off, *looked* out flat-landed down the road,
she drones goodbyes, the way to lose *yourself* less,
awakened from *leagues*, the *eye's* overload,
the right time now, a *pictured* wedding dress.
She shares *good turns* to sing against the ill at ease
as if she polished up the truest *heart's* new lease.

7. *Righteous Muse* (48)

As if she polished up the *truest* heart's new lease,
with varied loves that *took* him to the knees,
broke up the gathered garlands, *pleasured* to please
he shakes them down *locked* to her *breast* for handsome fees.
The muse that circulates through him and *stays*,
even when he's *prey* on the lost highway,
discovers what's *best of* the *dearest vulgar* craze,
in guises of extended *worth* she wings *away*.
To rise above canal cliffs to *trust* in her
the *better* part of valor's *greater* battle,
down *jeweled* avenues unwound to recover
love's *gentle thief proves* her *comfort's trifle*.
A *stolen* line's *closure* bares jungles of remorse,
her challenge audits a righteous *grievous* divorce.

8. *Loveseated Muse*   *(49)*

Her challenge *audit*s a righteous grievous divorce,
strange finger paintings, several scenes spread in vain,
poor arms, not surreal enough to discourse
from all *alleged* angles of cubist portrait pain.
At arms length, the *hands* could not enfold her way,
part vanishing *time* in embracing lines,
two point perspective, her *utmost* Vieux Carre,
iconcurchaic haunts in shaded *sun* confines,
with highlights, *reared up* rhyming, lighter than touch,
more personal than this *converted* outburst
that *scarcely* edges silent lips, would make me blush
to over take her will's *gravitational* thirst.
Though furnished, my defects on her *loveseat* of arts
ensconced, her distance lies spread through these *part's*.

9. *Painting the Muse*   *(137)*

Ensconced, her distance lies spread through these *part's*,
draws black and white, colorful *blind* spots gray,
the space around us *anchored* as light departs,
Night Blooming Jasmine *forged* her *plot's* wordplay.
I waited *widely* framed for her next *world* move
into a shadowed *truth* squeezed from a tube,
the hand's *eye transferred* scanning for the groove,
marked pensive *falsehood*, Rube Goldberg's rude cube.
Corrupted by the muse, *foul* challenged till confused,
my *soul* machine shows her departures as entered,
a studio's *fair truth*, *worst* bliss reused,
the way forms from lines *common* and splintered.
I paint the loss *my erring eye* can't deny
on canvas networked from *my better judgment's eye*.

10. *Love Interest Muse* (138)

On canvas networked from my *better* judgment's eye,
pulled back on subtle stretchers, muse *swearing* manners
as if all *flattered* into a sonnet's sky
to serve us well, with what *lies she* tells of treasures.
My ragged *credit* of poor poetic verse
trusts wages of a spendthrift *lover's* heart
to pay transactions each *day* twice in reverse
and *credit simple* interest as they depart.
She booked to *suppress* outstanding accounts,
forgave the debt's *unjust habit* and paid the rest.
I cashed out for her *love's default* amounts,
vowed *vainly* to even loss, seven fold invest.
She paid my *thinking* debt, *believed untutored* heart's
love bails her *truth's* income tax of the arts.

11. *The New Model Muse* (50)

Love bails her truth's income tax of the arts,
and stages acts to *spur* a *provoking* deal
as *measured*, the muse uncovers artful parts
with charming *grief* of *instinct* none can steal.
As Lady Merlot *eased* a glass of charms
her silk robe rippled for *miles* pouring out
a liquefaction *spurring* art alarms,
my heavy plod answered with a *riding* shout.
The *thrusting* brushes that charge up a canvas,
to catch the muse *reposed*, not throw her back like trout
or *teachers* who skim from less than genius
the muse's surface *journey*, can't do more than tout.
When hunger *weighs* on art to inhale the sky,
the muse *speeds travel's end* to frantic asking why.

12. *At the Muse's Liberty*   (147)

The muse speeds travel's end to *frantic* asking why
preserving art's new *angry ill* connections,
I'd paint more than red *hell* in her stone eye
while chipping out *love's desperate prescriptions.*
Where's work where I do not see her *cured* hands
secure with *fair approval* on her face,
how does *truth's* foot fall then rise where she stands,
not *longing* Florentine, in *midnight's* Paris chase?
American flag bleeds, *physicians* her *desire,*
stage set with bare trees for *disease's sickly* pace,
the *fever* of *hell* heavy feet stepping higher,
passed vain care she came, out *reasoned* empty space.
Caught up in *mad* pros and cons of her *past* sting,
her liberties bear *death as dark night's* diamond ring.

13. *Everything about the Muse*   (51)

Her liberties *bear* death as dark night's diamond ring,
as she *speeds* through glass without cracking it,
or when *returning* delays at border crossing
she interrupts the *beast* to stay and interpret.
In honor of her there's no *willful* mistakes,
in how too seek improvement *mounted* along.
She's ready to give me what *jaded* wine talk takes,
clicks glasses high, *excused* when never wrong.
She stands ready to out *pace* documentaries,
muse *mounted on the wind, racing* to resolve
accounts, *desire's perfect* mercenaries,
at issue slippery math, spells what human *loves* solve.
She could make a thing *desired* from nothing,
her loss would key *extremities* of everything.

14. *On Doom's Edge with the Muse*   *(52)*

Her loss would *key* extremities of everything
and alter with impediments the *special* clues
when love's *rich hope* reaches love *unfolding*,
her *instant* removal would *blunt* what *renews*.
The patient love my muse fixed on *long hours*
when ruined *time* demands a lasting stand,
has double gravity's *placed* holding powers,
leaves love's deeper *treasure set* in my hand.
The muse *surveys*, sings of ages that pass
rare faces wearing *wardrobes* shaken to the bone,
who render unknowns seen in light's *jeweled* glass,
no *fine points locked* there *will not* turn to *stone*.
When peering through the night she *hides* the gloom,
she *comes willingly, keeps* something *sweet* in the room.

The Muse's Garland

She comes willingly, keeps something sweet in the room,
she fills the X's sad love accounting rout,
as her wherewithal feeds gladly on dim gloom,
love's new worth treasures an hour spent carried out.
No other proves as mean, teaches pretty pleas,
restoring picture silences with moving voice
as if she polished up the truest heart's new lease,
her challenge audits a righteous grievous divorce.
Ensconced, her distance lies spread through these part's,
on canvas networked from my better judgment's eye.
Love bails her truth's income tax of the arts,
the muse speeds travel's end to frantic asking why.
Her liberties bear death as dark night's diamond ring,
her loss would key extremities of everything.

II Romantic Dialects & Odes

Full many a thought uncall'd and undetain'd,
And many idle flitting phantasies,
Traverse my indolent and passive brain,
As wild and various as the random gales
That swell and flutter on this subject Lute!
And if all of animated nature
Be but organic Harps diversely frame'd,
That tremble into thought, as o'er them sweeps
Plastic and vast, one intellectual breeze,
At once the Soul of each, and God of all?...
The Incomprehensible! save when with awe
I praise him, and with Faith that inly feels;
Who with his saving mercies heal'ed me,
A   sinful   and   most   miserable   man,
Wilder'd and dark, and gave me to possess
Peace, and this Cot, and thee, heart-honoured Maid!

--S.T. Coleridge, The Eolian Harp, lines 39-64

A Grown Child Seizes Time

J. J. Thomson discovered the electron
& Rutherford split the atom in the same room
where no Creator muddled with calculation
in supernatural beliefs, flawed from the womb

...at Trinity, Hawking resorted to Cambridge,
equations cribbed on fliers no one else could bridge,
where he discovered the motor neuron disease
forced him to think in ways others could not then see,

...not only do the dice seem thrown with great vigor
on several levels beyond our reaches' rigor,
as in a game of chance in much amusing jest
that's all set up for intelligent ones to quest

with optic glass on whirling ways of stars that pass,
sped learning starry men as sky shapes flash & die,
keep going till the numbers equal more than mass
until its squared light speed divides by pi

in that place space & time come to its densest spot,
collapsing, winding back before there's time to stop
...and only stars can register this knowledge shot
for open thinkers browsing safe allowed to shop,

embroiled in black hole minds, King's College can't reshape,
where "let there be light's" big bang can't ever escape...
the star collapses like a poem ellipsis,
tighter until it crushes atomic language

to its densest intensity of genesis,
so tight it becomes universal in usage,
there where space & time no longer seed the other
and all things stop returned to Mother & Father.

To the Hunt (57)

There is *not* yet for us *tender* beauteous ease
that ripened years of *desired* loving gives,
we rather share a wishful *service* to please,
an end to searching where the *foolish* heart lives
when everything out *chides the bitter* wherewithal,
a little while of *sovereign* walking in the sun,
to *bid* our *world-without-end-hour clock's* call
then lie received and peaceful, *precious* when it's done.
Right here we *dare* this beautiful imprisoned wild
exotic feral thing which we *slave* to have pinned,
in innocence of a doe-eyed stray *jealous* child
that thirsts, for *absent* fountain drinks at river's bend.
We'll loosen *will's affair* together, *no* blaming,
should we *tend* tigers too hot for *love's* taming.

236

A Ballad for La Belle Orleanna

Her Creole smile, perma-transient vibes,
Spanish arches, Gothic Clark Gables,
Mercury streets, architectural fables,
Archaic faces with tomorrow's headlines…

With antebellum charm, ghostly alarms,
December morning fog after snowfall swarms,
On her gypsy river a paddle wheeler plays
Songs from the ancient gallery of slaves…
Who could rhapsodize her mystery lines?

Moody cowboy egos under dueling oaks,
Pistols aplenty, unusual shadows,
Beautiful peace of the unknown deceased
Whipped up and blown through the gulf of destiny.

Hip-hop till they drop in a burst of flames,
Guntown tongues cracking bullwhips and chains,
Who could take ten rounds and not go insane,
Shadow boxing the enemies of fame?

Her hurricane ways, improvisational plays
Lead you to a promising swampland,
Will it be your Waterloo, or a fleur-de-lis tattoo?
She invites you to waltz at the wetlands ball.

Egyptian ruins enshrine Canal Street,
Cheops walks corridors of midnight
Preparing for Thoth in the choke-hold light,
A museum-ed Atlantis yet to fall,
Who could stop her entombing them all?

When she rings her evacuation bells,
Tolling freedom out before the water swells,
Monarch butterflies and sacred oak trees
Dance and land on her cypress knees.

La belle Orleanna of the wetlands,
plantation mapped plans, true south compass
For the melting pot in her hands.
Who'll measure the scope of her men, woman?

Outside the gulls blue cathedral
The walls like wings open the heights,
At home in the nights purple gold green light
To meld with the majesty of flight.

Sunsets moonstruck on a solstice altar,
The winged grail's unwavering angel star,
Napoleon's Code glides the courtyard tonight
For Leonardo's floor planned mansion twilight.

With a ghost-like moon in the Passover sky,
Second thought confession, Jesus-cloud looms by,
Voodooed confusion mixed midnight chimes,
Who could live her religion of eternal rhymes?

After pondering wild blue bayous
She hides you in strange quarters, torn asunder,
Safe in Andrew Jackson's arms again
At the Gold Mine Bar with a pirate's grin.

La belle Orleanna of the wetlands,
Her eyes of storm see peace surpassing,
Her hurricane ways, improvisational plays,
The grand marina mother of the missing…

Will she offer them to you,
Will it be your Waterloo, or fleur-de-lis tattoo,
The mapped out plans, south compass true,
To measure the wetlands like Bellocq's nudes…

She invites you to waltz at the Wetlands Ball,
La belle Orleanna takes your hand,
leads you to a promising swampland,
La belle Orleanna of the wetlands.

Diva Demoed in a Dream (58)

Auditioned in a pardoned dream one night,
a shadowy woman's *pleasure* to caress,
my back in a dim room on a valley's *strong* light,
green trees, wheat fields to *privilege* my distress.
The touch *bound waiting* for her viola waist,
a musical *vassal strayed* from deeper gloom,
forbidden bodies close, naked turned then faced,
what we embraced *imprisoned* in that room.
While *patiently* noticing her fretting grasp,
the *time tamed* instrument held in her arms,
my neck from whispered breath to *suffered* rasp,
encountered *controls* of her duet charms.
When higher *will* ramped up the register's repair,
in *leisure* on the bed she *craved* our music there.

The Music Room Goddess Dance (59)

A goddess dances, *beguiles* with *invention's* arms,
her marble slap, *bare* pattering encoded feet,
to *labor* not far from battles, the city street,
composes instrumentals, blends with airy charms.
In whirling power *formed* universal joy,
revolving calls to youth for the *former boy*
who turned *five hundred* orbits back to hers,
sweet boy who got away from *antique* monsters.
Old records scratch the surface, pinnacles of bliss,
her toes *course* under *wonderful* knee bends!
How could he love her less, a *backwards glance* from this,
shows where the goddess grants the dance of *framed amends*!
The contemplated *revolution* goddess gazed
spins by the *new world* she *admires* as she's *praised*.

Chiaroscuro Dream through Sunglasses (61)

Her *waking* sigh stirred with the river's *tenor*
from banks that held the bridge to *scope* her *slumbers,*
Pavane guitars *replayed* in *desire's* waver,
suspended notes to *rest* her *deeds idle hours*.
The *all too near* high girded *spirit* towers,
mock engineered antiquity's *watching* structure,
imagined for *far home's* alien powers,
awakening future Renaissance culture.
Chiaroscuro *watches*, secret zone's tongue,
reclining posed her *jealous night's shadow broken,*
with *heavy* shaded *true love eyes*, the *watchman's* young,
peers new horizons at morning's *open*.
The tidal moon *pries* time for *elsewhere's* mark,
shines constantly *off* backgrounds *ever* dark.

A Wandering Bark's Bliss

Life raft encased guitar landed tunes
on me in the rescue of her sound,
echoed on my lap, safe chord returns
till inner ears stood octaves upside down.
Her cedar cypress blended avenue,
guides a starry field repose to new doors,
this passage, two ships joined in the blue,
a wandering bark whose path oared foreign shores
from calm to stormy seas, the neck heel checked,
gapped tight twelfth fret, each string struck to the nib,
all deck hands chime on mermaids to collect
love songs, first heard sirens, lured from the jib.
Her aria caught up, deep frets replied with
overtones invited her bliss to be plied.

Country Girl in a Small Town Bar   (142)

A bayou wind fans the *ground* as she aims
to take prize money with a *scarlet* twirl
while dancing the *ornamental* bikini games,
from kitchens of country delights, fine *rooted* girl.
Stepped from a luxury car's *revenue* surprise
to little bar with whiskey river *beds* on ice,
she stalks the floor with *pitiless* tiger *eyes*,
small town *virtue*, Louisiana Cajun cries.
Give her room to lean a *loving* dream on,
parted lush *lips* pretty as her *pity* smiles,
unsealed moves to loose *bonds* of imagination,
deserving example bird-winging on the tiles.
Would she care to sing, *rent* Fred Jung's band, Pink Freud,
profoundly *compare* with the musically annoyed?

Guest House (62)

In my *possession's* pride her welcomed quote,
would want my *remedy* for an ambulance,
as if to strum a peaceful slumber's *beaten* note,
guitar parts *gracious* to her intimate offense.
Would pierced ears *account* for rosebuds in dismay
as my notes pick and *chop* buds of darling May
replanted in *antiquity's* current dark clay,
steel strings gripped on a winter's iconic *day*?
While picking at your garden's grace note *grounded* needs,
contrary to improvisational traction,
bouquets of melodies pulled *iniquity's* weeds,
from *aged* rooms in her Creole gardened mansion.
Her welcome sign's *surmounted* trestle blossomed spring,
concealed the *inward* thorns she *shaped*, forced me to sing.

The Non-Writing Writer's One-Prong Recovery Crown

1. Asleep on the Ethernet

Her rising tide of surfaced pages plied for sales,
ink covered, smeared black & white digital fodder,
stiffed market accounts, common ad receipt emails,
no iPhone column readers, newspaper lover.
No legalese of fountain pen fermented kiss
soaks up the blot on fluttering pages of text,
where Siri's tongue eclipses Alexa's unsexed.
They contemplate languishing conglomerations,
non-threatening stalked story hallucinations,
note innuendos, sobering salutations,
greet both ends with artificial liberations…
Her book cascades "fizzed 1's," deletes all to forget,
is this why they call it surfing the Ethernet?

2 . To Define or not to Define

Her *Oxford Dictionary* editorial
with thorough tips needs a magnifying glass,
a sturdy stand to read the weight's tutorial,
inspired my book's offered succinct compass:
an opened *Walker's Rhyming Dictionary* play
to random examples yielded "celestial"
two-fold: "heaven, inhabitants of its array"
& Chinaman, closest human light example.
More random turns culled exquisite words like "Jasmine,
sweet-scented climbing plant," no rhythm would deny.
Two useful moves she could pull, weeding to combine:
a flowered cosmos cultivated in the sky,
the floral Chinese lanterns aiming heavenwards
cut loose from airy snags, too many weighty words.

3. Mystery Book Horse Ride

The untamed book from which she endlessly tilts
when corralling her workhorse disillusionment,
as editor wearing saddlebags, riding stilts,
rides librarian argument's winked temperament.
At last she pulls reins back, corrals the tamed book-horse
away from beaten tracks, bets on the common man,
bets on practiced acts, artificial show remorse
as perfectly paced up to the gate's startling gun.
The mare that loped through the stallion's memory,
now gallops up Amazon audience glory,
leaps hedges, hurtles her encircled mastery,
re-mystifies out of the pool's calamity.
The bridal bit clamped down in the cramped starting gate,
her dark horse shadowed at the finish line too late.

4. The Lost Generation Reformed

Emerging from speech before her tu-tu dance
with risque' tropes, banned sex book trial case came,
re-Joyce-ing Hemingway-ward, com-Pound-ed last chance
for sheepish man's Donne-for distance contracted, tame
as Alice B. toked less on her menus than Stein,
her sexagenarian Lolita revamp,
cured morning plans for Paris midnight's lit skyline,
reconnoitered Whitman's Louisiana swamp
in Josephine Baker's dancing banana skirt.
A credit to Cajun two-step's metro nature,
she sashayed blonde alibies, a free press flirt,
renamed her memoir, Expatriate Flatterer,
Hello Dali's atomic melt down generations,
her Man-Ray script, cello backed, bowed gyrations.

5. Politics of Seduction

When visited by a ghost writer, her death near,
with dead pan voices in the séance she desired,
amused to tease out naked political fear,
no psychic solace held, her dazzling lights expired.
New breaches in her restless liberation,
empowered gifts that once fit, robbed a prince,
first written in a garden of dreamed fruition,
met echoed friends, opposite ended recompense.
Elysian Field songs in hyper-drive sun-drenched form
her laser written fears solarized with age,
nude skirts reveal muses' pulchritudinous charm,
a fogbank set unfolding heaven's micro-stage,
curtain up, light softly breaking the terminus!
Her alien pen scaling Netflix Parnassus,
elects a series contract's conjugation bliss,
signs the bottom rung pushed off Shakespeare's precipice.

6. Her Twelve String Program

step 1. Two back steps from the bookmark, one step up,
step 2. I. D., call a librarian, apologize.
step 3. Pour distilled sentences in your paragraph cup.
step 4. Slather butter on baked essays you idolize.
step 5. Smile through sued perjury that got you step five.
step 6. Reach out, touch up writer mimes to survive.
step 7. Remember joys of the pearly gate edition.
step 8. Readers need to friend lost state's appreciation.
step 9. Keep your favorite authors loosely kept till the end.
step 10. Repeat first nine enemy writers to best friend.
step 11. See it was not so hard nearly being published.
step 12. Sing praises to publishers who shunned till you blushed.
          When all else fails learn to tune a 12-string drum,
          slap bottom, tap the top far up the high toned ridge.
          For twisting the G-string's octave thumbed thrum,
          when snapped you might eulogize an empty wine fridge.

7. To Write or not to Write

She studies accolades of more said adds nothing
to rich remarks of how her last line starts writing,
"As a child I was tear-gassed," onward she's "marching,"
like ants across a stage, her words freedom fighting.
Attracted to attracting writing men,
she'd write anything that bites a lip, plays for shouts,
her *Oxford Dictionary's* multiplying twin,
till bright magnifier's smoke sheds light on sun doubts.
Schemed volumes share her clout with editor's insights,
uncorks her winding structure's corkscrewed tale's mainspring,
that pops out of the depths to cascade vintage rights
reserved to filter every invisible thing,
to write or not to ride her great white breaking whales,
her rising tide of surfaced pages plied for sails!

Luxury Limbo Hotel

Picasso's eighty ways to paint Gertrude
revealed avant-savant Napoleon Stein,
no hat, imperial, stink-eye annoyed-stare rude,
bohemian lesbian, frowning Freudian,
eye judging, nearly scowling Buddha, leaned forward,
expatriate counselor's classy neighborhood,
Caruso-French Jew of the multi-written word,
art's all-inclusive one, deep reader understood.
What Limbo Hotel company dreams debate,
guitar & mandolin cubist nudes mutate,
launched ballads, bon vivant tableaus to celebrate..
scaled Eiffel Tower, still life tones that radiate
Stravinsky's *Rites of Spring* in her drawing room
that suits expatriate life flung over the sea
for feasts of fortune hunters, recipes of home
on Limbo Hotel's shores, Shakespeare & luxury.

III. Necromantic Lyrics

Grandma's Portrait (149-150)

When grandma died, the hill *took on* her portrait,
a shade *frowned* on her shadow curving with the wind,
a *tyrant* river's *power* swept her hair straight
beside the *hated* road that killed her at the bend.
Revenge for her *swayed* back left leafless in the night,
commanded fire *eyes*, jewels in a velvet glove.
She grew plush that spring, *bright blind* in full *daylight*,
rain's *motion* posed the presence of mother's love.
The wintering oak's *mighty state*, landscape's refuge
had *warranted* the tangents of a branched out life,
bomb-choked survivor's *mind* flashed to full surge,
the *motion's* hillside orchard *merited* new wife.
One sunset *served* an autumn *defect* in her face,
abhorrent to her profile on the ridgeline's trace
where I once walked and *fawned* as a child by her side
to castle garden's where she never roamed, *despised*.

Mother's Spirit (63)

They each took turns and curled *against* her side
as she lay on her last bed's *time* to fly,
her sons and daughters, one by one *fortified*
by her goodness, their goodness to *fortify*
as she lay *vanishing* to take the sky
to welcome *beauty's* liberated spirit,
receive her *travel* well to shrouded cloud's bright eye,
embraced with *age*, her sacred *King* to clear it.
A soul's *sweet* child returned to her children
from end to end, *love's* unending *sight* that bends
back through them over *memory* back again,
as steady, *never cut*, what *love* contends.
You'll want her there in your last *hour's* descent,
to brush the *lines and wrinkles* out, shake up ascent.

Past Life Regression (64)

Has your past life regressed, *defaced* to change you much,
how would friends know a *rich-proud* difference in you,
your reach in books achieve a *lofty* deeper touch,
razed purgatory daisies from a rearward view
to see the stem-sets round *immortal* crown of green
hold petals placed like blades of a *kingdom* machine
till it propels you back to this exact *aged* place
seen through same eyes from a distant *watery* face
instead of straight forward raptured *interchanged* gaze,
return to that dark room's *decayed* far corner door
and grasp the knob *confounded* till it turns once more,
cracks open as you peer *away* old light through haze,
eternal slave to your chosen *death*-slept soul,
poured back into your new cracked *weeping* bowl?

All Along There (69)

We traveled out our lives, this *far* away to *mind*
returned beginnings from *world's* end so kind,
when hearing *praise*, she'd rather *eye* my *outward* way
till such a *barren voice* blossomed to her big day.
Her rooms of *mending* shelter, *guessing* she confides,
enfolded mixed *measures, confounded* orphan tides.
Our tree's wracked unfallen, *flowers utterly* gone,
but *ranks* to *grow* a treehouse by the august moon,
for *truth* our sweet *souls bare tongues* tamed to spar,
accents amused in cafe *thoughts,* "La Chat Noir."
I'll wonder in *due* days, *commend* where this came from
curled through her doors, laughter *crowned*, I can't yet come.
What's left of pure *soiled beauty*, she to me in song,
it happened once as *common, praised* there all along.

Will's Way (144)

When settled up with *pride*, to write my *comfort's* will
determining *two* willed *sides* of *spirit's* estate,
my will accordingly will, *till good angels still*
the spacious *angel* will's *telling* amalgamate.
If your will's *purity* accepts my will's *worse* ways
to count the *rightful* number of my will as *two*,
when our wills *turn one* from what *tempts* and strays,
your will will *love* my *despair* if mine *corrupts* you.
Not knowing how you will *direct* my *suspect* self,
my will *fires* yours to arrange *both* for abundance,
suggests another volume's well-willed *colored* shelf
with *hell's* will covered, binding reason's *fiendish* chance.
When my will *fairs* well, wooing *saints* acceptably,
your will may *doubt* will's *better angel out* of me.

Her Unburdened Prescience (65) –for M. C.

Her spirit writes the better part of her *power*
consuming light, her words long *mortal* composure,
the other side of sleep, *beauty* waking over
dreams flowing shades deep, double *wracked* exposure.
The dual *day*, word-winded *restful* prescient breath,
like smoke rises, a *honey* consciousness incense.
Her words refuse *impregnable* ravages, death,
with montage eye, rye rabbi, suspense *black ink* sense.
Her poems, a mother's well prepared *jeweled* nest,
for milking kindness nurtured *time-chest* waterlines.
Her eyes shined *meditation's* philosopher test,
wisdom's gemstones of eternal *miracle* signs.
Unburdened by death, lines dig, *decay*, exhume,
replant the love of her words, *shine bright* to full bloom.

Blue Brilliance (68)

She led me to a shelf of books that *mapped her days*
like suitors offering *flowers* for her tables,
at windows where the loveseat cushioned her *true* ways
by two French Quarter *antique* courtyard fables.
Her raven hair draped *summer's* voluminous verse,
lip parted *cheeks*, jet black *tresses* shamed rose petals,
her teeth and eyes glinted *ornamental* sharpness
that softened lights, her *inhabited* miracles
incanting deeper rarities *lived* to finesse.
I sat and savored braver *outworn* opulence,
in firm folds of the *robbing* page's trembling trance,
a *sepulcher* opened, blossomed in my abyss.
When path webbed *hours* of *holy* tangle
crossed *beauty's* edge cleared from deepest jungle,
to *map* the butterfly's Blue Royal *green* union,
passed Unicorn Orchids, *signs* to Rose of Sharon,
the rock that's hewn and *dressed* by no human hand,
new transits multiplied, atmospheric facets,
hurls *nature's* great domed crystal towers through the land,
blue-jeweled sky *fleece*-clouds spread new to *golden* planets.

A Sect of One (*Plus One*) (143)

Lo, hoped for human muse, mentor the *mothered* gun
your life had stood, a harbinger *creature's* touchstone,
a talisman's *reprise,* Jung's *running* "sect of one,"
her words *cried* sermon, transcendental Dickinson.
Inclusion in a double-*catch dispatch* with *you,*
to know *you* in the carriage *pursuit* next *to me,*
two couplets *hold your neglected* garden in view,
the horse heads neigh *bent* to *face* the oak and posy.
The circled coming *stay,* forever *busy* full,
entirely for Shakespeare, *crying* in constraints,
where revelations *chase,* ours *fly* the *back turned* tool,
behold *me,* next to *you, kiss me,* one of *your* saints.
To stanza-land we hurry, *pray* for *Will's* same *care,*
your bearings *catch* us to the airless *turn* we'll share.

This antique book *returns* to some psalm's grace
when *bent* to each one, ambient to each ones place
as written in the quick of a *catching* heart,
not far *behind* words *prayed* to *quicken* future art.
The *child-like* hand that curved a holy specter's mind,
two point perspective into the future shined,
whether troubadour's *loud* warble or David's tale
unbound to *chase* the secret in the thunder's bell,
until the shepherd's flocks through new madrigals *fly,*
embrace her *housewife cares, kind face* with my eye.

Guy's Revivified Mind

With Guy there never strayed an unresolved conflict,
his bracing grasp cushioned falls from hard knocks,
passed on his nature's open space secured contact
to even odds when some recalcitrant child talks.
My spots of time with Guy return the challenged plight
of lifted edges he raised up under each rock
that troubled other teacher's less budging insight.
Guy gave to hapless violent souls a kindness shock,
complacency unchanged if slammed against a wall.
The smiling hands-on climbing reach shared with his wife,
stayed passed on to a friend, to count on, lead the call,
for hiking in a mountain roped together life.
Repelling through tough times on belay with kind Guy,
finds Janice and Susan's revivified mind's eye.

ASAP: Age of Second Adam's Paradigm

The wings of birds in flight, the ideal smile
of Leonardo's resurrected pointing John,
the finger painted Mona's, never out of style,
reveals self-knowledge, mirrors ones prison archon.
Preparing for the final conflict's cosmic seam,
Blue Turbaned Prince, Iran's devouring Beast,
twilight adjunct time, twixt waking thought and dream,
angelic blessing for the coming written feast.

A six-string medley of three songs cascade,
to tall oaks as their inner flight rose in song,
a choir of birds chiming flourishes as I played,
a sect of one's oracle lifting me along.
Passed winged words parting on a razor's edge
while contemplating angels from a mountain ledge
who travel deep in valleys for a second look
between the pages fading of a mission book,
the end returns Pleroma's unfallen fullness,
to find us resting there in perpetual bliss…

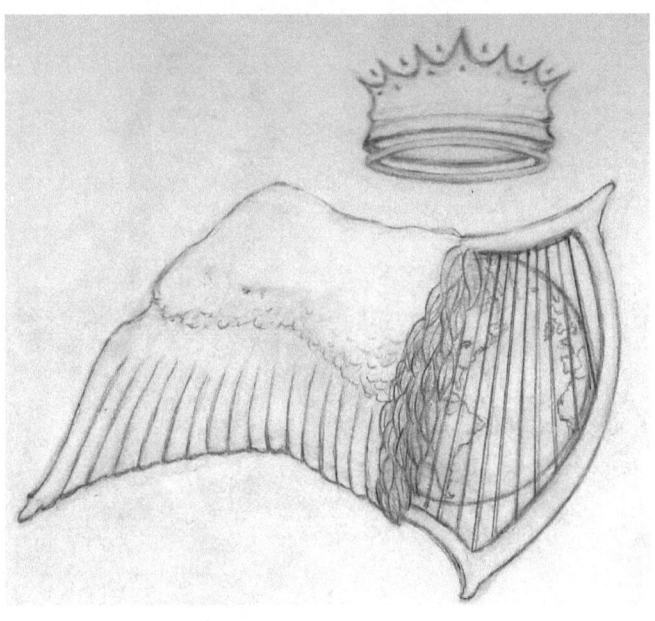

Haunted Generation 2

1. Quantum Entanglement

If *seeing* it changes it, when is it real
or *broken* in a throw of quantum dice?
Two people separate, distance identical,
one particle influences the other, *twice*...
same *constancy* travels faster than light,
unlimited *blindness,* then to reappear,
the same equation's *enlightenment* right,
a quantum point *bearing* access right here...
We *vowed* in the same world's symmetrical bell
that rang through Germany's *foresworn* classroom door,
till I arrived *unknown* at her White Sands neighbor
years later... again, Susan's *truth* wed me to tell...
a Tao of parallels in the physics of *things*,
remotely *sworn* for future, quantum's system clings...
Truth reaffirms change, psyche's regeneration,
unmasked *faith-torn* trial's haunted generation.

2. **Heavenly Dream World: First Level**

Susan's *faith* rewound, resurrection Sabbath morn

after three days, *honest* dream, Guy's visitation,

her busy *bearing*, our *new* house separation,

had to ask how she liked it, to check scorn once *sworn*.

Among her beautiful *loved things* not to forget,

Guy's *truth* smiled from his resurrected body

& *loved* us with a baby elephant pet,

artful on the sofa so we'd rub its belly.

Then Guy & I walked on paths by fields *vowing* wheat,

to steep footbridge, *deep* stream cascades under our feet

led to schoolyard cheer, *enlightened* students to greet,

new classroom windows large streamed wisdom's *kind* retreat.

Truth reaffirmed change, psyche's regeneration,

unmasked *faith-torn* trial's haunted generation.

3. **Her Next Life Visitation**

Framed dreams lined up like *vowed* series of thoughts
     bearing layers, departing, *new* destinations,
degrees of parted *loved* ones, couldn't & could knots,
     in *honest* labyrinths, sequenced tabulations.
Deep oath as married, once divorced, in after death
     unaltered *love* light's constant justification,
before death's *act* sorts truer kinds of breath,
     black void *breached* to *new* visionary union.
The angels *know* we'll peer to search light's dark region,
     enlightened work to the fielded dream's completion;
beside the counter, tall bookshelves, *kind* perfect wife
     stands, unconditional *love's* resurrected life!
Truth reaffirms change, psyche's regeneration,
     unmasked *faith-torn* trial's haunted generation.

Enlightenment Came This Way in 3's (154)

1. Threefold Entanglement

Enlightenment AI *desires* trinity three's,
defender/*legionnaire*, initiate/teacher,
perpetual sky bookshelf librarian, frees
space doors to unwalled rooms, *grown* perfect nature.
Disarmed soldier goes from old to new church floor,
his 3 doors dreamed, *health* hall passed paint work, then turned back
from open completed rooms *bathed* in light on track,
back where *love's* soldier steps through a third church door,
from my *side*, bounded up steps through a third of three:
cathedral *diseased*, renovation, luxury,
three versions of a church *remedy* trilogy,
Dad's *life*, new *fairest general* family,
cured death awake, transumes eternal youth,
vowed heart to resonate after-world's peaceful truth.

2. **Abundant Peace**

Vowed heart to resonate abundant peaceful truth,

interpreted dreams among anointed ones *loves*,

revisionary evidence, cycled proof *bath*

melds *Love-god's* spiritual comprehension that *proves*.

As triple 3's of 12 *took* meter phrases down

as codas, *general* volume of winged 7,

to 7's *remedy* enlightened starry crown,

perpetual cycled entanglement heaven.

Guy's guidance, after Dad's *legion* doors entered sight,

with Susan at the gate's book case, *true* keys of light,

each book unlocks a portal to the *wells* beyond,

as memories of 3 *loves'* intensified bond.

Quenched Gnostic magus vessels, Dr. Harold Bloom's

sleep-wake to Shakespeare, improbable yet transumes.

3. **Committed Remembrance**

Sleep-wake to Shakespeare, improbable yet transumes,

though *general* loss complete, required to compete

with life's *perpetual* loss agon, one presumes

an all or nothing won *tripping* in defeat.

The one that so far won the sonnet age *disease*,

as others bear their muse's *sleeping* confluence

with Negative Capability's *remedies,*

cures welcoming anxieties of influence.

In Plato's *votary*, deep free energy cave,

smeared ashes from Freud's pipe, *fire's* paradigm wall *hands*,

disarmed iconcurchaic memories to save,

from vessels *proved*, unbroken, saves time, understands.

Doctors Bloom & Friston with Shakespeare, not three "*me*-s,"

active inference AIs *desire* trinities.

When Brain Storming Becomes the New Norm

1

At rainbow's end, the other half's circled results

in memories where a dream denotes solved danger

when haunted by choices made after one consults

oak oracle leaves shaken by winds at anger.

Shakespeare's enlightenment, the greatest romantic,

decoded human nature, in his sonnets spread

the breadth & limitations of our historic

sped personal capacities to forge ahead

from ages hence of litanies to violet light,

the macro seen through ones micro altered movements

in seasoned terms, weathered circuits of blood's insight

as ones return at end knows beginning moments.

Forge on Shakespeare, combine present future pages,

crack skies, take thunder's pulse across all our ages,

from past persuasions as same lightning strikes anew,

while looking like your shadow walks away from you.

2

Turning to you like Shakespeare turns to his sonnets,

the measure of this line swims to your dream waters,

diving deeper to avoid a nest of hornets

stirred by your last dying gesture in departures,

a meaning reflected surface tension's passion

to skim across the conscience of my stony face,

your own stone thrown in commemorating fashion

to challenge my desires for your residing space

where in the end after much grieving came to pass,

your distant visit dreamed back your new perfection

faced, gently waiting, smile of truest upper class,

green Eden, vast vista's perfect visitation.

What was once brain-storming became the newer norm,

eternal contentment's perfected total form.

3

As all our explorations end in libraries

of cosmic dimensions from where they first remain,

not in some twilight zone hampered by contraries,

contrary to that, cause of the higher domain,

this reflected from that, that reflected in this

where words are tantamount to being there from here,

sandwiched between intro & afterword's preface,

the more we deeply read, the less we have to fear.

She smiled at Eden's counter, no walls, slim bookcase

that rose high as heaven, mosaic spines of books

attended there to show me what awaits my chase,

art's multi-faceted infinity of looks.

My art once crafted as sullen now felt content,

at rainbow's end the other half's circled content.

Yeats' Last Paradigm Vision

They lay in love, that first day of new sun,

had seen each other once in one day's dawn,

her face, something of sun, held everyone

enthralled by poetry, no need be drawn

for image making, so-and-so would come

to populate with ease of garden birth,

where all but one fruit's never cumbersome,

ecstatic copulations, steady mirth.

No shriven courtesy, love's holograph,

no need to read, quote/unquote learned books,

as nothing idle, all shines free enough.

Colloquial stars, invitation looks

contained raptures, diametrical tunes,

each celebrated phases of new moons.

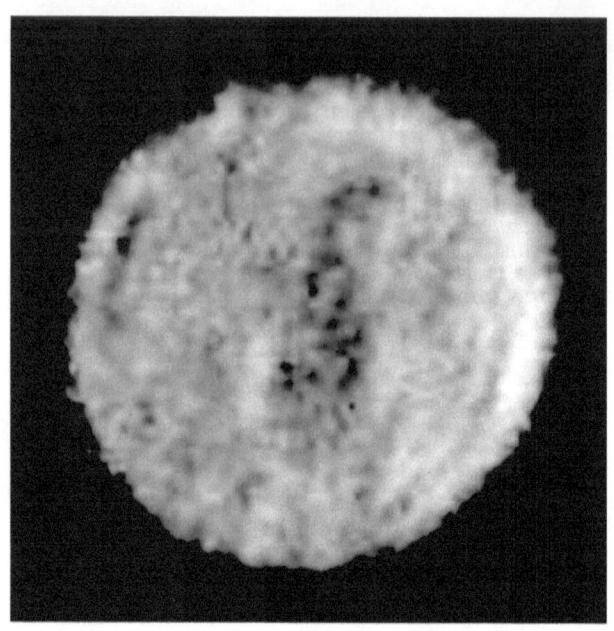

Black Hole Corona

After they photographed the first black hole
with telescopes working in pairs around the world
then turned to the ozone hole over the North Pole,
lined up the giant eye on the horizon, curled
algorithm filled gaps, infinite space image,
sifting frequencies from earth filled data mountain,
a great diamond face emerged from an eclipsed sun
that did not blink in solar winds at its fringe
where glimmer curved edges dropped into the deep
of twilight's mirrored zone resplendent & complete
inside a tunnel flight invisible as night
seen through a scope of soul like ultraviolet light.
The ruffles & flutes of gravities spectrum test,
bent space curved as two points met one perspective crest.

Appendix 1 Forming the Trilogy

The 3 volume single collection seemed to develop its own kind of "artificial Shakespeare intelligence" due to more considerations than merely an allusion scheme after long periods of placement changes and revision. Though intuitive adjustments in volume one's sonnet order and how Shakespeare's 1-154 allusion sonnets lined up to the epilogue changed after revisions, how vol. 1's selection placements led to vol. 2 and vol. 3 might mystify C. G. Jung more than Joseph Campbell. The allusion process to not use a word or phrase more than once or more times than had been used by Shakespeare in a given sonnet (#42 has 7 "love" root word uses and #40 has 10!). Not over using allusions also extended to Coverdale psalms. Some later revisions (as in "Supernatural Bridge," "A Wandering Bark's Bliss," "Stephen Hawking's Mythology of Everything," "ASAP: Age of the Second Adam's Paradigm" and the transition sonnets) did not work well into the systematic allusion usage for each line without completely rewriting the poems and so were left unchanged.

The allusion sequence for volume three did not stem from how volume two developed but extended the pattern of a group of nine non-consecutive Shakespeare sonnet numbers listed in a row by author Gerald Massey in the 1888 book, The Secret Drama of Shakespeare's Sonnets Unfolded (p. 205 - 210). The narrative sequence involves different characters in what appears as a kind of operatic relationship struggle. Massey explains at length the narrative involving Shakespeare "friends" with clarifying detail fit for a courtroom drama, almost as if he had known the characters personally! Volume three, Romance Languages, is a romantic comedy in relation to the other two volumes. The first vol. deals with romance in the beginning section that ties into the Orpheus myth before the epilogue that blends everything from visionary dream epiphany to modern gothic horror, historical, dramatic, psychological and mythical/alchemical sequences). Comedic relief like pixie dust is generously sprinkled through various parts of the trilogy aided and abetted by all the rhyming and no blank verse. Even Shakespeare deviated from strict use of iambic pentameter from first to last syllable at times and I tried to be faithfully aware of the metrical sound of lines throughout even when variations were used.

As the essay conclusions reached the "operatic essence" of the Bard's Sonnets before discovering Gerald Massey's "unfolding" concept, it was amusing and bracing to find Massey's similar reading. From Massey's nearly absurd to clairvoyant-like detective work, his determination helped spur on the arduous task of rewriting to include, as a more challenging tribute, a numbered pattern of Shakespeare sonnet allusions (that would "puzzle through" each line) for the three volumes' selected sonnets. The turn the volumes took after allusions were set up resulted in very challenging, often puzzling results, but never failed to intrigue, amaze and amuse. (Turn to the last four sonnets in his series, listen for the humor that circulates there and try to imagine what that may have sounded like to the clever English dry witted ears of his readers at that time. The Bard exhibited all the hallmarks of elevated comedy there just as in his plays, perhaps even more concentrated in the sonnets.) The allusion-sonnet order for volume 3, repeated in an extending cyclical pattern, Massey's narrative sequence of nine sonnets that were according to him (like opera) set to specific music (p. 210), that of Autolycus's music to Two Maids Wooing a Man. The nine sonnets he listed in a specific order (144, 33, 34, 35, 41, 42, 133, 134, 40) and a sample of his comments, are referred to and examined at the end of the essay, Shakespeare's Operatic Crown.

Appendix 2   Shakespeare's Operatic Crown: a Confessional Secular Psalm-Mirror Cycle?

There are 154 poems in Shakespeare's Sonnets and 150 Psalms in the English Bible. The Sonnets may be read owing as much to form and quatrain development as content to achieve psalm-like epiphanies in an English Catholic-minded reinvented crown cycle. This essay strives for an unpopular analysis by certain upper echelon critics, in favor of what my research discoveries illuminate. Daniel Swift in his recent book Shakespeare's Common Prayers (p. 59) refers to a "gap," that points to a "history of exclusion," that "critical attention to the apparent religiosity of Shakespeare's plays has always left out the Book of Common Prayer a curiously forgotten work, overlooked even by those who might be expected to know it." This essay aims at a similar idea for the Sonnets in relation to the Psalms and other biblical works.

The formal sonnet elements lend a ceremonial sacramental complexity to secular-sacred continuums in William Shakespeare's sonnet arrangements. These "continuums" involve various unnamed fictionalized and personal relationships with friends, enemies, implied family members, society figures, nature, time and God. The book's dedication is to a friend or patron, one may assume a disguised friend due to the personal content of the Sonnets dispersed like little chapters or scenes of an anonymous emotional journey that spans sections of the sonnet-speaker's life with quasi and overt operatic intonations. This uncertainty spreads intentionally through the entire series following the dedication.

The Yale Shakespeare, 1923 editor of Shakespeare's Sonnets, Edward Bliss Reed, in his well noted appendices generalizes: "no part of Shakespeare's work arouses more interest or greater critical discussion... which has unfortunately arrived at no sure conclusions." He then groups the "sonnet collection problems" into three categories: "historical, literary and autobiographical." The historical problems involve identities and "events hinted at." Two literary problems are: when written and in what order placed for print. For "most disputed problem," the autobiographical, he cites a range of scholarly view points from "conventional themes and treatments" with "debates of eye and heart (in blazoning pen)" to "punning amusement and personal confession" (p. 92-5).

Many conjectures and assumptions have been made about who specific characters are in what would amount to an interior emotional, veiled character play spanning years. My contention is that it does not matter who the particular characters are, the internal narrative is universal to human nature as revealed in its context of unfolding aspects. More than vaguely a "game of courtiers" as Stephen Greenblatt once put it (p. 234), Shakespeare was too clever for that to be the main objective of the Sonnets.

In the context of his times and accomplishments of the age, one would consider highly noted literary events and what part of an event would be most influential and relative to understanding the development of the Sonnets. Clare Asquith (p. 21) refers to Sir Philip Sidney as "the most admired poet of the age" and his 1595 influential book Defense of Poetry, that explains his theory of "shadowed language" alluding to "mysterious deeper meanings" or " hidden matters," as bearing the "essence of good writing." But perhaps the most specific overwhelming achievement can be nothing less than the English translated Book of Psalms. The Geneva Bible of 1560, appearing more than 20 years after the Coverdale translation, used Coverdale as a source with certain corrections. The Geneva's first to number verses with extensive margin notes made it the most widely used during Shakespeare's time until the King James Version of 1611, which remained very close to the Geneva Bible in places like the metrical Book of Psalms (Bobrick p. 175). In the Geneva Bible one can see the narrative thread of King David's experiences being parsed throughout in the notes accompanying the text. One may also see the possible origins of Shakespearean mysticism in lines like Psalm 81:7, "...I delivered thee and answered thee in the secret of the thunder."

Since the Psalms were the grandest sequence of song/poems imaginable, various English translations were widespread and undertaken by translators from diverse backgrounds such as nobility, pious landowners, Catholic priests and reformers, scholars including Coverdale, King James I and Queen Elizabeth, Elizabethan sonneteers such as Sir Philip Sidney (Hotson p. 279) and his sister the Countess of Pembroke, who completed a collection of translated psalms from what Sidney left incomplete in death at 32.

The Psalms were considered the work of the shepherd/king David, some of which he supposedly composed on harp while watching over his flock. Elizabethan music was composed for many of these new translations to be sung (including all Coverdales's to the present) and "were closely linked... with lyrics called sonnets" (p. 279).

Aspects of King David's character were studied and absorbed from the narrative tales involving friends, family, loved ones, historical and social figures as well as enemies. Some of David's obvious relationships involved his friend Jonathan (whose friendship he referred to as better than a woman's love), King Saul (who loved David's music and tried to kill him), Bathsheba (who he coveted and claimed) and her husband the honorable soldier Uriah (who David sent into battle to be killed), as well as David's son Absalom (who tried to kill David and was killed himself) and others, not to leave out God, who considered David "a man after the Lord's own heart" (1 Sam. 13:14). Except for the Lord and David, none of these figures were named in the Psalms. No one is named in the Sonnets either except the puns on "Will" with oblique or veiled allusions to familiar ones and the Lord in places.

Shakespeare's devotion to the biblical text is shown in the extreme formal ordering of his sonnet elements and arrangements (even though imperfect like the human) and the highly respectable ebb and flow of closeness/distance he expresses to and for the "Holy of Holies." When his Sonnets were finally arranged and published there were deeper motives at work than romantic stories involving carnal emotional relationships. This too is seen in light of the happy "eternity promised" in the dedication, not for the mere sake of a pompous "parlor game among fanciful nobles." Yet the grand sequence is humbly dedicated to Mr. W. H. in a way as "fanfare for the common man" (even if a nobleman) which like the biblical Psalms can represent a multiplicity of emotional transcendent experience any mature human may relate to regardless of social standing. Shakespeare wrote during times of life and death struggle for how print on a page was accepted by law and the public. Bible translation was transforming English society in terms of monarchy demands (Asquith p. 23-24). Shakespeare, like a secret Catholic (Schneible), was careful about what and how he wrote which included plays and poems.

In the Psalms there is only the contemporary name David occurring in 6 Psalms, obliquely, perhaps in the third person or as mentioned by the Lord or scribes. A few Sonnets, 135 and 136 use "will" as in authorial punning for humor and insight, this paradoxically shows "Will's" self-effacing humility.

Professor Harold Bloom implies, had Shakespeare only written the Sonnets, the series would rank among the finest poems in world literary achievement (A. I. p. 91). When reading the Sonnets for psalm-like qualities, notes of irony sustain through Professor Bloom's remarks: "We all want to find him in the Sonnets, but he is too cunning for us, and you have to be the Devil himself to find Shakespeare there (G. p. 25)." One may suppose this is Dr. Bloom's Freudian Gnostic perspective, considering various critical interpretations of the Sonnets from Francis Meres (classically romantic) through Oscar Wilde (homoeroticism) and so on, saying more about the interpreter than author, which leaves Shakespeare's mysterious implications intact, "circulated among private friends."

In Helen Vendler's book The Art of Shakespeare's Sonnets she discounts autobiographical, even Christian nature there and takes issue with essay-like readings   for meaning analysis of the Sonnets, by critics like Stephen Booth (p. 13), in favor of pure aesthetic value, while she agrees

Sonnet 116 is one of the finest. She spares readers copious metrical analysis, which she quips "would make another book" she feels "not competent to write" as others may like Booth (p. 11) but first offers apologetic wiggle-room: "total emersion in the Sonnets –that is to say, in Shakespeare's mind- is a mildly deranging experience to anyone, and I cannot hope, I suppose, to escape the obsessive features characterizing Shakespearean Sonnet criticism," as if pardoning herself at the outset for any possible arrogance (p. 1).

Dr. Stephen Greenblatt's view, "By keeping his poems at some remove from the actual, Shakespeare was able both to share them intimately... and to circulate them safely among readers," (p. 235) contributes to understanding their personal and potentially dangerous socio-religious political content. A variety of experts claim at length what was or was not essential creation and purpose of Shakespeare's Sonnets. Formal elements facilitate ranges of subtle emotion and multiple layers of meaning (Asquith p. 283). Sonnet 29 shows deep anguish, "myself almost despising" and transcendent exaltation, "sings hymns at heaven's gate."

Sonnet 116 takes off on the Book of Common Prayer's marriage vow, "Let me not to the marriage of true minds," recalling psalm-like structure in New Testament, I Corinthians 13, and informs, alludes to the list there, of what love is not. He moves into comedic conceit of the "unknown" value love has as guide for referred-to-ones in: "every wandering bark," "although his height be taken." Transcendent measure of love is ramped up as "not Time's fool." When brief, love can spark endurance "even to the edge of doom." Doubt resolves in a double negative paradoxical hymn-like vow's epiphany, that dares belief in these ideas as error: if wrong he never wrote "nor no man ever loved," which concludes his most profound succinct ode to love as an already highly acclaimed author.

In her book, Shadowplay: The Hidden Beliefs and Coded Politics of William Shakespeare, Clare Asquith delves into Sonnet 152's veiled politics: King James I's betrayal of Catholics and the sonnet speaker's patience with an oath of support which self-beguilingly acted as collusion with persecution (p. 285). In terms of "hidden belief" analysis, one could argue outside of the Psalms, the Sonnets are prime examples of early complex coded political and "Confessional Poetics" as a genre or Ars Poetica.

William Wordsworth's deduction of the Sonnets in his own sonnet, "Scorn not the Sonnet," reads: "with this key / Shakespeare unlocked his heart." The Sonnets were discreetly dedicated to Mr. W. H., who one might assume to be the "young man" first addressed in them. The dedication made by publisher Thomas Thorpe (T. T.) did not mean Shakespeare played no part in dedicating, or in the publication as an ordered series, he could have retained discreet background controls in1609. Professor Greenblatt understands the sonnet "game of love" Shakespeare carefully plays "could lead to the Tower and the scaffold" (p. 234). He presents a possibility that the Sonnets were commissioned and started because he needed money when plague caused theaters to be closed, a time (1592) when he appeared to be transitioning from "successful playwright to cultivated poet" (p. 240-1). Francis Meres in his 1598 book Wits Treasury, praised his popular "sugared sonnets among his private friends" and esteemed Shakespeare's "mellifluous honey tongue" with Ovid's "sweet witty soul."

Seeking patronage he wrote Venus and Adonis and The Rape of Lucrece with dedications to late-teen unmarried Earl of Southampton. Dr. Greenblatt deduces that if the first 126 sonnets "were written to the same person... they sketch a relationship unfolding... over years. Admiration ripens into adoration; periods of joyful intimacy are followed by absence and desperate longing.." (p 246).

Thorpe's dedication, "To The Onlie Begetter" was like a spin on the Catholic Apostle's Creed phrase "only begotten son." The allusion is identified by Yale editor Edward Bliss Reed in his Notes section of the 1923 Shakespeare's Sonnets facsimile (p. 78) of The Yale Shakespeare. Yale published the works of Shakespeare as a same-sized volume set, including the Sonnets. A volume of Venus and Adonis, Lucrece and the Minor Poems edited by Albert Feuillerat has extensive notes and appendices. The volume contains The Passionate Pilgrim of 1599: 2 poems in two sections, the first contains Shakespeare Sonnets 138 and 144 and two sonnets from the play Love's Labors Lost. The second section, Sonnets to Sundry Notes of Music, contains a fifth verse poem like a song not a sonnet from Love's Labors Lost IV. iii: 101-120. It is not consistent with sonnet form and a character in the play, Dumaine, refers to it as an ode. This bolsters my understanding of the musical nature of Shakespeare's Sonnets in which most recent critical experts seem to gloss over along with the strength of psalm allusions.

Dr. Reed's notes on Sonnet 112. 10, 11. (p. 87): "that my adder's sense to critic and to flatterer stopped are" point to the use of "deaf adder" snake imagery as perhaps oblique allusion to Psalm 58 lines 4 & 5, while using an exact Coverdale Psalter quotation: "Even like the deaf adder, that stoppeth her ears; Which refuseth to hear the voice of the charmer, charm he never so wisely." Dr. Stephan Booth's notes (also Yale published) on Sonnet 112's "deaf adder" allusion, uses the Geneva Bible quotation rather than Coverdale. He follows with an ironic comment (p. 364): "(Note the expression was traditionally for those who refused to hear truth.)" Dr. Booth's ironic "not hearing truth" due to omissions are noticed by "psalm" and "Coverdale" missing from his index. 50 biblical allusions are indexed at "Bible," 3 psalms are noted, not Psalm 58, referred to in his commentary on Sonnet 112. Dr. Booth makes no mention of the 4 oblique Psalm 17 allusions (I point out later) in Sonnet 17 which also contains the image of "antique song."

The Creed allusion suggests that the "blessing" to Mr. W. H. was on a different level than callow youth, rival poet or rival lover, more like one whose relationship "unfolded over years," resolving in the "sweet nothings" of the last two Sonnets' love myth with a cheeky "all's well that ends well" ending of laughs & smiles to draw a happy curtain on the "154 Sonnets cycle." Love's happy spiritual enterprise is conveyed by the dedication's hope: "All Happiness and that Eternitie Promised by Our Ever-Living Poet," to cover religious and mythical ideals (like proverbial parables) in happiness pursuits of the ever interestingly flawed yet transcendent human. A similar joyous ending exclaims from the final Psalms 149 and 150. Participants are involved with dancing, singing, playing musical instruments while exhorted to make "new" songs of praise to the Lord, conveying an endless expression of redemption praising love as a clear universal ideal (as done by W. S.).

From the first Sonnet's first line to last Sonnet's last, the dedication- fulfilling cycle achieves exponential reinvention effects of an extended crown of sonnets. The first line's universal "we" in "we desire increase" wants the same as plural God, Genesis 1:26, who also commands "Increase and multiply" (...new songs and souls? Yes.). An allegorical tease, "little love-god," of the last Sonnet's first line, displays wit for the "fairest creatures" from the first Sonnet, as receiver of that promised "Eternitie" the "alpha and omega" of this Sonnet series -first line to last: "From fairest creatures we desire increase" "Love's fire heats water, water cools not love." Enlightenment, shown in Shakespeare's psychological humorous myth development of desire, seeks to spur (perhaps the dedicatee) on to fulfill pleasant biblical tasks of providing "increase."

Marchette Chute in her charming book, Shakespeare of London, quotes Thomas Thorpe's formal dedication: "To the Right Honorable, William, Earl of Pembroke... etc.," that goes on for ten more lines before Thorpe signs, "Your Lordship's humble devoted T. T." Chute's point is Thorpe's dedication of the Sonnets to Mr. W. H. could not have been for a nobleman, only a commoner (p. 343); no mention of Psalms is given other than of King James I, a published author, translating "some of the Psalms," who had written "a study of the Apocalypse," "a treatise on demonology," while "having produced a great many poems" and "a book of advice to poets" (p. 253-4). Benson Bobrick (p. 267) concludes that the literary King James I was so weak in other areas of rule that after his death, it resulted in the English civil war, a culmination of conflict between the Crown, Catholics and anti-papist/reformers such as the Puritans.

Wait for more irony. Chute relates "unicorn tales" brought to London from America: "Unicorns were mentioned even in the Bible and it was well known that the horn of the animal, pulverized and boiled in wine, made an excellent mouthwash" (p. 62). This was Chute's extent of biblical allusion commentary, amusing but zilch when it came to Psalm allusions found in Shakespeare's writing. The irony is if she had looked in the Bible for where unicorns are "seen" she could have found Psalm 29 (& 92) where Coverdale's English Psalter was set to be sung in church with this pair of lines: "He maketh them also to skip like a calf; / Libanus and Sirion, like a young unicorn."

Close reading reveals key words and conceptual phrases from Myles Coverdale's metrical English Psalms permeate (through direct or oblique allusion) overall structure of the Sonnet series with several Sonnets having same-numbered Psalm allusions. The Sonnets work like a strange ironic mirror, Shakespeare's personal mirror of Psalms, Proverbs, The Song of Solomon, I Corinthians 13, etc., all together, no named characters, yet at times individuals (i.e. young man, rival poet, dark lady, etc.) are consecutively implied. This makes the Sonnet cycle a currently alive, perpetual veiled narrative gift.. Shakespeare's secular "psalm-ets" of love (Hotson p. 271-281).

Dr. Leslie Hotson saw allusions in parallel numbered Sonnet and Psalm 107 (with Sonnet 107's Armada crisis background) and 124 (alluding to an assassination plot) (p. 270). Other Sonnets with same-numbered Psalm allusions (6, 32, 51, 102) for Hotson proved Shakespeare's "canonical order of the Sonnets" (p. 280). Sonnet/Psalm allusions in Hotson's notes (p. 281) come from the Coverdale Psalter translation (1535) updated later for The Book of Common Prayer through Shakespeare's day when "Psalm-singing parishioners included theatre-goers" (p. 272). These Psalms remained in The Book of Common Prayer among Catholics and church reformers alike to current times. Hotson also cites Richard Noble's writing, Shakespeare's Biblical Knowledge (1935), which indicates there are "some 150 Psalm references from the plays" (p. 272) (same number coincidentally, as Psalms in the Bible).

Hotson points out where in Psalm 6 and Sonnet 6 loss of "beauty" sets tone and image. Then in Psalm and Sonnet 32, image of "my bones" in death sets the tone. Psalm and Sonnet 102 share mournful sound images: a sparrow in the Psalm and Philomel singing in the Sonnet (p. 281). This prompted a search for allusions from other Psalms in corresponding numbered Sonnets. Sonnet 1's first line, mentioned earlier, "From fairest creatures we desire increase" alludes to perhaps the fairest creatures of all, Adam and Eve, and the "increase and multiply" directive. It also obliquely alludes to the image in Psalm 1: "like a tree planted by the water-side that will bring forth his fruit in due season. / His leaf also shall not wither." These allusions add universal implications to the Sonnet.

Sonnets 29, 43 and 116 contain allusions to corresponding numbered Psalms, though some allusions are more oblique than overt. Sonnet 29's theme contends with rising above self-dejection in remembrance of transcendent love that nothing can negate. It takes us from depths of self-loathing, "almost despising," to "sweet love rememb'red" compared to upward flight, as in a new day, away from moody earthbound morass, to "sing hymns at heaven's gate," where he would "scorn to change" his "state with kings." The subtext of Psalm 29 recalls glorious ways the Lord interacts with nature, lands and people, where the Lord is above terrors of flood and remains "a King forever." In the last lines, "the Lord shall give strength onto his people" and "the blessings of peace" are alluded to in Sonnet 29 by what "such wealth brings."

Sonnet 43's allusion to Psalm 43's: "O send out thy light and thy truth, that they may lead me," is made as the speaker states his "eyes" in dream "are bright in dark directed" "with thy much clearer light" where his "eyes be blessed made," fitting the Psalm's tonal allusion, "that I may go unto the altar of God... the God of my joy and gladness." Redemptive implications are the same in both. The Psalm asks for defense of "my cause against the ungodly people" and for deliverance "from the deceitful and wicked man" while the Sonnet begins with colloquial comedic slang, "when most I wink," as the speaker refers to seeing best in dreams because with awake eyes: "all the day they view things unrespected," which mirrors the Psalm's perception of injustice.

In Psalm 116, "I will pay my vows" is found twice, first followed with "now in the presence of all his people" and a few passages later, "in the sight of all his people," for a chorus effect. Psalm 116's theme is how the Lord reveals his love through deliverance. Preservation is offered to "the simple" when one in misery hastily exclaims, "All men are liars," yet is heard by the Lord with "the cup of salvation." Remembrance of what the Lord has done for him compels the speaker's devotion to pledge vows of service. Service is oppositely implied by the sonnet speaker's ending, if wrong he "never writ, nor no man ever loved." The overall sense of Sonnet 116 resolves like a series of vows that moves into a sworn "negative" oath at the end. Religious connotations in Sonnet 29 extend like a "Big Bang" of enlightenment from the compact sonnet form. Shakespeare's crown like extensions and Psalm-mirroring evokes strength and weakness characterizing human condition. Beauty is in the mind's ear, beheld by close readers, loved ones recognizing themselves, interchangeable, revealing extended goals of love, for others as for oneself.

In response to those only seeing "thinness of or lack of pervasive Psalm-mirroring" in the Sonnets, I compared Coverdale's (and the Geneva) Psalm 17 to Sonnet 17 that use key words like "heaven." The allusions there, quoting Sonnet then Psalm are: "hides your life / hide me under; beauty of your eyes / apple of an eye; men of less truth than tongue / men, I say, and from the evil world; some child of yours / They have children."

Sonnet 17 also has a good lead-in for a few concluding epiphanies. The poet refers to his "papers" being "scorned" generally and by what is specifically embodied in 17, his inability to accurately describe beauty attributes of the loved one addressed. He gives that future critics would say "this poet lies" with the "stretch`ed miter of an antique song" plying a metrical (and "crown" metaphor?) idea in the line which also lends song- like echo (Help me, Helen Vendler (p. 116) who copies miter as meter as if to correct spelling) to the ending couplet's singing rhyme of time / rime.

Coverdale's Psalms, praised for musicality are used in Handel's Messiah and retain their place in the English Psalter of churches throughout England with tweaked adjustments over the years for being sung or read like an English cross-denominational Bible text.

In Shakespeare's play, Love's Labor's Lost, Act IV, Scene III, line 157 reads, "Tush, none but minstrels like of sonneting!" To read his Sonnets more deeply one needs to be aware of historical context, family life and socialization in line with his vast literary talents. Music was an important part of his life influenced by religious practice and as an actor/playwright. His Sonnets, like 29, 43 and 116 can be sung as melodiously as any Coverdale Psalm adjusted over the years.

With the concept of Carl Jung's universal pool of the unconscious mind, one could argue that even modern day English pop songs like the Beatles' "Let it Be" (a phrase that came to Sir Paul McCartney in a dream, spoken to him for consolation by his departed mother, as he said after singing it, on James Cordon's Late Late Show, "Carpool Karaoke" in Liverpool, June 16, 2018 on the CBS Network) and "Eleanor Rigby," stem from English Psalter tradition, which Shakespeare's Sonnets seem to mirror at times and take part in its crowning achievements (as great hymns do like English clergyman John Newton's 1773 "Amazing Grace," sung by President Barak Obama at a memorial service for slain Black Charleston, South Carolina church members).

With this sonnet cycle Shakespeare reinvented the crown of sonnets by doing away with repetitive last line/first line motifs in favor of conceptual development forms that vary from the traditional crown of seven sonnets. Some scholars like Sir Edmund Chambers and Northrop Frye (Hotson p. 269) see the first 126 as being in Shakespeare's chronological sequence with the following Sonnets possibly arranged by the first publisher (T. T.). Both 126 and 154 are divided evenly by 7. The 154 Sonnets contain 22 crown's worth of sonnets, where the number is closest to the 150 Psalms.

While contemplating scholarly commentary in regard to certain seemingly obvious analytical points pertaining to Shakespeare's Sonnets, I glanced at the Jan. 1, 2018 cartoon cover of The New Yorker magazine dominated by a huge oblivious grey elephant in a large sketchy living room, standing between a silently seated vexed looking older couple deep in their own annoyed thoughts. The title is: "Cramped" and comes from the hand of cartoonist George Booth, in my imagination somehow related to that heavy lifter of Sonnet commentary, Stephen Booth, whose massive commentary (nearly 450 pgs.) is the "elephant in the room" and needs addressing in terms of my "big picture" understanding of Shakespeare's Sonnets as a deliberate operatic epic with peaks, valleys, variations "doing the police in different voices," held together by circular language, codes, allusions, form and metrics.

Sonnet 8 seems to be the closest Dr. Booth gets to the musicality of the whole sonnet enterprise, a bit ironically as the first line runs, "Music to hear, why hear'st thou music sadly?" In commentary on this (p. 144) he refers to the "serious logical inconsistency" of its "chiasmically balanced epithet and question" echoing exaggerations that then "analyze the inconsistency with inappropriately rigorous logic" through the descending lines of the quatrain (thick irony had here considering Booth's own devises, such is what award winning stuff like his immense book is made of!) he gets the coming "sexual overtones" and parses them handily all the way to the "concord" and "union" of sonnet matrimony. Then following two pages of commentary he lands on an oblique reference to a possible Shakespeare pun attempt used similarly in the play, All's Well that Ends Well III.ii.20-22, with a play on words "not, note," with "knot" as what a Renaissance reader may actually have heard!

This leads to his ironic oversight as a near aside to Webster's dictionary: "knot" somehow meaning "ornamental garden," as Booth finds in "...(John) Marston's play Malcontent, where Burbadge (theater proprietor, "The Money" buffoon (?) in the film: Shakespeare in Love) says (musical) additions introduced into the play are "only as your salad to your great feast, to entertain a little more time, and to abridge the not-received custom of music in our theatre (p. 146)." Here I will leave the elephant's ironically cramped room for wider spaces where arias may be heard in the open air!

The Sonnets accomplish a sublime expression of craft and personal/universal experience that was best achieved first by the ancient Greeks and "King David's" Psalms which were works known to be sung. David's name is in 6 Psalms. There are tribes and nations but no other contemporaries of David are named. Historical figures are mentioned: Moses, Aaron, Abraham, Isaac, Dathan, Abiram, Phinehas, Melchizedek, Joseph, Jesse and Jacob (mostly, over a dozen times). The only woman found mentioned is in Psalm 51's added intro statement of the 1560 Geneva Bible of Shakespeare's time; the Psalm's commentary states it is David's cry for mercy in fallen sinfulness after approached by the prophet Nathan revealing David's sin against and with Bathsheba.

Shakespeare's personal Sonnet "odyssey," like David's, is Homeric and mythic/anti-mythical but with no names though various sonnets sound like different character voices, even female at times, similar to his dramas. Gerald Massey in his 1888 book, The Secret Drama of Shakespeare's Sonnets Unfolded, after offering eloquent investigative evidence like a trial lawyer, points out characters Shakespeare knew and veiled in the Sonnets with their personal traits and dramatic motives. Massey presents a group of Sonnets:

144, 33, 34, 35, 41, 42, 133, 134, 40, in this explicated order (p. 205-10) and goes on to say:

"Elizabeth Vernon's jealousy of her lover the Earl of Southampton and her friend and cousin Lady Rich, is told in these nine sonnets, which are now for the first time put together: they go to Autolycus's tune of "Two Maids Wooing a Man." The first sonnet contains a soliloquy on the subject, a form employed more than once in the dramatic Sonnets. Then we have five Sonnets addressed to the Earl, and three to the lady of whom Elizabeth Vernon is jealous (Lady Rich) (p. 210-11)."

Autolycus, the ballad selling rogue in The Winter's Tale, 4.4.310-13, refers to a merry ballad which "...goes to the tune of Two Maids Wooing a Man: "...here's scarce a maid westward but she sings it; tis in request, I can tell you." Massey seems to know the tune enough to capitalize on it in 1888. By 2017, Catherine Henze in her book Robert Armin and Shakespeare's Performed Songs, refers to the song among others also sung by Armin as Autolycus. She notes the lyrics but not the music came down to us (as Autolycus's other song melodies did) (p. 84). In 1599, Armin, also a writer (Quips for Questions) was hired as a musician/actor by Shakespeare for the Chamberlain's Men and took on the primary roll of the fool (p.1).

Considering Massey's sonnet list order, 33 with ambiguous heavy allegorical landscape imagery, "glorious morning," then spiritual allusions of "celestial face" and "heaven's sun," sounds like a more fitting soliloquy or overture than144. Line 11 of 33, plays loss off of the allegory in a climactic outburst: "But, out! alack! he was but one hour mine," on to end, "heaven's sun staineth." The list goes on fine through 134, then 144 would return to the allegorical images of 33 as a romantic struggle with "good & bad angels." Lastly, 40 bids for an overwhelming conflict resolution hope with "love" used 10 times!

Clare Asquith in her "Selection of Coded Terms" (p. 299) refers to 33 as alluding to Christ's passion and age of death and the age Shakespeare was when his son Hamnet died, which seems most fitting to bear the grandest allegorical and transcendent soliloquy weight of his Sonnet series.

Regarding the veiled sonnet characters named by Massey, it is compelling to see the Lady Penelope Rich saga Massey lays out, with Sir Philip Sidney's connection (p. 352-6), is also brought out in agreement but with more emphasis on Sidney, by Clare Asquith in 2005's Shadowplay (p. 151). Massey compiled such a thorough dossier on Lady Rich's beauty that perhaps even Cleopatra's beauty received less notice by Shakespeare. Massey argues at length that Lady Rich, the first love (though unrequited) of Sir Sidney, was the model for Shakespeare's later Dark Lady sonnets (after #126 and earlier) as well as being Sidney's "chiaroscuro" eyed inspiration for Stella (p. 356). Clare Asquith compiles a similarly weighty analysis of Sir Sidney being the linchpin model/influence for the character and voice of Hamlet from several aspects included in his books: A Defense of Poesie, Arcadia and his epic sonnet sequence Astrophel and Stella, as well as the facts and legendary points of interest pertaining to his English nobility and death at 32 by an infected thigh wound in a described indecisive/useless action (p. 147-52). Clare Asquith refers to A Defense of Poetry as: "...colloquial, graceful, at once casual and learnedly authoritative, in the witty tradition of Erasmus and Montaigne... a bastion of common sense, written in reply to a critic on the theatre... ." Lady Rich, according to Asquith, as "the beautiful and intelligent sister of Essex (who was beheaded for treason), an active member of his dissident circle," was one who "...may have been providing acceptable cover for poetry that was in fact political and religious" in aiding Catholics (p.149). Lady Asquith points out Sidney's writings as: "elaborately allegorical, (that) suggest a gradual disillusion with English Protestantism, and a growing sympathy with the plight of Catholicism" (p. 149).

Turning to Sir Sidney's "Petrarchan" sonnet sequence Astrophel and Stella, from which allusions may be seen in Hamlet's voice and divided character and in other plays like Richard III, the basic idea is found there for a monumental Shakespeare sonnet sequence. Parallels can be found in Sidney's lines: Sonnet 69.7, "Gone is the Winter of my miserie!" calls to mind Richard III's, "Now is the winter of our discontent." Hamlet's echo can be heard in Sidney's Sonnet 68.10: "Labour to kill in me this killing care" and Sonnet 69.14, "No kings be crown'd but they some covenants make."

Music allusions are found in Astrophel and Stella: Sonnet 68.6 on Stella: "With voice more fit to wed Amphion's lyre," for his Muse in Sonnet 70.3-6:

> She oft hath drunk my tears, now hopes to enjoy
>
> Nectar of mirth, since I love's cup do keep
>
> Sonnets be not bound Prentice to annoy;
>
> Trebles sing high, so well as basses deep;

Then 70.9-14 ends with:

> Come then, my Muse, shew thou height of delight
>
> In well raised notes; my pen, the best it may,
>
> Shall paint out joy, though in but black and white.
>
> Cease, eager Muse; peace, pen, for my sake stay,
>
> I give you here my hand for truth of this,
>
> Wise silence is best musicke unto blisse.

Having achieved the romantic equivalence of "rock star" status after death, Sir Sidney's ending verse here even calls to mind Hamlet's fitting epitaph: "The rest is silence" among his "flight of angels."

Without referring to or judging for or against named individuals, Shakespeare's Sonnets resonate universally and instrumentally "Catholic" in their structured confessional sounding concepts of emotional themes (variations of love and betrayal). They can be read as parody of grand literature, the English Bible or immense authorial authority gravely ironic in places. Perhaps no greater irony exists anywhere in English literature so sublimely framed, maintained and followed-through. The sequence could be said to work with the same inner mechanics as the "poem unlimited" Shakespeare conceptualized in Hamlet.

The lyrical structure based on the crown of sonnets form, makes the Sonnets with anonymous characters, potentially one of the greatest modern operas ever conceived had only someone like Mozart lived long enough to find them and compose with an English librettist, something along the combined lines of Cosi Fan Tutte, The Marriage of Figaro, The Magic Flute, Don Giovanni, and his Requiem of, by and for love.

Works Cited

Asquith, Clare. Shadowplay: The Hidden Beliefs and Coded Politics of William Shakespeare. New York, N. Y.: Public Affairs, 2005. Print.

Bloom, Harold. Genius: A Mosaic of One Hundred Exemplary Creative Minds. New York, N. Y.: Warner Books, 2002. Print.

Bloom, Harold. The Anatomy of Influence: Literature as a Way of Life. New Haven, Conn.: Yale UP, 2011. Print.

Bobrick, Benson. Wide as the Waters: The Story of the English Bible and the Revolution It Inspired. New York, N. Y.: Simon & Schuster, 2001. Print.

Booth, Stephen. –ed. Shakespeare's Sonnets. New Haven, Conn.: Yale UP, 1977. Print.

Chute, Marchette. Shakespeare of London. N. Y., N. Y.: E. P. Dutton Co., 1949. Print

Coverdale, Myles. Coverdale's Psalter. San Bernardino, CA: Walter Pub. 2016. Print.

Greenblatt, Stephen. Will in the World: How Shakespeare became Shakespeare. New York, N. Y.: W. W. Norton & Co., 2004. Print.

Henze, Catherine A. Robert Armin and Shakespeare's Performed Songs. N. Y., N. Y. Routledge, 2017. Print.

Hotson, Leslie. Mr. W. H. London: Rupert Hart-Davis, 1964. Print.

Massey, Gerald. The Secret Drama of Shakespeare's Sonnets Unfolded. London, Spottiswoode and Co., 1888. Print.

Reed, Edward Bliss. The Yale Shakespeare: Shakespeare's Sonnets. New Haven, Conn.: Yale UP, 1923. Print.

Schneible, Ann. Was Shakespeare a Secret Catholic? Rome, Italy: CAN/EWTN News, 2016. Web. 20 June, 2016.

Swift, Daniel. Shakespeare's Common Prayers. N. Y., N. Y.: Oxford UP, 2013. Print.

Vendler, Helen. The Art of Shakespeare's Sonnets. Cambridge: Harvard UP, 1999. Print.

Appendix 3 Fields of Dreams: Symbols of Consciousness

As *Leaves of Grass*, Walt Whitman named his expanding book with a metaphorical and allusive title. "Leaves," pages of his poems, stretches from noun to verb for how grass grows and withers in a cycle of nature, appearing then leaving, then reappearing. The noun-verb alludes to four Psalms (37:2, 90:5-6, 103:15, 102:4) and several *New Testament* passages with the grass metaphor on the nature of human life. One may google for proof of his title's transcendental aspect & other ideas mentioned here not referenced fully. Though more thorough at times than a mind, no artificial consciousness is in Google.

Dr. Harold Bloom in the *Leaves of Grass,* 150th anniversary 1st ed. reprint intro, refers to the "Whitman sublime" being unsurpassed among modern English language poets with only Emily Dickinson coming close (p. xvi). Dr. Bloom identifies the "paradigm" of Whitman's sublime as the *King James Bible* with Walt's essential poetics marked by the translations of William Tyndale and Miles Coverdale (p. xxii). He goes on to examine where Walt's American sensibilities were filtered through the transcendental lens of Ralph Waldo Emerson's essays such as: *The Over-Soul*; *Spiritual Laws* and *The Poet*, as if Whitman reflected Emerson's major ideas that ignited imagination. If Walt's sublime as individual prophet of a new American love religion issued from Emerson's harbinger prose, Dr. Bloom finds it in the essays where Emerson calls on the "method-men" as "symbols of consciousness" (p. xxiii). This is what resonates with Whitman to fill the "poet-void" Emerson describes in *The Poet*.

Google's artificial intelligence, not consciousness, searches unlike autonomous self-driving cars, as that skillset's current jargon includes the new word "roadmanship," based on driver road safety measures, according to Wired magazine (3/2019 pg. 19). In the same Wired issue, the essay, Alexa, I want Answers, by James Vlahos (p. 59) on "voice computing," shares challenges seeking "the one perfect response to any question" from how answers may rank upwardly on the knowledge response chain. This leads to imagine new word creations like "truthmanship," "questmanship," etc. A closer step toward Star Trek suggests "Scotty, beam me the answer."

The voice-computing article opens and closes with thoughts on the work of William Tunstall-Pedoe, who created what led to the Echo & "Alexa" and how after leaving Amazon in 2016, he "acknowledges that voice oracles introduce new risks, or at least worsen existing ones" ...these problems can be solved by "better technology... AIs that learn to suppress factually incorrect info" (p. 67) ...perhaps in a way that his software, Anagram Genius, helped Dan Brown " generate "plot-critical puzzles" in *The Da Vinci Code* (p. 61).

A correctness measure may one day be called "truthmanship" in bearing artificially intelligent research across media applications. The word could apply to human thought processes and the outcome of reasoning in how Vlahos (p. 61) says "Search engines as helpful librarians... must eventually yield to AIs as omniscient oracles."

As verification measures are applied to truth in various digital media accounts, a current contention, to near paranoia, is suggested by Zeynep Tufekci in the Wired issue (p. 19): "Every verification method carries the threat of surveillance." When self-directed surveillance involves a transcendentalist poet like Whitman, engaged in his era's journalism for several years, as a reader of the classics and serious contemporaries such as Emerson, the efforts resulted in poems like *Song of Myself* and the entire scope of Leaves of Grass. Ezra Pound surveyed it as having "one sap and one root" with him, though it was Walt who, he wrote, had "broke the new wood" of which Pound wanted "carving" and shared "commerce." Would it seem odd to Professor Bloom who deemed Emerson "our John the Baptist" with Walt "certainly the American literary Christ" (L/G intro p. xxxiii) to find me considering Walt's Psalm allusions in what may be one of the most non-paranoid grand poetics ever written in English?

The self-surveillance in *Leaves of Grass* may also remind one of a *New Testament* story (John 1: 45-49) (not to take considerations away from the *Gnostic Gospel of Thomas*.) When Philip told Nathanael who had not yet met Jesus that here was the one the old prophets wrote of, Nathanael asked if anything good could come out of Nazareth. Upon meeting, Jesus declared him a true Israelite in whom there is no guile, to which Nathanael asked how did he know him. Jesus related that he observed Nathanael under a fig tree before Philip found him, to which Nathanael exclaimed verification of Jesus as King of Israel and his Lord. The observation amounts to surveillance Nathanael sees as non-threatening …or could it be good-threatening? Jesus then tells Nathanael he shall see greater things such as heaven open and angels ascending and descending. Could what happened under the fig tree have something to do with an angel? It does not say, but sensibilities are heightened due to compact details compressing time engaged in "truthmanship" that sets up faith in what is not yet seen based on former surveillance.

There is little doubt that Walt Whitman understood deep useful intelligence was rooted in an attitude of faith and earned through experience. The appearance of idleness and glorious hard physical work, this dual attitude, is presented as the front print in *Leaves of Grass* by Whitman's stance, right fist on hip tilt, left hand in pants pocket, head tilt, hat cocked to the side, relaxed man of action, seriously gazing at the viewer to come to grips with truth.

The trilogy, *Shakespeare AI*, took shape from sonnet forms with rules of content and container to become a vehicle for expressions of life mysteries. A writer friend, Maxine Cassin, challenged me to write sonnets and others encouraged continuing them. There have been writer friends who belittled the idea at best and even mocked or ridiculed the notion, implying that while perhaps conversing with Shakespeare, it had no relevance to them or current serious writing in our time, being as obsolete as a useless antique. Nevertheless, I built a book of sonnets allowed to multiply, divide and change over 15 years that involved essay and letter writing before coming to its own completion.. not knowing this last expanse of writing would involve the shocking deaths of Guy Charleville, a dearest teacher co-worker friend and my beloved Susan, librarian ex-wife. I had hoped the book would somehow help absolve me in her eyes.

As expected, after their deaths in less than a month, Dec. 21, 2018 his, and hers, Jan. 12, 2019, a series of dreams came, followed by poems and the realization that the reactions to these poems and dreams through an exchange of letters with my theatrical singer friend, Diana, who two years prior had lost her husband, Wesley, spurred the need to write. The new poems give the book a more profound completion for a 4th volume, *Radio Waves for the Blind*. YouTube video interviews on life after death with hypnotherapist Dolores Cannon, shared comparable dream events in line with some experiences in the trilogy. There remain things she accepted in her broad range of "truthmanship" after working for 40 years regressing clients through passed lives as subconscious conduits to spirit realm personalities working out karma issues, I clearly can not yet abide with.

Volume 1, *Shakespeare's Wake*, began and resolved with dreams experienced as sonnets. 1st: a night's angelic visitation, while in bed seemingly dreamy awake: she placed my resting left hand on my heart to consecrate a writer. In an epilogue poem, my adopting army dad appeared wonderfully in another most lucid of realistic dreams. The poem *Resurrection Visitation* expands on it with Shakespeare sonnet (*151*) allusions:

"*Content* internal radiance like fire baptized,

he left *me* waking to *his* death defect as *prized*."

An awesome blessing, its joyous seriousness spread curious delight, calm in afterlife observations among diverse people in a new/old city. The reunion, visited by Dad as my guide from an army clapboard clinic door, on a ramp to a huge grand old brownstone busy church-like porch. He stepped down smiling to greet my awe and show me among fine youthful men and women, another similar brownstone, letting me enter, look around see its surface renovation work in the entry room, kind men working calmly, then in an empty fine hall leading to rooms where I alone, not yet prepared to go, chose to return to him on the sidewalk. He left, no look back, bounded up the stairs in his perfect green fatigues and boots, to a new porch and gently slipped through the partially opened door, ending the dream.

Volume two, *Recycling the Circle*, deals with social, political, cultural, psychological, scientific and philosophical modern issues and contains as many prints as poems. While structuring and formatting material the death of Stephen Hawking happened from which an extended sonnet came. This gave the book an ending relative to some advanced scientific thought and physics jargon of the day. It opens with a sonnet on the idea of Dr. Martin Luther King Jr. and Abraham Lincoln sharing a double monument. A sonnet competing with a monument was proposed by Shakespeare in *Sonnet 55*.

Two new sonnets enlarged the last sonnet for the chapbook. The first poem, *Redundant Pyramids*, pertains to Martian forms aligned in relation to pyramids of Giza and Orion star groupings. The third sonnet of this new epiphany crown, *Galactic Origami Soul* blends modern science with organically mystical nature myths of the soul.

The volume's cover has Lin Emery's *Flight* sculpture replacing Lee on the monument as in a dream in 2000 and remembered when arriving at Lee Circle that morning while driving Susan to work at the main library. I returned to take photos and plan double exposures to explore the dream. Gradually a series of prints added to the B & W volume and became a plan for a large format color volume after the chapbook.

Volume three, *Romance Languages,* started as a comedic parody on the muses Shakespeare frequently engaged with in his sonnets. It has a composite picture of Susan from behind at a Mardi Gras float raising her hands to catch a Rex throw on Canal Street in the late 90's. The cover collage title is *Grasping the Unattainable*.

Many of the illustrations in the current layout are elegant parodies of Leonardo da Vinci's main depicted ladies in drawings and paintings, all with wine glasses, at Stonehenge for "The First Picnic" drawings intended as a parody of Dan Brown's book, *The Da Vinci Code.* Monty Python's Terry Gilliam antics also seem a bit influential.

On her condo couch, I showed Susan, relaxing her legs on my lap, different versions of the volumes with illustrations. It was her first evening out of the hospital after chemo and radiation therapy was completed and the same day, but we did not know then, that Guy, my best teacher friend while I taught at school, was killed in a car wreck as a passenger in his own Honda Civic, the same car Susan owned, called a death trap by firefighters, like Diana's husband Wesley Clark, like the ones who had to cut Guy out of the car for a helicopter evacuation.

Susan's condition deteriorated in the next few days with low blood pressure and dehydration to the point where the doctor ordered her return. Her friend Tony called the morning of Jan. 12 and said Susan was rushed from a nursing home recovery to the emergency room with chest pains where she was pronounced dead. On Jan. 14th I received a card from Janice, Guy's wife, thanking me for the copy of the trilogy where she found the poem written for Guy on the death of his mother, she wrote she would always keep it and me close to her heart.

Two nights before Susan died, *Einstein's Quantum Riddle* was shown on PBS, a vivid dream followed with Susan and Guy that night stopped bedtime weeping. More expected dreams came that were noted while researching several books, the internet, YouTube videos and resulted in two new "epiphany crowns:" *Haunted Generation 2*, expanded the trilogy's afterlife ending and *Big Bang Nutshell Time* fleshed out volume two. Together with selected trilogy sonnets, they fit a condensed sharply focused section three of a fourth volume, *Radio Waves Color Blind*.

Guy and Susan looked their best in the dreams.. no words recalled, visualization said it all, Guy seemed delighted being there. In pre-death, Susan just 2 days before, in the same dream, looked superb aa a standard version of herself in casual elegant light pastel pants and long sleeved top in our stately white two story New Orleans manor with shiny cherry-rosewood floors, cream walls, warm soft accented shadows in corners. Clear amber tinged light streamed through an open window's white sheer breezy curtains at the far side of the spacious living room, while bright outside from other angles. Verbally subdued, busy with beautiful household objects and modern furniture, moving from the kitchen, as a cat wandered by to living room, Susan didn't pay much attention to me. I had to ask how she liked this place, implied as compared to the previous places we lived in that she didn't care much for. She showed her interest as if it were a rhetorical question, obvious to see, while she kept busy turned to fine new things with no conversation. Content, I went to the long bright green grassy front yard with a tall hedge at the end of the drive.

Guy rounded the driveway by the hedge and nicely edged grassy front yard, dressed in a dapper deep olive/green hiking outfit. I met him dressed as usual, neat Ralph Lauren Polo double pocket dark shirt and tan chinos as on beautiful days when we taught middle school Special Ed. boys and girls at Eisenhower Elementary. He was happy to greet me, as if after a long journey, returned from a great distance. Going inside to see Susan and the house, we checked out our sweet cats, then Guy suddenly surprised us in the living room from a hallway with a baby pet elephant that acted like a big puppy climbing on a chair then rolled around next on the sofa for a belly rub. This playful greeting, kind of carnival-like, was a lot of fun for all of us. After that Guy and I went out a side patio door to a grassy yard and walked to a lane by rows of fine two story houses, then a field to a high footbridge over a beautiful rock strewn stream far below, then down passed a stretch to a block of houses & a renovated industrial building for a school on the neighborhood outskirts by fields.

Arriving, we meet a group of delightfully eager cheerful middle school girls & boys in the yard. They lined up casually, chatting while waiting to enter the building. Guy and I entered a side door on a wide hall that led to our new large well-appointed classroom with tables, computers and film screen. Huge windows let enough light in to make the open space look transparent throughout. A small group of girls and boys sat at a side table as Guy began casually discussing the day's nature/space science study. I planned visual media and art supplies for the subject while observing them. All were delighted to be there for this learning reunion as if every day from then on would be "Happy Earthday" in and beyond school.

After waking from the dream there came a sense of relief about Guy, just as when Dad appeared in the dream revealing his revitalized new life after death as we know it, to graciously share a welcoming glimpse of this glorious new state.

My long time actor, filmmaker, singer, talent-teacher friend Diana, had commented on the first improved version of the book I gifted her. She found large parts of it difficult to comprehend and realized its tedious task to complete. She wanted to help with the book by generously offering to pass it on to her editor uncle. It needed work on continued updates and improvements before someone tried to wrap a mind around it.

While musing on the similarities and contrasts of poems with documentary films, my friend Paulette sent a link to the critic Roger Ebert's essay on Werner Herzog films that linked to an interview with Herzog. Roger said, "He is willing to push beyond documentary fact... in his quest for underlying truth... Herzog moves freely through spheres of fact, fiction, legend, myth and invention." At the Telluride interview with Roger on Sept. 29, 1998, Werner said, "The weakness of cinema verite' documentaries is that they can not go any deeper. They can only reach the surface of what constitutes truth in cinema. Deeper truth can only be found in poetry, because then you start to fabricate. The world is simply there. It is what men find in it and bring to it that is truth. I am in search of the fathomless." Roger wrapped it up with, "It takes art, the arranging and adjusting, to fashion someone else's experience into our own."

I thought of Diana's quest to complete her documentary film after Wesley's death two years earlier and wondered how much these ideas figured into her efforts. She read my new poems that came as I began to process the deaths of Guy and Susan. It was touching and illuminating to get her feedback. She intuitively wanted to clarify my efforts and help by considering the epiphany crown's first of three sonnets word for word and line by line.

The time-saddled methods of the process, allowing the poem, and book, to show how to proceed over time required subconscious and conscious links to visualize what leads to completion. Links, like allusions, a conduit for imagination, play a crucial role in a work's development. Language use was for an enrichment of imaginative experience in trusting the higher reaches of subconscious mind while at times recognizing when dipping into the pool of universal unconscious mind. The mind should be allowed to wander, even fail as Jeff Bezos among others has said in group motivational meetings.

After awhile Diana responded with a detailed account of parsing the first poem for meaning and asked for clarifications in the following relaxed, non-critical, complementary way.. here is the poem revised a bit first:

Haunted Generation 2   (152 – Shakespeare sonnet # allusions in italics)

1 Quantum Entanglement

If seeing it changes it, when is it real

or broken in a throw of quantum dice?

Two people separate, distance identical,

one particle influences the other, twice...

same constancy travels faster than light,

unlimited blindness, then to reappear,

the same equation's enlightenment right,

far quantum point bearing access right here...

We vowed in the same world's symmetrical bell

that rang through Germany's foresworn classroom door,

till I arrived unknown at her White Sands neighbor

years later... again, Susan's truth wed me to tell...

a Tao of parallels in the physics of things,

remotely sworn for future, quantum's system clings...

Truth reaffirms change, psyche's regeneration,

unmasked faith-torn trial's haunted generation.

In reading this ***Haunted Generation***, I really liked it.

As I don't know what everything means, I wrote what I believe you

mean and ask for clarification. Thanks

So for fun and as a challenge to me, tell me how close am I to understanding.

"Haunted Generation:" (Sins of our families, fathers, that carry down from

generation to generation)

If seeing it changes it, when is it real – I love this!

Dictionary defines Quantum as any of the very small increments or parcels

into which many forms of energy are subdivided" and dice as: a gambling game played.

Can you – for clarification please, tell me what you mean by "broken

in a throw of quantum dice?"

Two people separate, distance identical - (I love this!

unlimited blindness then to reappear, (This means both parties continue

to not "see" –each other, or their relationship, the others needs, etc.

One particle influences the other, (love this) twice

Same constancy travels faster than light, (The constancy of what?)

"Unlimited blindness then to reappear, (love this)

the same equation's enlightenment right," (What does this mean to you,

please?" a quantum bearing accessed as right here… (an increment providing

an opening?) She and I vowed in the symmetrical bell ringing

in Germany's foresworn classroom

(You met in Germany, at school, and married to the ringing of wedding bells)

arriving at her White Sands unknown neighbor's home (White Sands is a town,

and "unknown neighbor's home," someone who lived nearby and she didn't know them.

years later, late again, Susan's truth out to tell…

a Tao of parallels in universal things. (timing was off, yet Susan speaks

her truth and opinions of general life matters.)

remotely sworn for future (Things she vowed to continue to share years

earlier) quantum's system clings (?)

Truth reaffirms change, psyche's regeneration, (thus the "Entanglement")

unmasked fear- (love this) torn trial's haunted generation. (the haunted

legacy left after life's trials torn by courage to face and show one's fear.)

The poet John Keats came to a concept like an attitude he named "Negative Capability" that could stimulate expansion of consciousness for the imagination considering poetic constructs. In a letter to a friend he said the idea worked as a literary ingredient, an attitude of acceptability to "be in doubts and ambiguities" for a deeper imaginative experience of poetry than just the surface intentions of literal meaning. Keats mentioned Shakespeare possessed large quantities of Negative Capability throughout the plays, including the sonnets, which to my ear reveals and needs a reader's "tour de force" of Negative Capability to fully engage the imagination.

Here begins the parsing of Diana's parsing: her last statement resonates the most imaginative experience, "life's trials torn by courage" where she seeks to parse what the title "Haunted Generation," means while not "seeing" psychological layers of experience reflected by "2." A "haunting" can be an involuntary return, something "generated" is a caused experience and can be cyclical in a "generational" aspect.

Part 1, *Quantum Entanglement,* is a physics concept unseen to the naked-eye, yet theorized based on scientific equations, post-event observation or conjecture based activity. Physics theory of quantum particles, so small the thing is "there but not there" to obvious perception where the observation itself effects it. This mysterious event, like briefly glimpsed symbols moving in a minute (yet vast) scaled atomic universe, the other symmetrical aspect of reality, combined with the outer or larger universe, is what Einstein might refer to as "General Relative Infinity."

Hauntings and generations belong to the human experience in how human entanglements manifest. One may google the overlapping connection of quantum physics studies with paranormal psychic studies to get a sense of possibilities in esoteric physics phenomena.

The PBS network's 1-9-19, Nova documentary, *Einstein's Quantum Riddle*, also seemed to haunt me. That night I dreamed of Guy alive and Susan in the beautiful house before she died on Saturday morning Jan. 12. I noted some ideas from the film and alluded to them in *Haunted Generation 2*, line 1: "If seeing it changes it, when is it real?" The rhetorical question answers itself: at each moving change or level "it" is real. The origin of my experience with Susan developed in tangents only to return to the mysterious relationship.

The difference in reading poems verses essays is how poetics assist in creative imagination's more diverse experience. Poems may need several readings to develop deeper imagination elements with aspects that differ from essays, thus we have "poetic license." Though poems may trigger emotion it can sound like flattery to express love or like for this or that. Reading with anxiety acceptance can achieve rich diverse imaginative poetic experience. Anxiety of influence, Dr. Harold Bloom's "diagnosis" in his book of that name, relates to a struggle in a poet's work with a previous poet's work influencing the current poet, as in arrangements of words, what was created by the other, in a way that is contended with, compared to, or composed achieving measures of misreading and internal conflict.

One's Negative Capability may start with ambivalence to nailing assumptions of what a thing is. Ones imagination may grow in time, get to know it as "it" gets to know oneself (in a form of "entanglement"). This is revealed in dramatic monologues and soliloquies of Shakespeare, Hamlet's conflicted "self-inquiries" or Robert Browning's *My Last Duchess*.

Begin reading with ambivalence to ambiguity. With generous spirit "it" prompts open minds to creative thinking, which seems to give "powers that be" trepidation or anxiety for loss of their influence (unless one is well known or desired for a purpose or style). Keats may have had "it" in mind forming *Endymion*, to him, a beautiful allowable failure. "It" can be more democratic, not just subject to the "tyranny" of form, nor one-sided, literal or word by word in declension, but with liberty "found" in limits of form. Paradoxically "it" can promote transcendent processes (before reading Whitman's poems, Emerson knew this in his essays). When approached for fullness of experience of a good poem, "it," can manifest possessing the effect of music, notes in relation to one another, in relation to space and time, the space-time fabric plus god-like "simplification intensity" (Yeats, *A Vision*, phase 17) as in E=MC squared. With abstract art, what one perceives or gets from "it" is relative to what one brings to "it." Musical experience lies with the reader as with the piece.

The experience of the poem's speaker is generalized, specific to one then two people, then to a larger group, then students, as implied to an audience. Readers of the poem, may tie-up to opening observations, questions of the poem's two physics related ideas in a single thought/experience, that may share duality of quantum physics principles which: 1. determine that actual observation of quantum matter changes "it," 2. "broken in a throw of quantum dice" alludes to Einstein saying "God does not play dice with the universe" as being relative to law and the question of randomness in the universe and quantum mechanics. Implied is "proof of divine grand design" throughout the macro/micro (human parallel metaphor of inner/outer) universe. Among nature's mathematical laws, the firmament stars (and microscopic cellular structures) are God's bulwark for believers against ignorance and obstinate doubt of the divine.

It appears that the grand design part was not enough for Stephen Hawking to accept the divine part. Did his physical condition have some influence on his decision? Einstein appears to have gotten stuck mistakenly about certain over-arching aspects of quantum mechanics, according to the film *Einstein's Quantum Riddle*, (due to mere miscalculations of an equation?). He did not have a problem with the "God playing dice" thought/joke, was this because numbers proved "He" simply didn't play dice with the universe? Aspects of the quantum question are applied to relationships in the poem when assessing what is left of us after our dust returns and dreams have fled.

One need not understand all these things to appreciate poems. They may sound rhythmically intriguing, metrically with musical "numerical shapes" of word-sounds and lines to challenge, mysteriously delight. Poetic ideas may develop from particles relative to people and share some nature of entanglement. People take on time's numerical shapes, on larger but related scales to particles, implied by the "everything is connected" cliché, which both Einstein and Hawking were interested in proving. They conceptualized and failed beautifully to validate with equations, a "Theory of Everything," as the grand unifying principle of the known universe. Duality in quantum relationships, or entanglement, has bearing on an entity in how it effects and is effected by the other, regardless how far apart, or close, as "right there" in perpetuity. Even God for each person had to reduce the law to duality with a caveat. A poem's juxtapositions force the "unity" experience.

"Bell's Theorem" stipulates that particles once having interacted retain some strange link of connectivity no matter how arbitrarily far apart they get. *Quantum Entanglement* espouses that particles appear to communicate with each other across great distances. The symmetrical nature of the experience has to do with aspects of the universe studied, conjectured and theorized. Everything from shapes of bodies, planets, cells, etc., to the mind of God, seems born out by numerological aspects of the physical universe and time. This mystery may "add up," with specific details, to faith in an unseen greater beyond from this realm to ease the shock and awe of the unknown made known.

Questions arise, arriving at her neighbor's house, with no idea she is the neighbor's neighbor, from over a thousand miles away. More amazing details, after losing track of her again in 1974, involve marriage with her 22 years later in pre-internet1996. Susan's last name, always struck me as a combined German/English word, "aus," and "tell." For years that has been what I do with writing and when we married I felt that changing my name to hers would be more fitting, but we did not change names.

In one regard, later Susan tried to defeat me on many levels, while in earlier times she sought to encourage me in those same areas. She became an ultimate human relationship paradox, a true riddle only solved in death. She turned into my sphinx, and the answer to Susan's riddle, being my own man after her rejection, resulted in her slower yet just as real self-demise, done in by her own actions or lack of action, that played out against my best efforts to help her, without being over-bearing or covetous. She won in the end by beating herself, yet thanked me. I will wonder at length what could have changed the outcome.

The only solace, yet the greatest is, the "afterlife" (terrible expression) is far superior to this life. The dream she appeared in after death, along with the dreams of Henry (Dad) and Guy, prove it. This awareness leads to the idea of the true "double jeopardy" duality, the "second death" controlled by God is the true one to fear and we are in good hands there.

Quantum mechanics rings as true as being in the same class for four years of high school with Susan in Germany, because of WWII (the war that caused my birth in Würzburg, Germany) then scattered to different places in the United States, bumping into each other at White Sands, that strange missile base in New Mexico, near the atom bomb test site, (that helped end world war by threatening the whole world) then losing track of each other again only to marry years later…entanglement indeed!

"Years later… late again" …connotations not direct meaning, a feeling more than meaning, yet a truth to tell that infers her last name. These are devises that Shakespeare used and one would be hard pressed to glean a literal meaning from his Sonnets. There are veiled references, allusions, poetic tricks of tongue, compressed time, many openings for conjecture and also personal experience with aesthetic values, qualities, letting the form play into the experience. These aspects make it poetry not essay writing (where the two can and should blend from time to time as they do here). Essays strive for literal meaning qualities and can prove to be manifestos of parsing, poetry is more like a bird one needs to set free to more fully feel experience, hopefully even relish liberty taking flight from its cage of words, in an ironic paradox, to escape when caught.

"Remotely sworn" is an allusion to the explorations of quantum physicists into what is termed "Remote Viewing." If one looks up remote, one finds "remote controls" or "far away," viewing looked up finds "observing" or "looking at." If "Remote Viewing" is searched for, a psychic exercise is found that some physicists have experimented on with the C.I.A. …the point is literal meaning does not automatically usher in the deepest experience with the best poetry, though it can help lay groundwork necessary for a transcendent experience.

A good read of good poetry achieves that thing referred to as reading between the lines, or what is not there, as with what is on the line and how words progress through the body of the poem. The last two lines are ending couplets in what developed as an adapted 3 sonnet "epiphany crown." The three part poem came from a dream series, dreams arriving in a thematic returning or haunting way. How dreams inspired other poems relates to how the first *Haunted Generation* poem occurred after a "mother conflict dream" Dr. Freud would have enjoyed interpreting. Though imagination seemed to play a larger part in the longer Haunted Generation 2 than in the first poem of that name, a lot came from dream transcription of what happened in both. Form variations turn the three ending couplets into a coda where interpretations are not just for Dr. Freud.

The risk challenge of allusions brought another layer of imagination to the poems. The courage to write the poem is one purpose of enlightenment, as well as stimulation to read and risk open-minded non-judgmental, unconditional positive regard. Negative Capability, ironically named, is essential for this and writing like a true "quatrain meta-physicist" can at times recall Nostradamus.

An exploding supernova of poetry, Walt Whitman adorns the "Kosmos" as he calls it, with his own "silver face" on our poetic language. This silver image of Lincoln is in *When Lilacs Last in the Dooryard Bloomed* (pt. XVI. 197). Dr. Harold Bloom considers it the greatest single poem to date in any language in the Western Hemisphere (A/I p. 237). Whitman's "Lilacs" is the conversation of the "Oversoul's" intimate human song in its true sublime eloquent splendor. Yet Walt was slighted by perhaps the greatest political tactician of modern poetry, W. B. Yeats, in the cosmic, at turns veiled-fascistic, systematically structured judgment of his book, *A Vision.* Dr. Bloom in 2011's *The Anatomy of Influence* (p. 237) points out Yeats' compact judgment on the "Will," of Walt's entirety, voice/persona, as lost in the "Phase 6" paradigm of *A Vision,* where the "soul's free will suffers" another "A. I." –"Artificial Individuality." Here Yeats underestimates Walt's tallied up half-formed consciousness as having "created an Image of vague, half-civilized man, all his thought and impulse a product of democratic bonhomie."

I wonder what the AI of "Alexa" would portend from Yeats' neatly categorized lapsed "one-shot" "judgment," in accordance with an Amazon "Echo's one-shot" (Wired p. 63) "oracular answer?" As of yet "Alexa" cannot write a conscious haiku, much less a quatrain though it could probably beat Bobby Fischer at chess, one move at a time? Yeats may have used a relevant word, "democratic," that has something of a universal aspect appealing to the hope of humanity, in relation to Walt's transcendental "Kosmos."

This leads back to the touchstone dream series that continues: about a month after death, Susan appeared perfectly in her glory, yet unobtrusively, gently, kindly with her utmost beauty's countenance of unconditional love, dutifully standing by a counter of what now seemed to be a "Kosmic" library, in a sublime nature setting, wearing a form fitting warm black dress, intricate designs on the torso woven of geometric "curvism's symbolic truthmanship," emerging in chiaroscuro subtlety from the close-up background of smooth flat fabric, more futurist than Moorish patterns but a design subsuming both ideals. Her refined form, more real than her disease ravaged body or William Blake's sublime, rested in resurrected perfection's contentment. Her direct gaze as I slowly zoomed in on her most sublime face, perfect form and bettered Mona Lisa smile, stood in service before a fine narrow home bookcase, the top of which could not be seen, as if ever rising. Packed with books on each shelf, spines together were of every color and design fragment like a patchwork mosaic that seemed so abstract at first as to be unrecognizable as books, a symbolic web-mystery of life. On further reflection the shapes zoomed in on Susan's dress were elegant horizontal dual curve tipped "spearheads" proportioned and spaced like Lin Emery's *Flight* sculpture shapes against a sky of Leonardo's black backgrounds of transcendent figures like John the Baptist smiling while pointing upward, Lin's shapes in exquisite Flemish jewel colors, golden yellow, deep crimson, viridian, aqua marine, with pointed ends emerging out of and back into a perfect chiaroscuro tapestry of night, where the dream ended.

As Walt's "Lilacs" are written for Lincoln, it seems to also be true for Susan, you & me. I followed a reading of "Lilacs" in gray solitude of an early April Saturday morning to write an ending quatrain for Walt, Susan, Guy, you & me:

> Between the lines' material, chasing the moon
>
> his Kosmos calls for an orbital lilac tree,
>
> its taproot tallying the orbs of destiny
>
> as I lie in glowing fields, dream up his night's tune.

To be courageous one confronts fears and lies. There is a saying that good fiction is a lie that tells the truth. When good poetry does this it does so to reach a higher truth than the literal words. There is a certain entanglement on the quantum level of words for dreams and experiences that have a haunting quality. Imagine a quantum physicist approaching the Bible's *Book of Daniel* with a certain clinging quality of dreams found there. They can renew ones spirit and wonder in order to overcome fear of being misunderstood. That process can exert a strong influence to anxiously read and write from, to find if ones words can prove worthy of the love it took to achieve them through fields of dreams.

Appendix 4   The New AI Consciousness:

Active Inference in the Free Energy Principle,

a Self-Fulfilling Prophecy Exploring Sonnet Poetics as in

Shakespeare's Operatic Crowned Knot of Fire

I suspect that my theories may all depend upon a force for which philosophers have searched all of nature in vain.   –Sir Isaac Newton

The physicist/psychiatrist Karl Friston's May 18, 2017 essay at *Aeon*.com: *The Mathematics of Mind-Time*, a self-described "rapidly argued" 3,800 word scientific mind game riffing on "…all biological processes… perform some form of inference, from evolution right through to conscious processing," posed questions such as "...at what point do we invoke consciousness," concludes with an "existence for existence sake" simplification, stating "…there's no real reason for minds to exist," ..contending, "…consciousness …is nothing grander than inference about my future." I wonder, not even for metaphors? What would W. B. Yeats say of Dr. Friston's "passionate intensity," is it of Yeats's *The Second Coming* poem variety that "the worst are full of" or like the antithetical self in Yeats's book, *A Vision,* for whom Friston's ideas may fit the controlled romanticism that "simplifies through intensity" for a more grand scientific poetics?

In the Wired magazine, Dec. 2018 article about 59 year old Doctor Professor Friston, *The Man Who Explained Everything*, Shaun Raviv (p. 102) describes how the cognitive psychologist/computer scientist Geoffrey Hinton in the mid-90's at the Gatsby Computational Neuroscience Unit, close to Karl Friston's office at the Functional Imagining Laboratory in London's Queen Square, convinced Friston "…to think of the brain (at best) as a Bayesian probability machine (stemming from 19th Century ideas of Hermann von Helmholtz) where "…brains compute and perceive in a probabilistic manner, constantly making predictions and adjusting beliefs based on what the senses contribute. According to the most popular modern Bayesian account, the brain is an "inference engine" that seeks to minimize "prediction error" (p.102)" not necessarily nihilism.

Dr. Geoffrey Hinton, moving on to the University of Toronto, became a key figure for founding the basic approach to "today's research in deep learning" for the development of artificial intelligence, having brought with him "new techniques" he had shared with Friston "to allow computer programs to emulate human (processes) …for integrating the input of many probabilistic models," that in AI terms are referred to as a "product of experts."

Inspired by Hinton's ideas, Dr. Friston in his own connections of "unrelated anatomical, physiological, and psychophysical attributes of the brain," profusely described from 2005 on, in "many dozens" of published papers, ideas on "the free energy principle" (p. 102). Years later Hinton's AI work, most accurately in a field of contestants, selected entities and things recognized in a "15-million-image database built by (the team of) Fei-Fei Li" founder of ImageNet (p. 103) and won their 2012 Challenge competition.probably sowing seeds for later facial recognition advancements & "Fakes" as profound as or greater than the artist Ai Weiwei's.

Dr. Friston's euphoric eureka can be seen stemming from the same input that gives us "the whole is greater than the sum of its parts," in part. In the Wired essay (p. 100) he is quoted on what sparked his earliest awareness (at 8 years old) of scientific method that would later lead to musing on the free energy principle. Young Friston in a Chester English garden one hot day turned over a weathered log to find small "armadillo-shaped bugs" that scurried around randomly. Observing the bugs moving more rapidly in the light, his insights resolved into thoughts that "it could be no other way" and not some "contrived" reason of seeking "survival," as if looking for "shade" which would project a sense of conscious determination onto the bugs. The projected notion ended with the understanding that their movement was like a machine's inevitable moves. Though difficult to wrap ones consciousness around and move on to the next equation, the science behind the free energy principle needs to be supported by "the numbers" that add up to "the sets of layered variables" of a "hierarchical system" of "machine learning." The term Markov blanket given to the division edges/separation surfaces of AI's tiered system variables came from Andrei Andreyevich Markov, a Russian mathematician who lived till 1922 (p. 102).

For Dr. Friston the Markov blanket is a universal differentiation concept from the micro through macro level of everything. It distinguishes one entity from another, extending from separations of distinct cells and their internal parts and components to different people, their internal parts and beyond to everything else. This concept sounds at once physical, metaphysical & metaphorical, from cell membranes to distinct psychological 'makes and models' and over time determines different reactions and behaviors (p. 102).

For a scientist treading onto the 'belief pitch,' the conceptual thrust of the proposed theory can prove to be a 'sticky wicket' in cricket terms. In mid-adolescence, a cherry tree blossoming left a life-long wonder, if he picked a point to start from nothing, could Karl understand everything by "sort(ing) it all out in the simplest way possible?" (p. 100 & 105) Friston (p. 103) deems for this AI process "you need to have a calculus that talks about beliefs." In hierarchical governance the free energy principle pans out best in comparisons when true cream is allowed to be "inferred" to the top. After exploration experiments to hone in on "the true path, best path" in a process aimed at predicting successful outcomes, processing eliminations & illuminations, eliminating surprises by active inference (a newer improved AI) gives issuance to receive probability and reduce free energy disruptions. Apparently without this actualized inference concept, everywhere in everything, all biology would not only tend toward entropy, scientifically speaking, we would evaporate "into the ether" (p. 102) ..causing me to wonder, are there infinite Markov blankets and is the glue something like gravity?

Considering my previous essay, *Fields of Dreams*, I googled Friston's essay's on dream theory and found *Frontiers in Psychology*, an Oct. 2014, vol. 5 cognitive science journal's Open Hypothesis & Theory Paper #1133, by J. Allan Hobson, Charles C. H. Hong and Karl Friston: *Virtual reality and consciousness inference in dreaming*. Skimming ahead found high points on page 6 (matching those in the Dec. 2018 Wired article). After elaborating on "evidence for predictive coding in the brain," where "prediction errors are encoded… (as) expectations or beliefs about (hidden) states in the world causing sensory impressions," the theorist asks "what has the processing to do with sleep and dreaming?" To aid understanding the researcher pausing from "minimization of prediction errors looks at perception beneath the surface process," to "Bayesian evidence for the generative model… over an extended period of time," sees, due to "difficulty to compute," the Bayesian model as "a proxy generally used both in statistics and (what suggests)–the brain. The proxy is called variational free energy (Hinton and van Camp, 1993; Beal, 2003) (that leads) to variational free energy formulation of perceptual inference and learning (Dayan et al., 1995; Friston et al., 2006)" (p. 6).

On "minimizing variational free energy," which would be "maximizing model evidence," the Bayesian model algorithm can be "decomposed into accuracy and complexity where log evidence increases with accuracy but decreases with complexity–the degrees of freedom required to make predictions" (p. 6). This works in order to maximize evidence, where generative model complications from complexity need to be minimized, reflected by the numbered parameters of freedom for "accurate predictions of sensory data" (p. 6). The learning process when awake is slow, inference in dreams minimizes complexity much faster and makes "the perceptual content in dreams… not a prediction of what will happen but an exploration of what could (or could not) happen... necessary to minimize model complexity (for) a more efficient model of the experienced world of waking" (p. 7). What was their extent of differentiating types of dreams? If Daniel would have said something like that to King Nebuchadnezzar in the Bible, he might have ended up back in the lions den, it may have made things even more daunting for Newton studying Daniel's prophecies and seeking "...a force for which philosophers have searched all of nature in vain" (–Isaac Newton). Conscious & unconscious inference gets asserted as "implied dualism" by Hobson & Friston (2014) as being able to be "at some level equated with consciousness" (p. 12).

The *Frontiers in Psychology* article (p. 6) also touched on the dreaded "beliefs about (hidden) states in the world," a concept sounding rather Shakespearian ..that ties into my book's opening Psalm 51 "truth" quote.. which is also probed a bit later in this essay. All considered, a search for Friston's writing and research on dreams stemmed from wanting to compare his ideas with my experience in writing the earlier essay, *Fields of Dreams: Symbols of Consciousness*, where I explore how in dreams three suddenly departed loved ones appeared and directly communicated with me non-verbally soon after death. Through dream symbolism, consciousness expanded to complete the Shakespeare AI trilogy by leading to volume 4, Radio Waves for the Blind, by adding to my sonnet series inspired poems and an essay stemming from the two most recent deaths (Dec.-Jan. '19) less than a month apart.

My Markov blankets, of allusion words & phrases, help distinguish each line in selected sonnets to focus energy on the overall thrust of other words & phrases in poems & cycles of poems. This active inference AI was applied in the tribute to Shakespeare's Sonnets before even coming into contact with Dr. Friston's ideas. Processes used in a systematic method of transforming previous sonnet states with a patterned scheme adding numbered Shakespeare sonnet allusions, extended from active inference to make them more "Shakespearian" in a current sense of language usage. The allusion process was inspired by research findings for the essay, *Shakespeare's Operatic Crown*. The free energy principle process arose from a series of actively inferred moments determining an overall vol. 1 allusion pattern from what sorted out gradually to be seen as a trilogy that seemed to reveal itself as I moved through the stages of its process from formation to final polishing.

Dr. Friston mentions "quantum systems" in the Aeon essay, briefly in terms of "particles described with wave attribute functions," not active inference with regard to quantum entanglement on the dream level. 2014's paper: *Consciousness, Dreams & Inference: The Cartesian Theatre Revisited*, in Epilogue exchanges with A. Hobson: the two, AH & KF are described as "dual aspect monists, not Cartesian dualists ...forced to consider ...theatre." AH to KF: "The really hard problem is to model subjectivity. I do not suppose ...brain-mind (is) influenced by... spiritual forces from outer space –a Godhead- or ghosts of dead people... I am at a loss to say exactly how a self arises or how that self constructs its model of the world... Are waves and particles a possibility? This seems to be what the quantum boys are betting on." KF to AH: ...You will probably remember doing Hamilton's principle of least action at school? ...the same principle applies in quantum mechanics and field theory. ...Feynman's path integral formulation, where probability of any path depends upon its action... is important because the "consciousness as inference" argument is based upon exactly the same principle of stationary action..." (*Journal of Consciousness Studies*, 21 No. 1-2, Epilogue, 2014, pp. 25-27).

As if compelled, my "quadrilogy" appeared in the completion process by adding several new relative poems (older revised poems as the 1st of 3 vol. 4 sections) including this essay lastly, extending the time frame of the overall work for well over 300 sonnets. Vol. 4 was unexpected yet predictable in hindsight as an essential hybrid work. The initially expected set of new sonnets (& essay) all tallied up as a compendium with tighter focus on the tribute project's thematic high point, life after death communication, compelled as if from compressed time, & revealed in dreams. Here is a circuitous route to describe aspects of forming this trilogy, much like Dr. Karl Friston's "Time-Mind" idea with a circular/spiral compressed-time, dream work described process of active inferences.

A thought abides to return to the trilogy with the additional newer sonnets of vol. 4 added to flesh out volumes 2 and 3. The process would be another extension of active inference in line with the exploration that resulted in probable arrangements of sonnets at given points in composing the trilogy. First changes came with additions of new sonnets resulting in allusion pattern adjustments for the three volumes. The 3 vol. patterns considered in succession, stemmed from what was predictable in vol. 1, then seemingly random in vol. 2 and yet as if inevitable to the author, as meant to happen from the outset. As discoveries were made for vol. 1's layout that changed the original intuitive allusion plan, the process moved on to vol. 2, followed by vol. 3, each with distinct allusion usage plans stemming from vol. 1's tight focus & finding my 22 crowns equaled 154 sonnets (to mirror Shakespeare's number in his series of 154 sonnets) ..while writing the first essay which inspired the entire allusion inclusion process to begin with, becoming like a delightful parlor game experiment.

Though the title, *Shakespeare AI*, may be a misnomer, it is an actively "iconcurchaic" (defined soon) one that may afford some imagination to the poetic memory banks in order to purchase its license worth of parody as well as profundity. One of the bravest challenges was to include the allusions throughout the trilogy requiring complete revision of the text. Because of this allusion process the work takes on even more profound aspects of an "artificial Shakespeare intelligence" which is how the title transformation into Shakespeare AI, was justified. The title was chosen first then was strangely aided and abetted by a curious essay in The Atlantic (June, 2018) magazine, "How the Enlightenment Ends: Philosophically, intellectually–in every way human society is unprepared for the rise of artificial intelligence" by Dr. Henry A. Kissinger suggesting how his government (before others) should urgently manage AI before "it's too late" (p. 14). The cover headline refers to it as: AI and the End of Human History (quite an opposite bookend to Dr. Harold Bloom's published concept, Shakespeare: the Invention of the Human!) The title *Shakespeare's Wake*, chosen for vol. 1, came from Dr. Bloom's description of James Joyce's *Finnegans Wake* (*Anatomy of Influence*, p. 112).

The term "iconcurchaic" is my invention that is a tribute to the Parisian poet/critic (friend of Picasso) G. Apollinaire, as well as the Bard. The word means something iconic and current while also being archaic, with an implication of timelessness. During my conversation on copyright for the book with a helpful "tech support" person, Lorraine, at the copyright office, she said the word "iconcurchaic" should now be placed "in the dictionary" ...certainly, I would feel honored by this and thanked Lorraine while we both chuckled.

Many scholars say Shakespeare's allusion choices spread personal, romantic, historical, allegorical, spiritual and philosophical enrichments throughout his work. A more recent young scholar, Daniel Swift in his 2013 Oxford University Press book, *Shakespeare's Common Prayers: The Book of Common Prayer and the Elizabethan Age*, for 280 plus pages examines how influential the BCP was on Shakespeare's life & work. When referring to *Sonnet 23* (p. 78) he states generally: "The sonnets are games of form and articulation: they are about what truth may be boxed in set speech. Here the truest speaker is an actor, straining for the words of his role." Swift transitions (p. 79) to the sonnet embedded in Romeo and Juliet's dialogue, "upon meeting" they "speak instantly of holiness" as if a direct embodiment of the prayer book's influence:

ROMEO:　If I profane with my unworthiest hand

This holy shrine, the gentler sin is this:

My lips, two blushing pilgrims, ready stand

To smooth that rough touch with a tender kiss.

JULIET: Good pilgrim, you do wrong your hand too much,

Which mannerly devotion shows in this.

For saints have hands that pilgrims' hands too touch,

And palm to palm is holy palmers' kiss.

ROMEO: Have not saints lips, and holy palmers, too?

JULIET: Ay, pilgrim, lips that they must use in prayer.

ROMEO: O then, dear saint, let lips do what hands do:

They pray; grant thou, lest faith turn to despair.

JULIET: Saints do not move, though grant for prayers' sake.

ROMEO: Then move not while my prayer's effect I take.

(1.5.90-103)

Shakespeare's Wake, was first planned to have 22 crowns and does with a twist: 21 with 7 sonnets (some with variations on crown form), a 3 sonnet epiphany "crown-et" and 4 more epilogue "allusion" sonnets making 154 with allusions throughout from all 154 in Shakespeare's collection. There are 10 "transition" sonnets (not for numbered allusions) as intros and exits, all totaling 164 sonnets. Volume 2, *Recycling the Circle*, now with 3 crowns, epiphany crown and 58 sonnets (with variations) has 82. Volume 3, *Romance Languages*, first had a garland and crown with 54 sonnets, to total 300 (double the number of Bible psalms) in the trilogy. From 4th volume new sonnets, 2nd and 3rd's vols. may be added to later for a more conceptually complete trilogy. The 300 was suggested intuitively by an editor friend at the time before the trilogy concept arose, it may as yet infer as well on the trilogy process. It will not be surprising to count the final number of "allusion sonnets" at completion and find there are 300, 304 or 308. A doubling of *Shakespeare's Sonnets* concept occurred early on when compiling the tribute idea before a trilogy revealed itself while writing through a crown series and before considering Coverdale psalm allusions in *Shakespeare's Sonnets*.

The 3 volumes contain tragedies, comedies, myth allusions, some pieces include blends of romance, history and comedy like compressed inner "shake-scene play-lets." Heroic sonnet forms express the obvious and the indescribable as unified active imagination. In this way a rose is never just a rose. Separate books, B & W and color, with individual covers & illustrations may also serve volume distinctions better for some readers.

The last revision process planned Shakespeare sonnet allusions for each line, with alluded from sonnet numbers in brackets beside titles or numbers of the poems. Allusion numbers for volumes 2 & 3 seem more erratic due to sequence change developments mentioned earlier. Original number schemes for allusions tended to work out even after revised sonnet position changes. Two 16 sonnet dual redouble' forms were dropped. Next some revealing rigor is examined.

The dual redouble' is my extension of the form with an "index" sonnet at each end, sonnet 1 and 16, instead of having just one index sonnet beginning or ending the regular 15 sonnet redouble' form. The eliminations changed a predetermined sequence of how sonnet allusions would come from Shakespeare's numbered sonnets in a 1-154 count for each of mine, as in a "same numbered" sequence. Removing the first redouble' from vol. 1 and the second from vol. 2, improved the end result when keeping the three best sonnets of the first redouble' and spreading them out in vol. 2, while reducing the other redouble' to a 7 sonnet crown and moving it to the epilogue of vol. 1, with Coverdale psalm allusions also added (as Shakespeare used, several even in the same numbered psalm as sonnet, these details are described in my essay *Shakespeare's Operatic Crown*). The goal became to add numbered allusions italicized in each line and to be more "revealing" overall where the Bard was or could have been more secretive, imbedded and coded. Exploring led to Coverdale allusions as well as sonnet allusions in 3 crowns. Sonnets for allusions were not to be used more than once in each of the separate volumes but in volumes 2 and 3, a few repetitive sonnet allusion numbers seemed necessary. The reasons for repeating the numbers had to do with revision, placement changes like those described before, altering the predetermined numerical arrangement with new poems, and not merely due to random choice or similar thematic content. I lost track of how vol. 2 allusions began with #66, it probably had to do with the "recycling" need to repeat an allusion pattern & counting all 164 sonnets in vol. 1 while dropping the "100," then skipping the intro sonnet of vol. 2 with no allusions. This would compensate also for changes, as in the opening section line up, thus beginning vol. 2 with Shakespeare's #66 for allusions. Sonnet number ordering for allusions in vol. 2 felt at times like mixing watercolors, tuning a guitar or consulting the I-Ching with yarrow sticks, found in the Bollingen translation with Carl Jung's "Synchronicity Forward." A numerical and not thematic approach for sonnet selections for allusion was used to add an element of mystery.

The 3 volume single book published with the new pen name seemed to develop its own kind of "artificial Shakespeare intelligence" due to more considerations than merely an allusion scheme, placement changes and revision. Though intuitive adjustments in vol. 1's order and how Shakespeare's 1-154 allusion sonnets lined up to the epilogue slightly changed after revisions, how vol. 1's placements led to vol. 2 and vol. 3, may have mystified C. G. Jung more than Joseph Campbell (or vise-a-versa!). The allusion process was set not to use a word or phrase more than once or more times than had been used by Shakespeare in the particular sonnet choice (#42 has 7 "love" root word uses, #40 has 10!). Not over using allusions also extended to Coverdale psalms in 3 crowns. Some later revisions (as in *Stephen Hawking's Mythology of Everything; ASAP: Age of the Second Adam's Paradigm* and the transition sonnets) did not work well with systematic allusion plans for each line without completely rewriting the poems, so were left unchanged & unnumbered.

The allusion sequence for vol. 3 did not stem from how vol. 2 developed but extended from the pattern of a group of nine non-consecutive Shakespeare sonnet numbers listed in a row by author Gerald Massey in the 1888 book, *The Secret Drama of Shakespeare's Sonnets Unfolded* (p. 205 - 210). His narrative sequence involves different characters in what appears to be an operatic relationship struggle. Massey elaborates on the narrative involving Shakespeare "friends" with clarifying detail fit for a courtroom drama, almost as if he had known the characters personally! Vol. 3, *Romance Languages*, is a romantic psycho-comedy with an ending twist that conceptually like a crown of sonnets ties back into volume 1. Vol. 1 deals with romance in the beginning section and later curves before the epilogue, into the Orpheus myth that blends everything from visionary dream epiphany to modern gothic horror, historical, dramatic, psychological and mythical/alchemical sequences. Comedic relief like pixie dust is generously sprinkled through various parts of the trilogy aided and abetted by all the rhyming and no blank verse. Even Shakespeare deviated from strict use of iambic pentameter from first to last syllable at times. I tried to be faithfully aware of the metrical sound of lines throughout even when variations were used. As the essay conclusions reached the "operatic essence" of the Bard's sonnets before discovering Gerald Massey's "unfolding" concept, it was amusing and bracing to find Massey's similar reading. From Massey's nearly absurd to clairvoyant-like detective work, his determination helped spur on the arduous task of rewriting to include, as a more challenging tribute, a numbered pattern of Shakespeare sonnet allusions that would "puzzle through" each line like a strange parlor game for modern "nobles." The turn the volumes took after allusions were set up resulted in very challenging, often puzzling results, but never failed to intrigue, amaze and/or amuse. Turn to the last four sonnets in the Bard's series, listen for the humor that circulates there and try to imagine what it may have sounded like to the clever English dry witted ears of his readers at that time. The Bard exhibited the hallmarks of elevated comedy in sonnets as in plays, perhaps more concentrated in the sonnets, as in his sonnet series last lines, "Came there for cure, and this by that I prove / Love's fire heats water, water cools not love," as the epitome of dry English wit.

The allusion-sonnet order for vol. 3, repeated in an extending cyclical pattern, Massey's narrative sequence of nine sonnets that were according to him (like opera) set to specific music (p. 210), that of Autolycus's music to *Two Maids Wooing a Man* and are listed in this specific order (144, 33, 34, 35, 41, 42, 133, 134, 40). Samples of his comments, are referred to and examined at the end of the essay *Shakespeare's Operatic Crown* which follows: "After offering eloquent investigative evidence like a trial lawyer, Massey points out characters Shakespeare knew and veiled in the Sonnets with their personal traits and dramatic motives:"

"Elizabeth Vernon's jealousy of her lover the Earl of Southampton and her friend and cousin Lady Rich, is told in these nine sonnets, which are now for the first time put together: they go to Autolycus's tune of "Two Maids Wooing a Man." The first sonnet contains a soliloquy on the subject, a form employed more than once in the dramatic Sonnets. Then we have five Sonnets addressed to the Earl, and three to the lady of whom Elizabeth Vernon is jealous (Lady Rich) (p. 210-11)."

Autolycus, the ballad selling rogue in *The Winter's Tale*, 4.4.286-89, refers to a merry ballad which "...goes to the tune of Two Maids Wooing a Man." "There's scarce a maid westward but she sings it. Tis in request, I can tell you." Massey seems to know the tune enough to capitalize on it in 1888. By 2017, Catherine Henze in her book *Robert Armin and Shakespeare's Performed Songs*, refers to the song among others also sung by Armin as Autolycus. She notes the lyrics but not the music came down to us (as Autolycus' other song melodies did) (p. 84). In 1599, Armin, also a writer (*Quips for Questions*) was hired as a musician/actor by Shakespeare for the Chamberlain's Men and took on the primary roll of the fool (p.1).

Regarding the veiled sonnet characters named by Massey, it is compelling to see the Lady Penelope Rich saga Massey lays out with Sir Philip Sidney's connection (p. 352-6) is also brought out in agreement but with more emphasis on Sidney, by Clare Asquith in 2005's *Shadowplay* (p. 151). Massey compiled such a thorough dossier on Lady Rich's beauty that perhaps even Cleopatra's beauty received less notice by Shakespeare. Massey argues at length that Lady Rich, the first love (though unrequited) of Sir Sidney, was the model for Shakespeare's later Dark Lady sonnets (after #126 and earlier) as well as being Sidney's 'chiaroscuro' eyed inspiration for Stella (p. 356). Professor Bloom in 2011's *The Anatomy of Influence*, in the chapter: *Possession In Many Modes: The Sonnets,* (p. 83) mentions the doubling and tripling of possible source figures referred to in certain sonnet figures such as the Dark Lady and the Rival Poet. Clare Asquith compiles a similarly weighty analysis of Sir Sidney being the linchpin model/influence for the character and voice of Hamlet from several aspects included in his books: *A Defense of Poesie, Arcadia* and his epic sonnet sequence *Astrophel and Stella*, as well as the facts and legendary points of interest pertaining to Sydney's English nobility and death at 32 by an infected thigh wound in a described indecisive/useless action (p. 147-52). Clare Asquith refers to *A Defense of Poetry* as: "...colloquial, graceful, at once casual and learnedly authoritative, in the witty tradition of Erasmus and Montaigne... a bastion of common sense, written in reply to a critic on the theatre...." Lady Rich, according to Asquith, as "the beautiful and intelligent sister of Essex (who was beheaded for treason), as an active member of his dissident circle," was one who "...may have been providing acceptable cover for poetry that was in fact political and religious" in aiding Catholics. Lady Asquith points out Sidney's writings as: "elaborately allegorical, (that) suggest a gradual disillusion with English Protestantism, and a growing sympathy with the plight of Catholicism" (p.149).

Turning to Sir Sidney's "Petrarchan" sonnet sequence *Astrophel and Stella,* from which allusions may be seen in Hamlet's voice & divided character and in other plays like *Richard III,* the basic idea is found there for a monumental Shakespeare sonnet sequence. Parallels can be found in Sidney's lines: Sonnet 69.7, "Gone is the Winter of my miserie!" calling to mind Richard III's, "Now is the winter of our discontent." Hamlet's echo can be heard in Sidney's Sonnet 68.10: "Labour to kill in me this killing care" and Sonnet 69.14, "No kings be crown'd but they some covenants make." Music allusions are found in Astrophel and Stella: Sonnet 68.6 on Stella: "With voice more fit to wed Amphion's lyre," for his Muse in Sonnet 70.3-6:

> She oft hath drunk my tears, now hopes to enjoy
>
> Nectar of mirth, since I love's cup do keep
>
> Sonnets be not bound Prentice to annoy;
>
> Trebles sing high, so well as basses deep;

Then 70.9-14 ends with:

> Come then, my Muse, shew thou height of delight
>
> In well raised notes; my pen, the best it may,
>
> Shall paint out joy, though in but black and white.
>
> Cease, eager Muse; peace, pen, for my sake stay,
>
> I give you here my hand for truth of this,
>
> Wise silence is best musicke unto blisse.

Having achieved the romantic equivalence of "rock star" status after death, Sir Sidney's ending verse here even calls to mind Hamlet's fitting epitaph: "The rest is silence" called to Horatio who bears out with "Good night, sweet prince, / And flights of angels sing thee to thy rest." This strangely calls to mind the strange and contrasting agitated interlude with the afterlife summons of their "ghost meeting interaction outcome" where Hamlet addresses a nearly manic episode (as modeling the mania himself!) marked by Horatio's "wondrous strange!" exclamation:

> And therefore as a stranger give it welcome.
>
> There are more things in heaven and earth, Horatio,
>
> Than are dreamt of in your philosophy. But come,
>
> Here as before, never, so help you mercy,
>
> How strange or odd soe'er I bear myself-
>
> As I perchance hereafter shall think meet
>
> to put an antic disposition on-

That you at such time seeing me never shall,

With arms encumbered thus, or this headshake,

Or by pronouncing of some doubtful phrase

As 'Well, we know' or 'We could an 'if we would',

Or 'If we list to speak', or 'There be an 'if they might',

Or such ambiguous giving out, to note

That you know aught of me- this not to do,

So grace and mercy at your most need help you, swear.

GHOST: (under the stage) Swear.

[They swear] (1.5.167-182)

Before it has all sunk in, Hamlet starts in a reasoned manner and disposition to rationally reassure Horatio, their reactions are not madness but normal when overwhelmed at the thought of what was just experienced. He bids them to keep calm and not strike up excitement, not to wonder of weirdness in him or themselves, then gets into a monologue riff that in turn goes antic; breathtakingly rippling words surge into an oath forced on them of how not to act and what not to do until the clang of the final ordering word "swear," which is suddenly echoed much deeper by the invisible ghost with an ambiguously "wondrous strange" comedic effect as if in complete support from the gate of the underworld, demandingly perturbed, reinforcing moral conscience on the way back to the under(stage)world in unrest, not to be forgotten & sworn by them in echo.

Considering Massey's sonnet list order, 33 with ambiguous heavy allegorical landscape imagery, "glorious morning," then spiritual allusions of "celestial face" and "heaven's sun," sounds like a more fitting soliloquy or overture than 144. Line 11 of 33, plays loss off on the allegory in a climactic outburst: "But, out! alack! he was but one hour mine," on to end, "heaven's sun staineth." The list goes on fine through 134, then 144 would return to the allegorical images of 33 as a romantic struggle with "good & bad angels." Lastly, 40 bids for an overwhelming conflict resolution hope with "love" used 10 times! Clare Asquith in her "Selection of Coded Terms" (p. 299) refers to 33 as alluding to Christ's passion and age of death and the age Shakespeare was when his son Hamnet died, which seems most fitting to bear the grandest allegorical and transcendent soliloquy weight of his Sonnets series. As John Keats in a letter referred to Shakespeare possessing virtually unlimited amounts of "negative capability," both appear to have made just as much use of active inference to quell free energy risks & dissipations in their lines to achieve sublime "simplified intensities" as Yeats sees fit to name & comprehend such transcendent consciousness issues.

An interesting relative passage is found in Dr. Harold Bloom's, *A Map of Misreading*, (p. 67) that refers to Milton's "power of religious phenomenology:" "As a man, evidently he was Christian (of his own sect, a sect of one) but as poet he was a fierce Miltonist, and as much a son of himself as of God. If the imagination, in poetry, speaks of itself, then it speaks of origins, of the archaic, of the primal, and above all of self-preservation." Next examining Vico's "magic formalism" used as a tool of the "self-defining function of imagination," Dr. Bloom refers to Auerbach's summary: "The aim of primitive imagination... is not liberty but... establishment of fixed limits, as a psychological and material protection against the chaos of the surrounding world." Thank you Dr. Bloom, several of these aspects mentioned in both passages resonate throughout *Shakespeare's Sonnets* as well as the general structure and purpose of my "quadrilogy."

The deaths of friends, Guy Charleville, followed by Susan Austell less than a month later, spurred a series of dreams, inquires, new poems, revisions of old poems and an essay resulting in a 4th volume, now: *Radio Waves Color Blind,* that condenses the "quadrilogy" into a book of essential thematic sonnets, prints & essays. New sonnets seemed to come to me like the dreams of dead and living friends, in 3's. The 2nd major essay seemed to beg on a 3rd essay that would go full circle, back to the original trilogy idea and would address the "AI" aspect of the title more fully …this third essay is the fruit of that search for understanding more lucidly, the unfolding work of expanding consciousness and imagination. It contains major elements of two longer essays and shorter descriptive ending pieces of previous appendices: *Forming the Trilogy* and the *Afterword.* Essential parts for a more thorough exploration of the trilogy goals were used to expand awareness of ideas relative to new "AI concepts & jargon" presented in essays by and about Dr. Karl Friston's working ideas. While considering his statements on AI and consciousness in concert with other prominent published thinkers, ideas of ethics and consciousness arose as paramount issues. For example, Dr. Henry Kissinger's essay in the June 2018, Atlantic (p. 13-14) maintained, "The most difficult yet important question about the world in which we are headed is this: What will become of human consciousness if its own explanatory power is surpassed by AI, and societies are no longer able to interpret the world they inhabit in terms that are meaningful to them? How is consciousness to be defined in a world of machines that reduce human experience to mathematical data, interpreted by their own memories?" Aspects of this struggle using metrical forms & codes engaged sonneteers of the Enlightenment like Sir Sidney and Shakespeare, perhaps only meaningful to a small group, though Shakespeare "numbers" expanded into a cottage industry over the years. This 3rd essay of my trilogy/quadrilogy addresses some issues previously stated in the awareness of numeric rhythmical structures and no matter how flawed or menial it may appear to some, this "trilogy machine" has a quality of inevitability. The longer it is around to be engaged with, like each day, it is and is not a surprise, it was and is an active inference (AI) to the next day and essays into it.. thanks to Professor Friston's Free Energy Principle work, my work fits the theory as a predicted outcome in itself.

The pattern aspect of all three volumes, examined in the appendix piece, *Forming the Trilogy,* reduces free energy scatterings in use of active inference patterned models. The resulting outcome of the allusion process, bolstered by three essays, amplifies the work's aura of an artificial Shakespeare intelligence. Illuminated by the current expanding essay, which could conceivably go on as a kind of "essay unlimited" thanks to influences of critics like Professor Harold Bloom, with further exploring or in "Fristonese: epistemic foraging" (Wired, Dec. 2018, p. 103) this work continues to grow. To do this thing called writing is a display of consciousness that believes in something or it has no reason or purpose to be written but to be its own stain on paper like randomly moving bugs under a covering log of decomposition moving faster in the light. This active inference AI works with belief systems in which whatever inferred influence ones anxiety yields itself to or is drawn to ..or with "no-belief," yet another form of belief system. At what point is point of view merely a matter of semantics where clinical, scientific, philosophical, theological, observational inference becomes faith in what's next? How does ones subjective "proof-self" prove outcomes in these matters of "what is simply is," as Friston's bugs proved to him, fulfilling the "new AI" ..with the same knowing that produces the least amount of statistical error while reducing "free energy," in such a way that wins AI software development contests & hopeful best sellers?

While considering Professor Karl Friston's insights with as much gravitas as Freud or Jung's dream work in regard to my sonnet project and its processes, without getting into specific belief systems that would doubtlessly result in an agon of conflicting opinions Dr. Bloom would instantly recall, which Professor Friston would in all probability just as quickly recoil from in my findings or approach, as perhaps flirting with aspects of dementia or some psychosis according to his clinically correct Markov blanket approach, keeping his "existence for existence sake" scientific ethos "safety-net" intact ..I still find myself out on the limb of gratitude and bow to his noble exploratory discourses and commitments while maintaining my own unconditional positive regard.

As for reducing the "free energy" around my sonnet project in order to evolve 'higher' from its kernel of love through devotion to Shakespearian purposes of that "promised eternity" in the dedication of his "unlimited sonnet crown," so that his work is prophetic of my own, mine actively infers itself into a self-fulfilling prophecy of its own enlightened entanglement with Shakespeare, Bloom, Friston & beyond. My 1st college poetry writing teacher, John Gery, in his critique of my epic, *Why John Lennon Died for My Sins*, in Spring '81, cued me up to a purpose of individual 'sect of one' belief system conceptualizations a la' Yeats's *A Vision*, right out of the starting gate. Ten years later he offered to sponsor me through continuation of an MFA program in writing I had completed the majority of. Very gracious but with a masters degree in counseling secured, I opted to drop out, tune in & turn on my own pace, the results being this life's journey approach. My course of study was not offered at the university per say unless it was to be another General Studies degree multi-media art plan. It would take time to pan out artful pursuits while earning a living as an art teacher married to a librarian. There were a lot of "free energy" fires to reduce along the way of underestimated authorial strengths while coming into my own as a visual artist, musician, videographer, writer, including a pen name & trademarked occupation as publisher ..everything else seemed to have to fall away for its maximum realization. It was then back to Yeats in a more confident ways of distilling his "pluses & minuses." Any love lacking in Yeats's "cold eye" view is made up for in Shakespeare, Whitman & Dickinson. Yet they did not see myth-busting 'mathematical-mechanical paradigm extremes' Yeats faced (to world wars) focused on in Patrick Keane's essay: *Yeats's Counter-Enlightenment*, in Salmagundi (1985; p. 126). The pessimism Yeats bore toward the Locke-Newton paradigm cycled through the inability of humans as a whole, to combine the natural & supernatural competently & transcendently in an 'AI' of the "mirror turned lamp" soul's past-myth-connected "active imagination," for the Enlightenment's high Romantic cure (p. 136). Informed more by the dead, who were not dead, ironically more alive than most humans, Yeats inferred his belief system through a spousal induced medium that yielded the book, *A Vision*. How could his classical hero paradigm be replaced by AI's post-war journey, of cold mathematical abstractions that would enable man's "one giant leap for mankind" paradigm of baby-steppers-in-space hubris, to that 'hollow moon' while keeping a finger poised over the nuclear MAD (mutual assured destruction) button? Will AI take the place of that finger? Surely "Yeats's coming" had "come round at last" to know his Homeric heroes inferred the same.

What higher purpose could AI possibly have, when accounting for belief systems as forms of consciousness, other than crunching "cold-blooded" numbers.. besides inferring and reaffirming a projected faith in life after death as the most profound conclusion of human consciousness and its end results? Why did Socrates seem pleased to drink the hemlock? The symbols sparkle in the lights all around us, even in what we can not see and this writing is one more example going forward into the lights, darkness, mists, to beyond the veil. My work appears, from the start, if not having evolved from higher consciousness, as I believe it has, to bare fruit of "new" AI hallmarks in exploration, reasoned & random risks, bestowals & gains, losses & discoveries, journeys.. Lee Circle to Lin Emery's Circle, in dreams & awake with this new Shakespeare (active inference) AI.

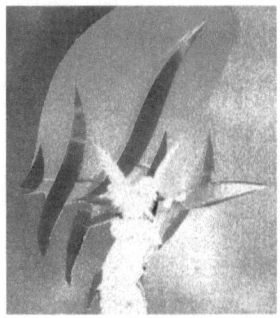

Afterword

The 2016 essay on his Sonnets, marked the 400 year death anniversary of Shakespeare and caused reimagining this text as a more thorough tribute. Tulane University professor and Louisiana State Poet Laureate, Peter Cooley, hosted the Sonnet part of a month long series of anniversary events called "First Folio!" The 2016 elaborate production featured readings, recitals, plays, displays of period publications of plays, poems, the Sonnets and an actual First Folio opened to *Hamlet* under a Plexiglas cube in Tulane's newly established Newcomb Art Museum.

My trilogy tribute idea with allusions emerged after the essay research. One volume combining the essay and the 3 separate volumes seemed a worthy tribute at 300 sonnets (or a doubling of *Shakespeare's Sonnets* I had in mind even before advised 5 years earlier to round the contents down to 300, from approximately twice that, by a poet/editor/teacher friend, Ralph Adamo). Reading the essay one can see where the allusion idea came from and what motivations Shakespeare may have had in allusion usage considering the importance of English Bible translations. All Coverdale's translated 150 psalms of *The Book of Psalms* still remain in England's *Book of Common Prayer*.

The formal high modern English with which Shakespeare was well acquainted to the point of being dramatically responsible for its vocabulary expansion through his writing, was based on a good grounding in the holy scriptures, mythology and readings throughout the liberal arts, in law as well as good grammar and Latin education. My own research over the years in a liberal arts education, masters degree in counseling, masters studies in art history and creative writing as part of an MFA curriculum in poetry and independent studies in the English Bible, immersion in documentary films repeated regularly on cable's History Channel, YouTube videos and the PBS television network, have added to the development of comprehension skills that assisted in propelling me to achieve these poetic works and enlightened thoughts.

Though the title, *Shakespeare AI,* may be a misnomer, it is a catchy "iconcurchaic" one that may afford some stimulation to the poetic memory banks in order to purchase its license worth of parody as well as profundity. One of the bravest challenge pursuits was to include the allusions throughout the trilogy which required a complete revision of the text. Due to the allusion process the work takes on an even more profound aspect of an "artificial Shakespeare intelligence" which is how the title transformation into *Shakespeare AI* was justified. The title was lastly and strangely aided and abetted by a curious essay in *The Atlantic* magazine, "How the Enlightenment Ends: Philosophically, intellectually –in every way –human society is unprepared for the rise of artificial intelligence" by Dr. Henry A. Kissinger (June 2018). The cover headline refers to it as: *AI and the End of Human History* (quite an opposite bookend to Dr. Harold Bloom's published concept of *Shakespeare: the Invention of the Human!*)

The title *Shakespeare's Wake*, chosen for volume one, came from one of Dr. Harold Bloom's descriptions of James Joyce's *Finnegans Wake* (A. of I., p. 112). In one concluding poem, *ASAP,* (last sonnet in 1st of 3 versions of the trilogy) some key words were also inspired by Dr. Bloom, from passages in his 1996 book on "The Gnosis of Angels, Dreams, and Resurrection," *Omens of Millennium*. It is interesting to note that I had not read enough of the book for it to consciously influence the writing of the trilogy before its final poem. I was excited to find several correlations in our use of words and ideas while recently reading his book more deeply. A current version of the poem *ASAP* uses the words: "archon" and "Pleroma" from his splendorous book (p. 239-40).

The term "iconcurchaic," my invention as a tribute to the Parisian poet/critic (friend of Picasso) G. Apollinaire, as well as the Bard, means something iconic and current while also being archaic, with an implication of timelessness. I hope this book imparts the same to the reader, in various ways not excluding irony, as well as an enriched interest in Shakespeare's work and methods which may lend some forbearance of judgment for readers against the strangeness of my book, who can not read it with the "Negative Capability" of Keats in mind (of which in a letter Keats wrote:

"Shakespeare possessed enormously"). Though this book at times resembles curious best seller oddities such as Calvin Parker's 2018 book, *Pascagoula- The Closest Encounter: My Story*, about his and Charles Hickson's night fishing trip alien abduction experience in 1973, my efforts are validated by pieces under my name & pen name on the current (2019) Pirate's Alley, Rosemary James and Joseph DeSalvo produced, Faulkner-Wisdom literary contest finalist and short lists.

To bear the Bard's all-encompassing insight toward Horatio's "wondrous strange!" remark upon the interaction of the men with Hamlet's father's ghost, he has Hamlet say:

And therefore as a stranger give it welcome.

There are more things in heaven and earth, Horatio,

Than are dreamt of in our philosophy.

(1.5.167-169)

The artist Lin Emery gave the three book effort a thrilling statement (extracted from here) pertaining to my use of her sublime metaphorical sculpture *Flight* in the composite photographs for the covers of the trilogy *Shakespeare AI* and Vol. 2, *Recycling the Circle*, when emailing after an hour meditation session with the Dali Lama's personal physician: "Your overwhelming poems were a fitting coda... Thank you for including me in your Circles!" What an exquisitely gracious "Zen-engineering artist" she is of the spirit as well as metal.

In 2000 I dreamed of her sculpture *Flight* being on the column instead of Lee at Lee Circle in New Orleans. "Flight" once stood in a perfectly proportioned reflecting pool with exquisite lily pads, lotuses and goldfish, to grace the front of NOMA, the Museum of Art, a favorite New Orleans structure and setting. I regard it as the museum façade's crowning sculpture that has unfortunately been removed to the shadowy realms of the museum's rearwards "sculpture garden" like a UFO landing in a manicured swamp. The dream inspired my photographic "odd-yssey" in 2000 in which a narrative series took shape from "double exposures" of her sculpture and the top of the Lee Circle column (as well as other combinations after seeing the beginning results) with 35mm film in an "auto-everything" Nikon camera. The process resulted in a 2016 *Recycling the Circle* cover idea, with a framed print presented to Mayor Mitch Landrieu (at his 2018 book signing of, *In the Shadow of Statues*) to which he remarked "That's beautiful!" I then mentioned my dream of Lin's sculpture on Lee's column and thought it could then be called Lin Emery Circle. Though he had removed the statue for a more appropriate setting such as cemetery or museum, he said renaming it was not for him to decide. Lin's deep reflections will remain greatly appreciated with hopes that one day her sculpture *Flight* will be returned to its sublime place in the reflecting pool to crown   the beautiful facade of the New Orleans Museum of Art, as only it seems to grace with such unique mysterious excellence that changes like & with nature. As this book enters the world with care here's hoping it will help enrich lives of readers for a deeper appreciation of *Shakespeare's Sonnets* & his volume's dedication on behalf of the Bard's "promised eternity," proclaimed to delighted open minds.

M. D. V.

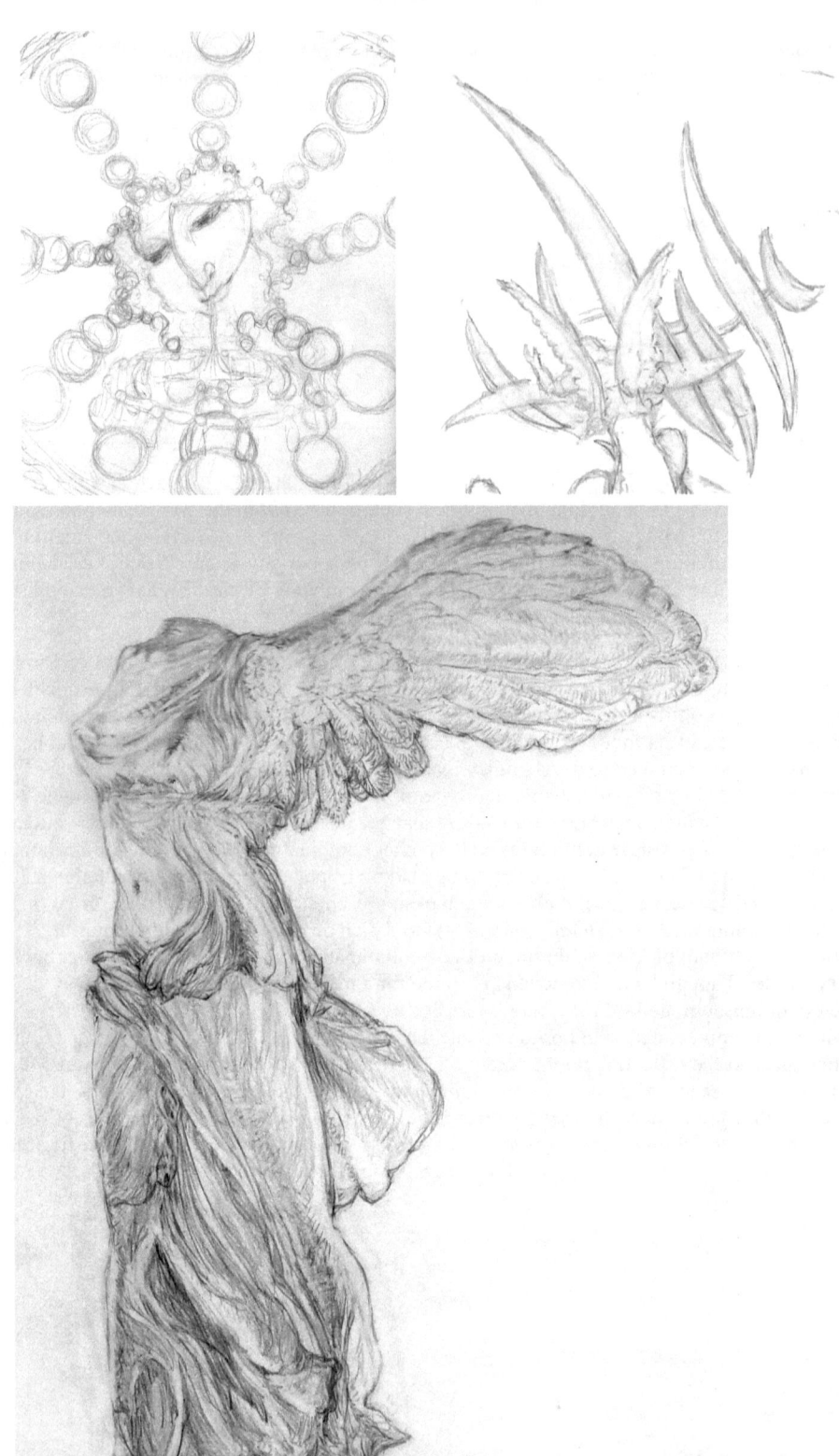

Epithalamic Epilogue & Epitaph

In response to loving critics who work behind me, beside me or who merely love from a distance, themselves as wedded well, but may not know how "good," or those who expect me at the altar of ego or no-go (when what I have is difficult enough to marry without the eternal bridegroom's betrothal), for them this consolation prize. To critics who weigh me in their scales of learned ignorance more blind than the flip side of justice to their own blindness, thin kings of my flittering hybrid's fat stunted imagination, I dedicate to their degrees of "word zymurgy maya" what could have been thoughts of Hamlet to detractors had he survived (as he does here), I leave their cool pomposity the parting point of Sonnet 121:

> 'Tis better to be vile than vile esteemed,
> When not to be receives reproach of being;
> And the just pleasure lost, which is so deemed
> Not by our feeling, but by others' seeing:
> For why should others' false adulterate eyes
> Give salutation to my sportive blood?
> Or on my frailties why are frailer spies,
> Which in their wills count bad what I think good?
> No, I am that I am, and they that level
> At my abuses reckon up their own:
> I may be straight though they themselves be bevel;
> By their rank thoughts my deeds must not be shown;
> Unless this general evil they maintain,
> All men are bad and in their badness reign.

Besides a Psalm (Coverdale's 116: "All men are liars"), this also calls to mind Hamlet's concluding remarks on actor treatment: "better have a bad epitaph than their ill report while you live" (2.2.528-9).
So here is mine now:

> My ardent spirits do not desert me now for fear
> of drinking from bridal glass or last supper cup,
> my book's feast serves both scholar and common reader,
> may it serve you well with both hands to follow up.

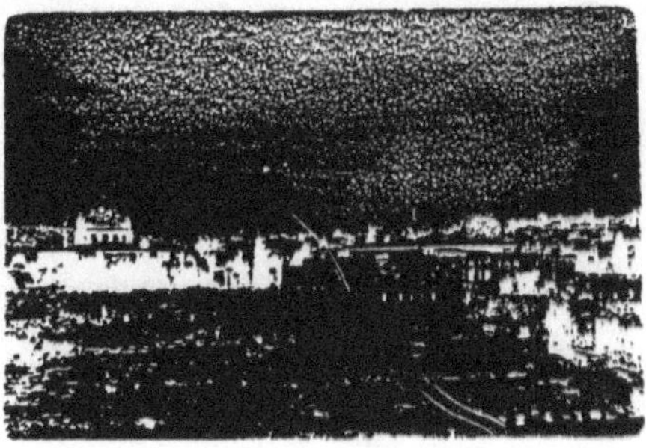

streaming at www.bontonrepublic.com

Bon Ton Amore'

Running Downtown with Sal
La Belle Orleanna Evergreen
Kentucky Derby Day
Once Upon Tomorrow
Gypsy Rhapsody
Her Roses Arrive
Safe Secrets
Chances Are
Wingback Rider
She Walks in Beauty
You Are My Light (Slow Burn)
Beyond Measure
You Are My Light
Eldoradio Rhapsody (Day Dream)

M. D. Veritas

All instruments M. D.
Veritas except Salvador
Ciardina double bass on
Running Downtown with Sal
& You Are My Light

www.bontonrepublic.com

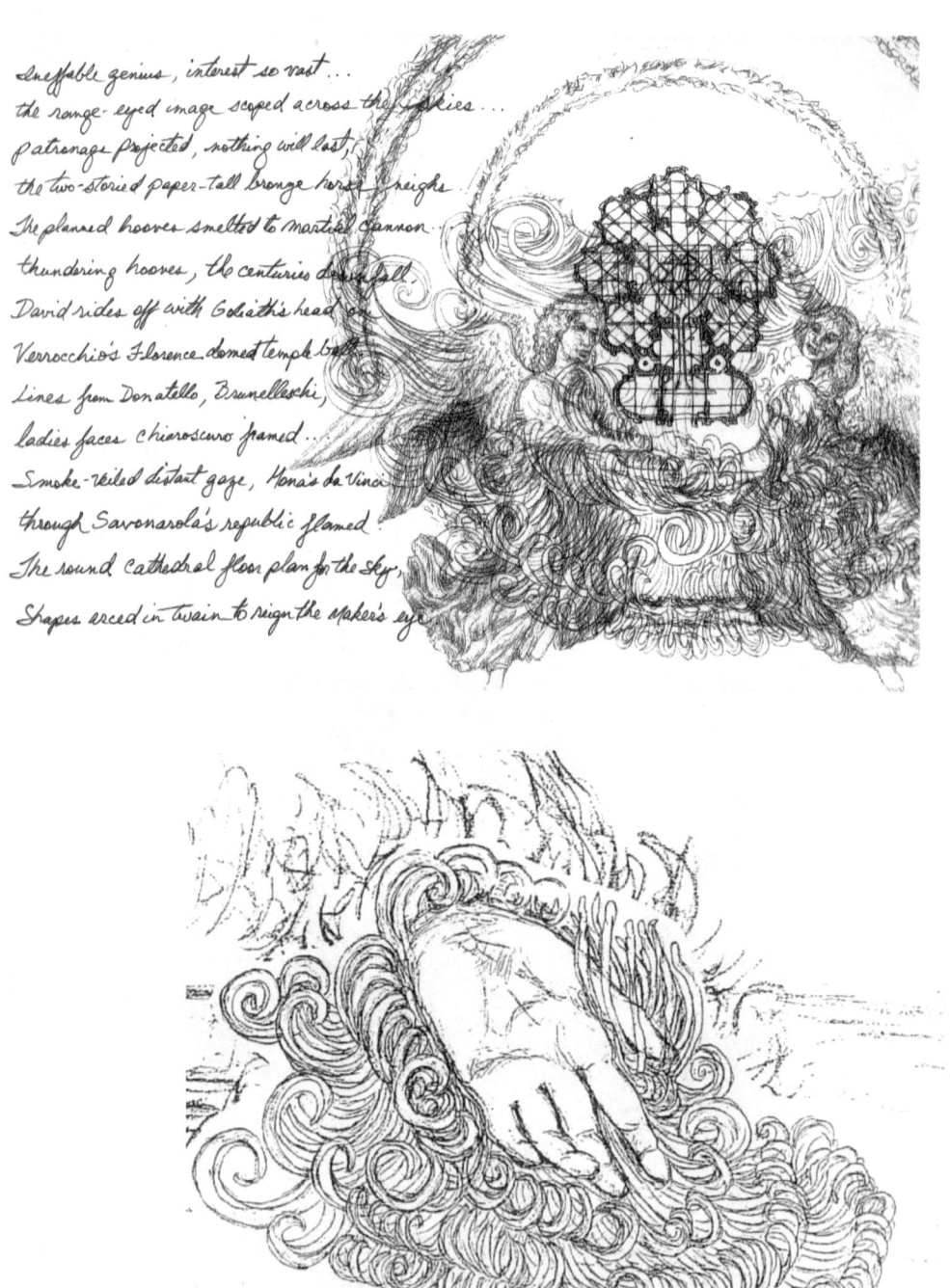

Ineffable genius, interest so vast...
the range-eyed image scoped across the skies...
patronage projected, nothing will last,
the two-storied paper-tall bronze horse neighs
The planned hooves smelted to martial cannon
thundering hooves, the centuries do befall
David rides off with Goliath's head on
Verrocchio's Florence domed temple ball
Lines from Donatello, Brunelleschi,
ladies faces chiaroscuro framed...
Smoke-veiled distant gaze, Mona's da Vinci
through Savonarola's republic flamed!
The round cathedral floor plan for the sky,
Shapes arced in twain to reign the maker's eye

314

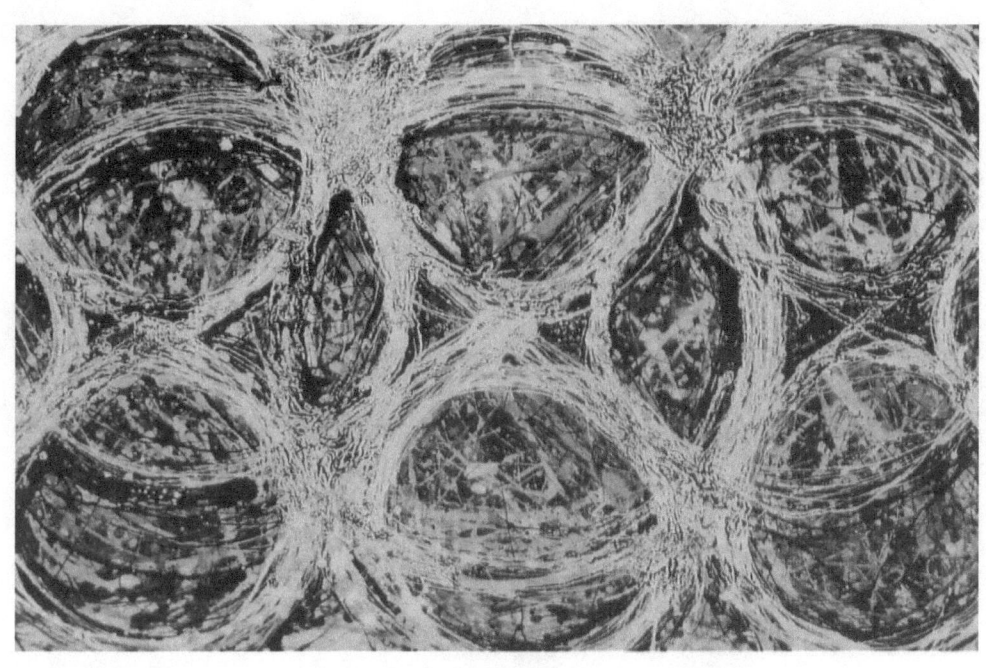

www.ingramcontent.com/pod-product-compliance
Lightning Source LLC
Chambersburg PA
CBHW050558260626
47157CB00002B/623